A Guide in Colour to

PRECIOUS & SEMIPRECIOUS STONES

A Guide in Colour to

PRECIOUS & SEMIPRECIOUS STONES

by

Jaroslav Bauer and Vladimir Bouska

OCTOPUS

Frontispiece: Amethyst crystals; Capnic, Rumania. Height about 60 mm.

Translated by Šimon Pellar
Translation edited by Sarah Bunney
Line drawings by Anna Benešová
Graphic design by Eva Adamcová

English edition first published 1983 by
Octopus Books Ltd
59 Grosvenor Street, London W1

ISBN 0 7064 1487 X

Printed in Czechoslovakia
3/07/12/51-01

Contents

List of tables

Introduction

Our early ancestors were the first mineralogists. Perhaps as much as 2.5 million years ago, people began collecting stones of special size, shape, texture and hardness for use as tools. At first the stones were used unshaped; then gradually they were fashioned with other stones into a variety of complex forms and used for specific tasks. Stones of a particular rock were sometimes collected from localities miles away from home base if they served a purpose well. This practice of collecting and shaping of stones for use as tools continued for hundreds of thousands of years, even until modern times in some remote parts of the world where people continue to have a hunting and gathering way of life.

Usually the only traces of Stone Age people remaining today are the stone tools left behind in caves, at riversides and other camp sites. By studying these tool kits, archaeologists can begin to understand how human cultures have evolved since our early ancestors first started utilizing stone as a raw material. In archaeological terms, it was only very recently in human evolution — about ten thousand years ago — that prehistoric people began to give up their nomadic life and to settle first in small, and then large communities. They found gold, silver, copper and tin, which they shaped into ornaments and utensils. Later, people discovered how to alloy copper and tin into bronze and to smelt iron.

Gem minerals, like the precious metals, would have been first found by chance. They were collected for their attractive colour, lustre and crystal form and were soon being used for personal adornment, or as charm stones or amulets. In this way gemstones became separated from the mineral kingdom and the first jewels came into existence. Findings from prehistoric cave dwellings in Europe show that amber was being used for simple jewellery several thousands of years ago; the use of serpentine and obsidian probably has a much older history. The main European source of amber was and still is the Baltic coast, but in prehistoric times amber would also have been collected from the coasts bordering the North Sea where it is still occasionally washed up. There is archaeological evidence of trading in amber in northern Europe in the fourth and third millennia BC. During the first millennium BC, the Celtic people of central Europe made bracelets from so-called 'švartna', which is a coaly claystone called sapropelite.

When man learnt how to shape gold and silver, jewellery proper came into being. Fine ornaments and cult objects were also made from the less-precious metals, such as copper and its alloy bronze, and these were often decorated with attractive pieces of rock or with semiprecious stones.

It is impossible to say exactly when gemstones in jewellery settings began to be used for ornament. The oldest records seem to be of Indian and eastern Mediterranean origin. Fine gold jewellery and carved seals (on Babylonian and Assyrian scrolls) were being made in Mesopotamia as long ago as the fourth and third millennia BC. Semiprecious stones were being used in gold jewellery by the Minoans, Mycenaeans and the Egyptians in the second millennium BC. Later, gemstone-working in the Mediterranean region became widespread, probably as a result of the eastern campaigns of Alexander the Great. Gem engraving or glyptography, for example, almost certainly reached ancient Greece from the Orient.

The making of furniture inlaid with gems, the carving of decorative objects from onyx, rock crystal and amber at the courts of the Hellenic rulers influenced the style of interior decoration generally and the crafts spread to Rome. During the late Roman Empire gems were being used not only for the adornment of the Emperor's robes but also to decorate harnesses, chariots and utensils in the Imperial household. The most prized gemstones of the period were agate, amethyst, beryl, chalcedony, amber, jasper, rock crystal, opal, ruby, emerald and coral. The gemmological knowledge of the Romans was relatively advanced. The great Roman naturalist and writer Gaius Plinius Secundus (AD 23-79), known to English-speakers as Pliny the Elder, wrote a work of 37 volumes called *Historia Naturalis* that covered the entire knowledge of nature, including rocks and minerals.

The glyptic art was at its peak in Roman times, an outstanding example being the famous *Gemma Augustea,* a sardonyx cameo in two bands depicting the triumph of the Roman commander Germanicus, step-grandson of Emperor Augustus. In the 16th century, Emperor Rudolf II bought the cameo for his private collection for 12,000 golden ducats. *Gemma Augustea* dates from the turn of the first century AD and was probably fashioned by the Greek engraver Dioskourides.

The typical Roman jewel was the intaglio seal ring or *annulus* made of agate. Originally, only patricians were allowed the privilege of wearing these rings, so that after Hannibal's victory over the Roman legions at Cannae in 216 BC the number and rank of the killed Roman commanders were established by the number of seal rings taken with rank insignia on them. Hannibal had the rings shipped to Carthage as war booty. In about 85 BC, the first agate cameo and intaglio collection — the so-called *dactyliotheca* — was founded in Rome. An even richer and rarer collection was put together from the spoils of war won by Pompey (Pompeius) after his victory against Mithridates VI. The collection was exhibited on the Capitol in Rome in 61 BC as a tribute to the gods for the victory. After the fall of the Roman Empire the centre of glyptography moved eastwards, mainly to Byzantium.

Two other gem-fashioning techniques with a long history are agate colouring and the making of glass imitations of gems, for which Alexandria became especially famous.

In the early Middle Ages interest in gemstones declined because Christianity emphasized the afterlife rather than worldly pleasures and personal adornment was frowned upon. Many ancient gemstone deposits were thus abandoned and fashioning techniques were forgotten.

A revival of interest in gemstones took place in the 13th and 14th centuries, first in France. Originally gems were only smoothed to remove all blemishes, then drilled through and polished, so that the stone remained as large as possible. This is the predominant character of jewels of the Gothic period. At that time the most fashionable gems were sapphire, ruby, spinel, emerald, rock crystal and amethyst. Agate gradually regained its popularity and the glyptic art was revived. In time the first facet cuts appeared. The main centres of the gem trade were Baghdad and Cairo where gems imported from the Orient were sold for more or less set prices. This is well documented in a learned treatise by Ahmed ben Yusuf al Teifassi, an Arab merchant who in 1242 made a survey of the gem trade and of the prices fetched at the markets of the world as it was then known. At that time, the best prices were fetched by rubies.

In the 14th century gems began to be used for the decoration of religious objects for the even greater glory and power of the Church. Several exquisite royal crowns decorated with high-quality gems date from this period. The fashion of wearing jewellery was spreading, both at the royal courts and among the nobility in general. However, the level of scientific understanding remained very low throughout the Middle Ages because ecclesiastical dogma hindered the advancement of research. Published works on gems are thus very scarce. Among the most important gemmological treatises are the *Etymologiae* by Isidore, Bishop of Seville (*c.* 570-636), a book by the Byzantine historiographer Michael Constantine Psellos (1018-1078), and a ten-volume work *De Natura Fossilium,* by the German mineralogist Georgius Agricola (1492-1555) (his real name was Georg Bauer).

During the Renaissance interest in the smaller precious stones grew. Diamond and other transparent and pale-coloured stones such as ruby, spinel, quartz, emerald and also the Persian turquoise, began to be used more widely. Information on the precious stones of the period can be obtained from the memoirs of the Italian artist Benvenuto Cellini (1500-1570) and from *Gemmarum et Lapidum Historia* (1609) written by the personal physician to Emperor Rudolf II and a great naturalist, the Dutch mineralogist Anselmus Boetius de Boot (d. 1634).

In the 17th century diamond gained the predominant position among gemstones that it still has today. New facet cuts were developed — for example, the rosette and the brilliant cut. Cardinal Jules Mazarin (1602-1661), the great French statesman and admirer of gemstones, is reputed to have been the father of the idea of the brilliant cut that enhances the lustre and the colour play of cut diamonds.

If the Renaissance period raised the status of gems, the Baroque devalued them, but not through any lack of interest. Quite to the contrary. What happened was that during the Baroque period the taste for rich ornamentation and lavish decoration led to the use of glass imitations rather than genuine gemstones. New decorative compositions were devised that utilized conspicuous pastel colour shades made possible by glass imitations of gems. Interest in genuine precious stones was almost entirely confined to diamond, emerald, sapphire, rock crystal and ruby.

The French Revolution gave birth to a new social class that brought a change in taste. The demand was not for splendidly luxurious, showy gems but more for personal jewellery that could be worn every day. The assortment of gems used for jewellery grew and interest has remained relatively stable throughout the 19th and 20th centuries. The synthetic production of gemstones has affected the price of some natural stones but it has never depreciated the value of natural diamond, ruby, emerald and sapphire. Synthetic stones may have reached an astonishing degree of perfection that often surpasses even that of the genuine article, but most people still prefer jewellery made with natural gemstones.

At one time, gemstones were classified into three groups: precious stones, semiprecious stones and decorative stones. However, this system of classification based on a complex value — a combination of rarity, properties and beauty — and used mainly by the trade has never been satisfactory because the lines between the individual categories were often meaningless. Moreover, some experts limited the term 'precious' to diamond, ruby, sapphire and emerald. Because of this lack of precision in terminology, gemmologists have abandoned the former classification and they now describe any stone as having gem quality if it has *beauty* (so that it delights the eye), *rarity* (so that it is unlikely that one's neighbours own one like it!) and *durability* (so that its beauty will last 'unto the third generation'). A gem must, of course, also be portable if it is used for personal wear.

Note that the term 'gem' covers cut stones as well as rough crystals and fragments of gemstone material. The term 'jewel' or 'jewellery stone' is more explicit and limited in its meaning because it designates a fashioned (cut) and/or polished stone prepared for setting in a precious or a common metal, or already set in a jewel. There are certain exceptions to the rule — for example, moldavite is used today in its rough, unworked form in jewellery.

As we have just seen, the possession of beauty is one of the criteria used to classify a mineral in the noble society of gemstones. But how do we measure beauty? Most people would agree that an attractive stone is one that possesses a high degree of brilliance and refraction of light, an attractive colour and transparency or translucency. Take, for example, the red ruby, the blue sapphire and the green emerald: they are all transparent, highly brilliant and attractively coloured. However, a gemstone need not be coloured for it to be attractive. For example, diamond is usually colourless but it more than compensates for this by its beautiful 'fire' or colour play on the cut edges of the facets (caused by a high refraction and dispersion of light), brilliance and transparency. One attractive property is sufficient to rank a mineral among gemstones; for example, turquoise is not brilliant or transparent but it has a beautiful azure-blue colour.

The cut gemstone must retain its beauty, especially its brilliance and transparency, even when set in a jewel and worn. The greatest danger to gems comes from mechanical damage and sometimes also certain chemical agents. A gemstone must therefore be as resistant as possible. Great emphasis is thus laid on hardness, formerly the chief factor in the classification of stones into precious and semiprecious categories. Minerals with a hardness greater than quartz (7 or more on the Mohs' scale — see page 51) were ranked among precious stones; softer minerals were classified as semiprecious. Some softer gemstones such as opal and peridot (chrysolite), although very beautiful, are not suitable for rings which suffer the greatest mechanical damage. If they are set in a ring, such stones will in time lose their brilliance and colour.

Rarity is the other important property a mineral must have if it is to be classified as a gemstone. However, fashion may play a big part in this respect. Bohemian garnets were very popular at one time, then they dropped out of fashion. Now the Bohemian garnet and other red stones are becoming fashionable once again. Only diamond, ruby, sapphire and emerald have never been threatened by the fluctuations of vogue. Some gemstones enjoy a considerable popularity in the countries where they are found; for example, the pink morganite or rubellite in France, alexandrite, malachite and rhodonite in the Soviet Union, and the pink kunzite and the green hiddenite in the United States.

Although a gemstone may be fashionable for a time because of its colour, certain rules should be observed with regard to the wearing of jewellery. Transparent stones of bright colour shades often suit women better than men and, as a corollary, stones with deeper hues of less conspicuous colour may suit men better that women. Jewellery must, of course, match one's clothes and be appropriate for the occasion. For instance, formal evening clothes for a theatre or a concert do not go with brightly coloured stones that loudly manifest their presence from afar. Similarly, a ring with a round stone will probably look wrong worn on a long slender finger. No jewel should be worn permanently because it loses its appeal in time, and it goes without saying that jewellery should not be worn if it is a hazard at work. If several jewels are worn together, they should match.

Gems shone on the necklaces and rings of the ancient Egyptians with the same intensity as they did on the hands and necks of the ancient Greeks. Homer wrote of the precious, priceless earrings of Hera and of the amber necklace that Eurymachos gave to Penelope. For thousands of years people have treasured gems. Is this only because gems are beautiful or does vanity lie behind it? Whatever the reason, since time immemorial mankind has loved beautiful things and it is no wonder that we have always been under the magic spell of gems.

Chemical composition of gemstones

There are about 3,000 described minerals and their varied chemical compositions include almost all the known chemical elements. About 80 of these minerals, in one form or another, have the necessary qualities to make them suitable for use as gemstones. Strange though it may seem, some of these gem minerals are also the principal constituents of the *rocks* that make up the Earth's crust. Varieties of quartz, feldspar and olivine, for example, are fashioned into gems; yet these same minerals are also among the 40-50 common rock-forming minerals.

Rocks are usually mixtures (*aggregates*) of several different minerals. For example, quartz and feldspar, together with mica, make up the well-known rock known as granite. These mineral constituents occur in varying proportions in different granites and even in different parts of the same granite mass, so rocks are nonuniform or *heterogeneous* — they do not have a definite chemical composition or structure. Exceptionally a rock will consist of only one mineral, an example being pure marble which is made up of calcite.

In contrast to rocks, minerals are uniform or *homogeneous* substances; that is, they have a characteristic chemical composition and definite internal atomic arrangement (structure) which may be expressed in typical outward forms called *crystals*. Minerals are usually compounds of various chemical elements, but may be composed of only one element (for example, gold, silver, platinum, copper and carbon). Carbon is better known as diamond — the hardest form of the element and the hardest of all gemstones — or as graphite, which is much softer. The basic constituent of the commonest mineral on Earth — quartz — is silica (SiO_2), a compound of the two elements silicon and oxygen. Most minerals are, however, composed of a greater number of elements bonded together in highly complex compounds. The gem mineral tourmaline, for example, is a complex borosilicate of aluminium and other elements (usually sodium, calcium, magnesium and iron).

All minerals are formed by natural processes. They are usually inorganic in origin, but some materials used as gemstones have organic constituents in them, being animal or vegetable products. Among these are amber, pearls, coral, ivory and the coal substances jet and cannel.

In the descriptive part later in this book, each gemstone mineral is given a chemical composition, but remember that completely pure minerals occur only rarely in nature. Normally minerals contain traces of other (foreign) elements, inclusions or liquids and gases or ingrowths of crystals of other minerals. These *inhomogeneities* change the mineral's chemical composition and to a certain extent affect some of its physical properties, such as specific gravity, hardness, colour and transparency. The foreign inclusions may, however, help to distinguish a natural stone from an imitation or a synthetic product, and because some inclusions are characteristic of certain geological conditions, they may also help to determine the origin and locality of the mineral.

A generalized chemical *formula* is usually given to each mineral compound. Sometimes one element in the compound is replaced by another element with the same valency and of similar size without changing the external crystal form of the mineral. This is called *isomorphism*. For example, in the olivine group the forsterite molecule $Mg_2[SiO_4]$ is replaced by the fayalite molecule $Fe_2[SiO_4]$; and in the garnet group pyrope molecule $Mg_3Al_2[SiO_4]_3$ is replaced by the almandine molecule $Fe_3Al_2[SiO_4]_3$. Isomorphism is also common in such mineral groups as tourmalines, plagioclase feldspars and pyroxenes. The characteristic isomorphism explains the range in composition and variation in properties in these mineral groups.

Mineral classification

Mineralogists have found it convenient to arrange minerals in groups sharing certain properties. Several classification schemes have been devised, most of them dependent on the chemical composition and the internal crystal structure of the mineral. (As we have seen in the case of carbon, the chemical composition alone is insufficient to characterize a mineral and its properties.)

One such crystallochemical scheme was devised by the German mineralogist Hugo Strunz, and is shown below. This system is widely used and is also recommended for the arrangement of small private collections of minerals. As can be seen, the minerals are subdivided into nine groups, which are arranged in order from the chemically simplest (pure elements) to complex compounds and, finally, organic substances.

1. *Elements* Diamond, gold, platinum, silver

2. *Sulphides* (also selenides, tellurides, arsenides and antimonides) Marcasite, pyrite, sphalerite

3. *Halides* Fluorite

4. *Oxides* (also niobates, tantalates and titanates) Agate, cassiterite, chalcedony, chrysoberyl, chrysocolla, corundum, cuprite, haematite, jasper, opal, quartz, rutile, spinel

5. *Carbonates* (also nitrates and borates) Aragonite, azurite, calcite, malachite, rhodochrosite, smithsonite

6. *Sulphates* (also chromates, molybdates and wolframates) Gypsum

7. *Phosphates* (also arsenates and vanadates) Apatite, brazilianite, lazulite, turquoise, variscite, wardite

8. *Silicates* Agalmatolite, andalusite, axinite, benitoite, chrysocolla, charoite, cordierite, danburite, dumortierite, euclase, feldspar, garnet, jadeite, kornerupine, kyanite, lazurite, lepidolite, natrolite, nephrite, olivine, phenakite, prehnite, rhodonite, sepiolite, serpentine, sillimanite, spodumene, staurolite, thomsonite, titanite, topaz, tourmaline, vesuvianite, zircon, zoisite

9. *Organic compounds* Amber, coral, jet and cannel, pearl

Not only do the members of each of these groups have similar chemical compositions, they also share properties, such as solubility in various chemical agents and resistance to heat. On the whole, silicates are hard and durable minerals and so it is not surprising that most gemstones belong in this group. Oxides too are generally hard and resistant to chemical attack. However, both carbonates and phosphates tend to be soft and easily damaged by acids or alkaline lyes and organic compounds such as amber are attacked by hydrocarbon-based solvents and detergents. A thorough knowledge of the chemical composition of gemstones is thus very important in the gem trade — without it gemstones may be totally damaged or permanently flawed during repair. The resistance of individual gemstones to chemicals and high temperatures is discussed later in the book (pp. 55-57).

Some gems do not belong to the mineral kingdom even though they are usually sold as precious stones. For example, serpentines and some marbles are metamorphosed rocks; obsidian is a type of volcanic glass; tektite is a natural glass which formed by the melting of rocks on the Earth's crust at the point of impact of a large meteorite; jet and cannel are coal substances; pearls are the products of certain molluscs; coral is mainly an animal skeleton; and ivory is obtained from elephant tusks.

As this is a book about gemstones, not minerals as a whole, the crystallochemical classification that has just been outlined is not the most suitable for use in a guide of this sort. Therefore, in the main pictorial part of the book, the gemstones are arranged in a special order devised by gemmologists just for jewellery stones. Further details of this classification are given on pages 77-78.

Origin and occurrence of gemstones

In the previous section we saw that gemstones do not form a uniform group of minerals related by similar chemical compositions and properties; some are oxides, others are silicates, carbonates, phosphates, and so on. Neither do all gemstones form in the same way, nor do they occur in the same rocks. Sometimes a mineral has a common variety that occurs widely and a much rarer gemstone variety that is found only in certain unique localities where special circumstances led to its formation. For example, the common olivine is the principal component of rock called peridotite and it constitutes a quarter of all basalt rocks, but its gem variety, peridot (chrysolite), is very rare. Quartz too is a very common mineral in the Earth's crust, but fine gem-quality crystals occur only rarely. Some varieties of diamond are much rarer than others. Since the origin and occurrence of gemstones cannot be discussed without reference to minerals as a whole, what follows is a general account of the environment in which minerals occur and in which they formed. The geographical occurrence of the most important gemstone minerals are given in Appendix I and illustrated in the maps.

All minerals originated by natural processes without any direct activity or interference on the part of man. Chemists can make a compound that has the same physical and chemical properties as a natural mineral, but because it is man-made it cannot be called a mineral. Nowadays, however, synthetic minerals are produced commercially on a large scale for use in industry and some jewellery stones are even made artificially, but these are not classified with naturally occurring minerals.

Many minerals are found in association with each other, and it is very likely that some of these originated side by side in the same, or very similar environmental conditions. Such a mineral assemblage is called a *paragenesis* (from the Greek *para* = alongside and *genesis* = origin). Certain minerals always occur in specific associations and experienced geologists and collectors know what minerals to expect in a particular geological formation and what minerals will be missing.

For mineral formation the right chemical elements have to be present at the right time; the process is also affected by factors such as time, pressure and temperature. Pressure and temperature can usually be simulated in the laboratory, but not time, although it can sometimes be compensated for by higher temperatures or pressures, or by some auxiliary factor such as water, gas or a catalyst introduced into the process.

Minerals originate in nature in many different ways. Sometimes mineral formation can be studied directly by observation of such natural processes as volcanic activity and smouldering coal heaps. Minerals also separate from hot-water springs and they form in the bottom muds of lakes and in mines and quarries. Mineralogists also gain useful information about mineral formation by studying the products of metallurgical and glass-making processes and chemical compounds synthetized in the laboratory. If a mineral is formed in association with certain other minerals during, say, a volcanic process, we can then reason that the minerals originated in the same or similar conditions in the geological past.

Some minerals — *primary minerals* — have retained their appearance since the time they were first formed. A larger group of minerals, *secondary minerals*, formed on the Earth's surface as the result of the transformation of the primary species. Minerals that develop deep in the Earth's crust in conditions of high pressure and temperature may be poorly suited for the conditions that prevail on the surface. So when such minerals are brought to the surface by geological processes and exposed to the effects of the atmosphere, water and aqueous solutions, they are gradually changed into other minerals that can withstand the surface conditions better. For example, limonite (iron hydroxide) is the rusty-coloured weathering product of iron-containing minerals such as pyrite, and the green malachite and blue azurite are formed in zones of weathering or oxidation in copper ore deposits. Secondary minerals usually contain the water molecule (H_2O) — hydrated compounds — or the hydroxyl ion (OH^{1-}) — hydrous compounds. Other minerals that are resistant to weathering at the Earth's surface may be eroded out of existing rocks and deposited in *sediments*.

Three main processes led to the formation of minerals and rocks: (1) the magmatic process; (2) the metamorphic process; and (3) the sedimentary process (Fig. 1).

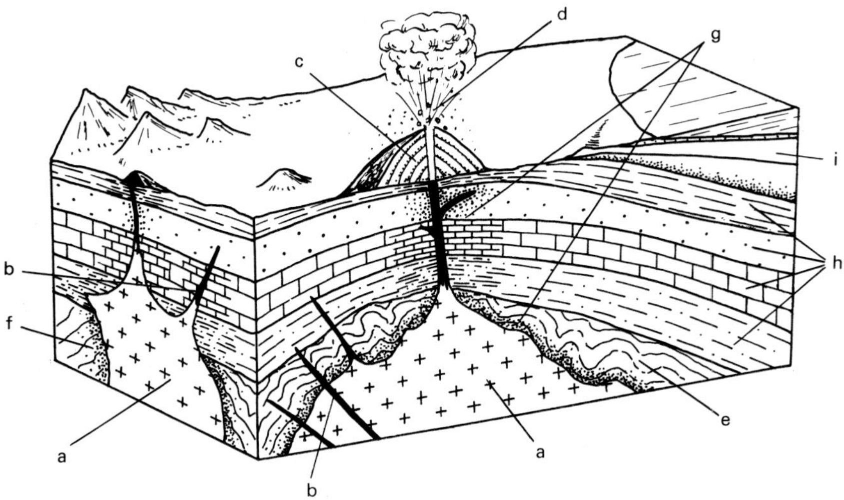

Fig. 1 Blockdiagram of the geological processes leading to the formation of the three main types of rock.

Igneous rocks: a, intrusive (plutonic) rocks consolidated at great depths in the Earth's crust; b, veins; c, effusive (volcanic) rocks; d, pyroclastic extrusive material blown from volcanic vents.

Metamorphic rocks: e, f, rocks changed by high pressure and temperature at different depths; g, contact-metamorphosed rocks.

Sedimentary rocks: h, i, deposits of different geological ages.

The magmatic process

The consolidation of hot molten silicate material, or *magma,* within the Earth's crust led to the formation of the great class of *igneous rocks.* Magmatic processes, which take place at temperatures of between 650 and 1,200 °C, cannot, of course, be observed directly, but some idea of them can be obtained by study of active volcanoes and of the final products — the igneous rocks themselves.

Magma is a complex material composed of different silicates, oxides and metallic elements, together with dissolved volatile components such as chlorine, fluorine, sulphur compounds, carbon dioxide and water vapour. The volatile components are retained in the magma melt under great pressure. Magma accumulates in reservoirs or chambers deep within the Earth's crust or upper mantle. If the pressure built up in the reservoirs reaches a critical stage, magma is forced upwards to cooler parts of the crust, or it may even penetrate the surface where it appears as lava. So there is good reason behind the adage that volcanoes are the safety valves of the Earth!

When magma reaches the cooler, upper parts of the Earth's crust or the surface, it crystallizes and solidifies into igneous rock. If rock forms below the surface and remains covered by older rock that prevents some or all of the volatile elements in the magma from escaping, it is described as *intrusive.* Such igneous rocks include granite, syenite, diorite and gabbro. If, however, the magma reaches the surface and is poured out as a lava flow, it solidifies to form *extrusive* or *effusive* rock. Such rock is also described as *volcanic.* Typical volcanic rocks are rhyolite, andesite, basalt and phonolite. These rocks differ from intrusive igneous rocks in structure and external appearance. Because they solidify rapidly at the cool surface, they are generally fine-grained and may even be glassy like obsidian.

Most of the important gem minerals are found in intrusive rocks, which are always crystalline, although their texture varies from coarse-grained to fine-grained depending on the size of the crystallizing body of magma and how quickly cooling takes place — in other words, how near the surface they form. Intrusive rocks that crystallize at great depths are termed *plutonic* and are usually coarse-grained. *Hypabyssal* igneous rocks form nearer to the surface and are usually medium-grained. They often form sheet-like vertical intrusions called *dykes. Sills* are more or less the horizontal equivalent of dykes — they conform to the bedding planes of the host rock, dykes cut across them. Dolerite is the hypabyssal equivalent of plutonic gabbro and volcanic basalt.

Particularly large gem crystals of such minerals as beryl and tourmaline are often found in pegmatites, which occur in thin veins and dykes formed when a liquid part of the magma, rich in volatiles and rare elements, leaves the original mass and penetrates fissures and cracks in the surrounding host or *country rock* before solidifying. Veins and dykes of fine-grained igneous rock associated with granite intrusions are called *aplites.* Igneous rock with a *porphyritic* texture is one with large crystals called *phenocrysts* set in a finer-grained groundmass.

Bubbles of gas escaping from volcanic lava cause spherical or ellipsoidal cavities or *vesicles* to form in the solidifying rock. The vesicles may become filled with minerals, so producing *amygdales.* Typical amygdaloidal minerals include quartz, agate and members of the zeolite group (for example, natrolite and thomsonite).

The separation of minerals from the cooling magma takes place in several stages. First to crystallize are the dark-coloured ferromagnesian (mafic) minerals — those mostly rich in iron and/or magnesium, such as the olivines, pyroxenes and amphiboles, and also calcium plagioclase feldspars and dark mica (biotite). These silicate minerals have a greater specific gravity and a higher melting point than other species and so they cannot remain in the molten state once the magma has started to cool. Being heavy they sink to the bottom of the melt leaving the lighter portion of the magma in the upper levels. As a result, rich heavy mineral deposits of, for example, magnetite (an iron ore), are formed.

Ferromagnesian minerals are relatively poor in silica and the rocks they form are described as *basic,* typical examples being gabbro and dolerite (and the volcanic equivalent, basalt). With an increase in ferromagnesian minerals at the expense of mainly calcium plagioclase feldspars and feldspar-like minerals (feldspathoids), basic rocks grade into *ultrabasic* types. Most ultrabasic rocks are plutonic in origin, a typical example being *peridotite,* which is rich in olivine and pyroxene and lacks feldspars. It is assumed that peridotite forms the upper mantle of the Earth.

In the next stage of *magmatic differentiation,* as the process is called, the lighter minerals start solidifying: for example, sodium plagioclase feldspars, potassium feldspars (orthoclase and microcline), quartz and light mica (muscovite). If the resulting rock contains more than 10 per cent of free quartz, it is described as *acid.* Typical acid rocks are granite (essentially quartz and potassium feldspars) and rhyolite (the effusive equivalent of granite). *Intermediate* rocks — between the basic and acid types — include syenite and diorite and the volcanic andesite. They contain less than 10 per cent of free quartz and are rich in sodium plagioclase feldspars and/or potassium feldspars. Igneous rocks — and silicate minerals — are also described as *alkaline* if they are relatively poor in calcium and rich in sodium and/or potassium. The alkaline rocks contain alkaline feldspars, feldspathoids, alkaline amphiboles and alkaline pyroxenes. The opposite of alkaline is *calc-alkaline.* Calc-alkaline rocks tend to contain calcium-bearing ferromagnesian minerals such as hornblende (an amphibole) and orthorhombic pyroxenes.

Sometimes igneous rocks contain concentrations of one mineral, a well-known example being the coarse-grained rocks on St Paul's Island off Labrador, Canada, which have vast accumulations of labradorite. This dark-coloured plagioclase feldspar is a characteristic mineral of gabbro. Similar labradorites are found near Kiev in Ukrainian SSR. The mineral is a popular gemstone because of its attractive play of colour.

Other minerals may occur in igneous rocks in such small amounts that their presence is not significant for classification purposes, although they may always be present in a particular rock. Such *accessory minerals* are found in granite (garnet, black tourmaline and zircon), in diorite and syenite (titanite and zircon) and in gabbro (apatite and ilmenite). Peridotites sometimes contain a magnesium garnet known as pyrope, and the dark brown to black melanite (a titanium garnet) is found in some alkaline igneous rocks (for example, syenites containing the feldspathoid nepheline). Cavities in peridotite on the Zebirget Island in the Red Sea contain crystals of gem olivine (peridot).

A special case of mineralogical association concerns the dark mafic igneous rock called *kimberlite,* named after the town of Kimberley in South Africa and famous for its diamond deposits. Kimberlite, or blue and yellow ground, as the weathered rock is also called, is a rock containing mainly olivine and pyroxene. Diamonds crystallized in the kimberlitic magma under very high pressures (5.5-10 GPa) and temperatures (about 1,200 °C). Similar extreme conditions are used in the production of synthetic diamonds for industrial use (see page 71). In association with diamonds in their primary deposits in South Africa and also in Siberia are the violet-coloured pyropes, so it is assumed that they also crystallized in similar conditions of high temperature and pressure. Such pyropes always contain some chromium (up to 7 per cent Cr_2O_3) which may be used for the prospecting of diamonds.

The dissolved volatiles in the magma play an important part in its consolidation: they lower the viscosity of the melt, thus making it more mobile; they lower the solidification point, thus allowing the magma to remain molten for longer and prolonging the period of crystallization; and they contribute to the better crystallization of the minerals. After the common rock-forming minerals have crystallized out of the melt at high temperatures, the dissolved volatiles, together with some metals and rare elements, become concentrated in a residual melt. In these rich conditions, in temperatures of about 600 °C or lower, the large crystals of *pegmatites* are formed.

On a worldwide scale, pegmatites represent one of the most important types of gemstone deposit. The largest crystals — occasionally several metres in length — are found in them. Pegmatites form veins or irregular lens-shaped (lenticular) intrusions within the main body of the igneous rock or closely associated with it. The granite pegmatites of Madagascar, Minas Gerais in Brazil and the Urals are among the richest known. Pegmatites are also associated with alkaline igneous rocks in, for example, Langesundfjord in Norway, Greenland and the Khibin and Lovozerets tundras on the Kola Peninsula in the Soviet Union.

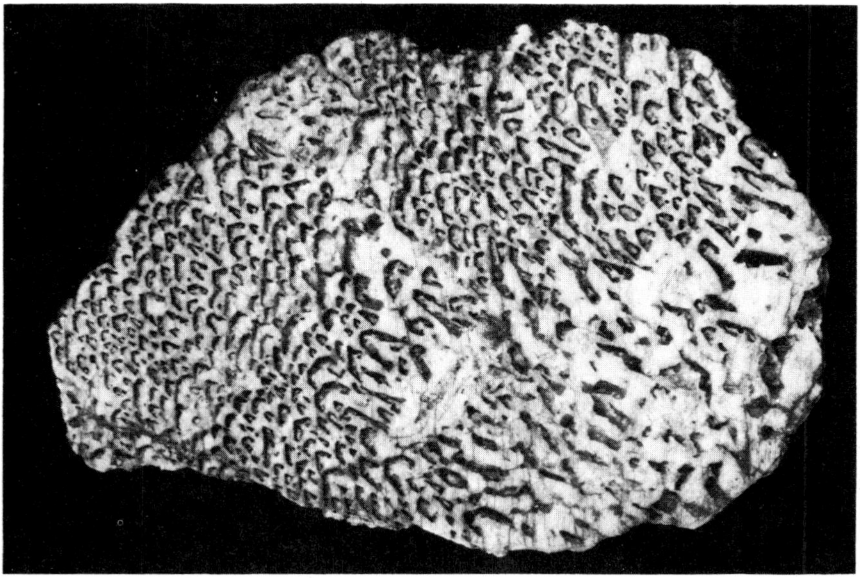

Fig. 2 Graphic granite (Shaitansk, USSR), 90 × 60 mm.

Pegmatite bodies are never very large, their maximum dimensions usually being of the order of tens of metres. In the marginal zone of pegmatites the orthoclase feldspar is often permeated by quartz to form the so-called graphic (alphabet) granite, mimicking Hebrew writing (Fig. 2). The appellation was suggested by the French mineralogist René J. Haüy (1743-1822). The stone is sometimes used for decorative purposes.

Economically pegmatites are important sources of many rare elements. Typically, granite pegmatites contain fluorine, boron, phosphorus, lithium, beryllium, lanthanoids, uranium, niobium and tantalum. Sometimes they also contain molybdenum, tungsten and tin, but these elements are more characteristic of pneumatolytic minerals (see later).

Among the many important gem minerals occurring in pegmatites are: rock crystal, smoky quartz, rose quartz, coloured varieties of tourmaline, spodumene, gem varieties of corundum, varieties of beryl, chrysoberyl (alexandrite), phenakite and garnet. There were once very rich occurrences of emerald in pegmatites in Colombia where these rare gemstones are found together with parisite ($CaCe_2[F_2|(CO_3)_3]$) and calcite. These associated minerals give the pegmatite a special character because they contain the $(CO_3)^{2-}$ anion group, which suggests a transitional stage between pegmatites and hydrothermal deposits (see below).

During the magmatic process, as the temperature and pressure continue to fall in the solidifying melt, the gases and vapours (mainly fluorine and boron fluorides) escape from the magma and bring about mineralogical changes both in the country rock and in the already crystallized intrusive mass. This process, termed *pneumatolysis* (from the Greek *pneuma* = gas), mainly affects feldspars and dark-coloured minerals in the surrounding rock. As examples, when boron-rich volatiles react with granite massifs and adjacent rocks, borosilicates such as tourmaline are formed; and the action of fluorine-rich vapours results in the formation of rock assemblages called *greisens*, which are rich in mica and quartz and sometimes topaz. Pneumatolytic processes take place in temperatures of 500-700 °C. Rich ore deposits can be formed in this way. Examples are the cassiterite (tinstone) deposits associated with granites in Cornwall in England and on the Bohemian and Saxonian sides of the Ore Mountains. Associated minerals include smoky quartz and its dark-brown variety morion, apatite and fluorite, often of gemstone quality.

Alterations of existing rocks are also caused by the action of hot water-rich solutions. This is the *hydrothermal stage* of the magmatic process. It either succeeds pneumatolysis or the two processes operate simultaneously. Many rich ore deposits are formed by hydrothermal activity at temperatures of 50-450 °C. The minerals are precipitated when the hot aqueous solutions start cooling in fissures in the surrounding rock in the upper parts of the Earth's crust. Usually the metallic elements (gold, bismuth, silver, nickel, cobalt, lead, zinc, copper, iron, arsenic, antimony and mercury) are bonded with sulphur in sulphides and sulphur salts, such as galena (PbS), sphalerite and pyrite. There are also many associated nonmetallic minerals. Although these hydrothermal ore veins, or *lodes,* are very rich sources of metals, their yield of gemstone material is usually rather poor. But gem-quality pyrite, sphalerite, quartz, haematite and fluorite may be found.

Hydrothermal deposits are often concentrated at the extreme tip of an igneous mass where they are zoned according to the temperature at which they formed; those nearest the instrusion formed at higher temperatures (500-300 °C) than those farthest away (200-50 °C).

Beautiful crystals of various minerals are found in subsurface veins in Alpine rocks. These deposits have a characteristic appearance and mineral content and their mode of formation has given rise to the term *Alpine paragenesis.* The types of mineral found in this paragenesis are related to the mineral constituents of the surrounding rock. Unsaturated aqueous solutions at a temperature below about 400 °C first leached constituents out of the rock as they passed through fissures in it. Then, nearer the surface the solutions deposited their mineral load to produce the characteristically subsurface veins. The veins normally contain quartz, feldspars and amphiboles; more rarely they contain pyroxenes, micas, chlorites, epidote, axinite, rutile, anatase, fluorite and haematite. In the Swiss Alps, gem-quality forms of clear orthoclase, rock crystal, smoky quartz, fluorite, rutile and axinite are found. Sometimes there is a gemstone variety of titanite in the form of yellow or pale-green sphene. Rock crystals from these Alpine deposits may contain ingrowths of small rutile needles, chlorite sheets or asbestos tufts. Veins of this kind are widespread throughout the crystalline core of the Alps, from Dauphiné in France via Switzerland and the Tirol to the Hohe Tauern in Austria.

The cavities — amygdales — formed in volcanic rocks by escaping gas bubbles are often the source of gem minerals. Attractive amygdaloidal agate and chalcedony come from southern Brazil, Uruguay, the US states of Wyoming and Dakota, India, the foothills of the Krkonoše (Giant) Mountains in Bohemia, and they came once from Idar-Oberstein in West Germany, a former important agate-mining locality. Zeolites occur in amygdales in the basalts of Antrim in Northern Ireland and elsewhere.

Crystal aggregations called *geodes* may also form in cavities in consolidating lava. These are hollow, globular rock nodules lined with crystals that project towards the centre. Geodes often contain fine amethyst and rock crystal and are much prized by collectors. Opal varieties such as precious opal, hyalite, fire opal and milky opal are sometimes found as veinlets or reniform (kidney-shaped) incrustations in volcanic rocks.

The metamorphic process

Existing rocks, both igneous and sedimentary, can be changed chemically and mineralogically if they are exposed to high temperatures and/or pressures within the Earth's crust. In the changed conditions, some of the original minerals are no longer stable and they recrystallize to produce new minerals that are in chemical equilibrium with the new environment. In the recrystallizing process, the texture of the rock may also change. This process is known as *metamorphosis*. The character of the new mineralogical assemblage — the *metamorphic rock* — is dependent on the temperature and pressure at the time of metamorphosis and on the chemical composition of the original rock.

In *contact*, or *thermal, metamorphism* temperature but not pressure is significant. The changes take place when a hot intrusive igneous mass comes into contact with, and acts directly upon, an already formed cold rock. Sedimentary rocks, particularly limestone, are the most affected by high temperatures. The changes can be traced in a zone or *contact metamorphic aureole* (halo) around the intrusive mass. The effects of thermal metamorphism are obviously more pronounced near the point of contact of the intrusive mass and the country rock.

Pure limestones are changed into marbles in this way; impure limestones — those containing dolomite and clay minerals, for example — are changed into calc-silicate hornfels, composed of various calcium and/or magnesium-containing silicates such as diopside, forsterite, garnet, tremolite and wollastonite. When sandstone is thermally metamorphosed, the constituent grains re-crystallize and become interlocking to form quartzite. Clayey or argillaceous rocks, such as shales, metamorphose into hornfels characterized by such aluminium silicates as chiastolite (a variety of andalusite with a graphite pigment), biotite or cordierite.

Dislocation metamorphism takes place in conditions of low temperature and intense localized shearing stress along fault planes and other weak places in the Earth's crust. The widest range of metamorphic rock types is produced by *regional* or *dynamothermal metamorphism*, in which heat and intense direct pressure act on great masses of rock over wide areas deep within the Earth's crust. This type of metamorphism is always associated with mountain-building events (orogenesis) and enormous igneous activity.

Rocks such as gneiss, schist and phyllite, which are metamorphosed shales, usually have a layered (*schistose*) appearance caused by the alignment of their mineral constituents (typically micas and amphiboles) in parallel planes at right angles to the direction of maximum pressure acting on them as they formed. The rock readily splits along these schistosity planes. Schists are usually named after the mineral responsible for the schistosity in any given case, so there is mica schist, hornblende schist, talc schist, and so on. Gneiss is a coarse-grained banded rock in which there is regular or irregular alternation of schistose bands of micas and amphiboles and coarse granular bands of quartz and feldspars. Gneisses often contain purple almandine or geniculate (knee-shaped) twins or columns of rutile. Mica schist, a slaty mixture of quartz and mica, often contains staurolite in typical twin crystals. Some marbles used for decorative purposes also belong to this group of crystalline rocks.

Metamorphism of ultrabasic igneous rocks produces serpentines and amphibolites. Serpentines are formed below 500 °C from hydrothermal alteration of rocks rich in olivine (peridotite). Varieties of serpentine are often fashioned into decorative objects; the massive light-coloured forms being especially valued. Sometimes chrysoprase (an apple-green variety of chalcedony) is found in nickel-bearing lodes connected with serpentinization, as in Szklary in Poland. Pyropes may also be associated with serpentines. The embedded crystals may have a fringe or *kelyphitic rim* consisting of a concentric zone of tiny radially arranged fibrous crystals, usually of amphibole, around them. The rim is formed by the chemical interaction of the pyrope with the surrounding rock. The rim could be said to function as a protective sheath around the garnets, preserving them from total decomposition. It shows up well on cut material.

The main mineral constituents of amphibolites are amphiboles and plagioclase feldspars. Groups of secondary minerals may develop on walls of cavities in amphibolites.

Metasomatism is a metamorphic change which involves the introduction of chemicals from other rocks. There may be a complete or partial change in the chemical composition of the original rock. Sometimes there is a complete replacement of one mineral by another without loss of the original texture. An example of this can be seen in the eastern Alps where layers of limestone and dolomite have been replaced by less-soluble components, such as siderite and magnesite.

The sedimentary process

Igneous and metamorphic rocks exposed for a long time on the Earth's surface to the effects of water, oxygen and carbon dioxide, to changing temperatures and to the activities of living organisms eventually *weather*. They crumble and the weathered rock is carried away by water into streams, rivers and finally seas; or it is transported by ice, wind and gravity (as happens when blocks of rock fall). The distance travelled by rock material when transported, for example, by a river will vary according to the strength of the currents and the size of the particles. When the velocity of flow slackens, the rock particles start depositing. First to settle are the larger particles, followed successively by finer and finer ones. During transportation there is continual abrasion of the particles as they rub against each other. In this way pebbles are formed. The accumulated sands and gravels are called *secondary* or *alluvial deposits* and in some parts of the world they are a rich source of gemstones. In time the sand and gravel layers become consolidated into rock such as sandstones and conglomerates respectively and clay material becomes cemented into claystones. These, and other rocks formed by mechanical weathering, are *sedimentary rocks*.

Other sedimentary rocks are formed by the chemical precipitation of minerals from water solutions, either as a result of evaporation or because of a change in the chemical composition of the solution. Sediments formed in this way include deposits of rock salt (halite), gypsum and anhydrite, and some ironstones and limestones. Severe chemical weathering of certain rocks can lead to the formation of residual clays rich in aluminium (bauxite deposits) and iron (laterite deposits).

Living organisms also participate in rock formation. Many marine plants and animals secrete shells made of calcium carbonate or silica. When the organisms die, their shells, either complete or broken up, accumulate at the bottom of the sea and ultimately form limestones. Coral limestones form from the mass of organic skeletal material that makes up the reefs of warm tropical seas.

Chalk is a pure-white, fine-grained limestone formed largely from the calcareous shells of certain unicellular microorganisms, among them foraminifera and coccoliths. The chalk sediments of western Europe typically contain bands or layers of irregular or rounded nodules called *flints*, which are composed of silica derived from the skeletons of minute marine organisms such as diatoms and radiolaria. These organisms lived in ancient seas in vast numbers and when they died the silica dissolved out of their shells and then redeposited in the insoluble form of flint. Flint was one of the raw materials used for tens of thousands of years by prehistoric people for shaping into tools.

Another type of sedimentary rock, *coal*, is derived from accumulations of woody plant remains, sometimes also from spores and algal material. The starting point for coal formation is usually partially decomposed woody vegetable matter such as peat. Coalification then proceeds through a series of stages corresponding to the amount of heating the organic material undergoes. The stages are represented by lignite or brown coal; sub-bituminous coal; bituminous coal; sub-anthracite; and, finally, anthracite. Collectively these are known as woody or humic coals. During the coalification process the percentage of carbon increases while the content of volatiles and amount of moisture decrease. Anthracite may contain as much as 95 per cent carbon.

The other main group of coals, the sapropelic coals (cannel and boghead coals), are formed from finely divided plant material, spores and algal and fungal remains. Cannel coal is rich in inflammable hydrocarbons and it burns like a candle. It has a different texture, lustre and composition from the usual types of bituminous coal, for example ordinary house coal. Jet — a black coaly matter formed mostly during Jurassic times (195-140 million years ago) — and cannel have a long tradition of being fashioned into decorative objects and jewellery.

Apart from organic materials such as jet, amber and coral (see the main pictorial part of the book for descriptions of how these last two substances form), sedimentary rocks also contain other gem minerals. Luckily many important gemstones have weathered out of igneous and metamorphic rocks and have been washed away into streams, later to be deposited with other rock particles as sands and gravels on flood-plains, below waterfalls, in pools and deltas, and other places along rivers.

For a valuable mineral to occur in these alluvial deposits it must obviously be highly resistant to water and abrasion and also heavy. This last property forms the basis of the age-old *placer* or *panning mining* method, which is still widely used today. The sand or gravel is removed from the deposits by hand or machine, and then washed in special baskets or pans; the precious metals and gemstones sink to the bottom of the pan, the lighter waste material floats to the top and is removed. Typical placer minerals include the precious metals gold and platinum and the gemstones diamond, ruby, sapphire, spinel and zircon. Vast gem-yielding alluvial deposits occur in Sri Lanka, Burma, India, the states of Rio Grande do Sul and Minas Gerais in Brazil, Madagascar, South Africa, and elsewhere.

Tektites

Tektite is a general name for a special group of naturally occurring glasses found in a few areas on the Earth's surface. They are usually given a name derived from the region in which they are found: *moldavite* (from Bohemia and Moravia in Czechoslovakia; in this case the name is derived from River Vltava (Moldua)), *australite* (Australia), *javanite, indochinite* and *philippinite* (Southeast Asia), *georgianite* (Georgia, USA), *bediasite* (from the territory of the Bedias Indians in Texas, USA), *ivorite* (Ivory Coast) and *irgizite* (Zhamanshin crater, Aral'sk region, USSR) are the principal varieties.

Tektites are rich in silica and superficially sometimes like obsidian in appearance, but they are not volcanic in origin. Just how they formed is still not clear, and there have been several theories to explain their origin. There is no doubt that tektites are remelted rocks — as their name, from the Greek *tektos* (= melted), suggests. Although all tektites have a broadly similar chemical composition and general rounded or elongated appearance, they differ in colour and considerably in age. The ages of some of them have been estimated by radioactive isotope dating techniques as follows: australite and tektites from Southeast Asia, 700,000 years; irgizite, 1 million years; ivorite, 1.2 million years; moldavite, 14.8 million years; and georgianite and bediasite, 34 million years.

Originally tektites were thought to be glassy meteorites, but their chemical composition seems to rule out either a planetary or a lunar origin. An alternative explanation of their origin is that they formed when giant meteorites or comets hit the Earth. The terrestrial rock melted at the point of impact and globules of the fused material were ejected into neighbouring areas.

Tektites contain bubbles of gas under very low pressure, and the question arises of how such a vacuum could have formed. One explanation is that it was created at the point of impact of a huge meteorite on the Earth's surface. As the meteorite passed through the Earth's atmosphere, it would have created a vacuum tunnel and when it hit the Earth an enormous vacuum bubble would have resulted.

To try to settle the problem of tektite formation, scientists have searched for meteoritic craters near tektite-strewn localities, or fields as they are called. In Ghana a meteoritic crater has been found some 200 km from the ivorite-strewn field and the composition of the rocks in the crater's vicinity corresponds to that of ivorites. Irgizites too are associated with a meteoritic crater. At Ries near Stuttgart, there is a meteoritic crater some 24 km wide, the age of which is identical to that of the moldavites found some 300 km eastwards. Upon impact of a huge meteorite in, for example, what is now the Ries region, a vast amount of thermal energy would have been liberated because all the kinetic energy of the meteorite would be converted into heat at the moment of impact. Moldavites therefore probably represent remelted surface sedimentary material transported by eddies and gas flows to the present locations in southern Bohemia and southwestern Moravia.

So far impact craters have been linked only with moldavites, irgizites and ivorites, but it is likely that all tektites have a similar origin. Of course, tektite formation presupposes a meteorite of sufficient velocity hitting the Earth at an acute angle. Such large bodies fall on our planet only very rarely geologically speaking — only once in millions of years.

Organic materials

Organic gem materials produced by living organisms include jet, cannel, precious coral, pearl, ivory and amber. The formation of jet and cannel, both varieties of coal, has already been mentioned in the section on the sedimentary process. Coral, pearls and amber are described in the main pictorial part of the book.

Structure and appearance of crystals

Minerals by definition usually have a characteristic internal structure, which may or may not be expressed in typical outward forms called *crystals*. The crystal form is the general equilibrium state of all solid substances. When allowed to solidify unhindered most minerals crystallize into distinct, geometrically regular, homogeneous bodies bounded by *faces, edges* and *angles* and with an ordered internal structure. This internal homogeneity is retained even if the growing crystals come into contact with each other in the solidifying melt and their growth thus becomes irregular. Note that the ability to assume a crystal shape is not exclusive to natural minerals because synthetic substances also crystallize.

Internal structure

The internal structure of a crystal arises from the orderly arrangement of ions, atoms and molecules within the substance. Although this internal structure is the fundamental property of crystals, nobody has ever seen an atom — they are so small that many millions of them occupy a cubic millimetre of space. In 1912 the German physicist Max von Laue first determined the true nature of a crystal's structure. He passed X-rays through a crystal and onto a photographic plate. The many symmetrically arranged spots that appeared on the plate (Fig. 3) were found to be visible evidence of the configuration of atoms within the space of the crystal. Further research has opened the

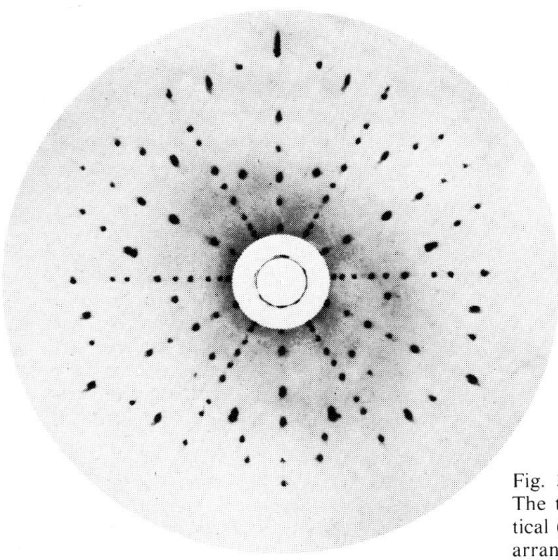

Fig. 3 Laue diffraction pattern of sapphire. The threefold symmetry according to the vertical (*c*) axis of the crystal is expressed by the arrangement of the spots.

Fig. 4 (a) Structural series, (b) structural plane, (c) structural space lattice.

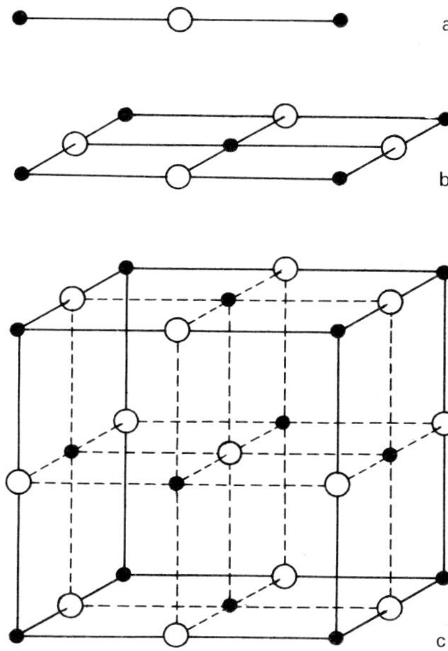

door to a vast field of knowledge about the internal structure of crystals. Today, the structure of all commonly used gemstones is known.

Within each crystal the particles of matter occupy positions or *nodal points* with definite geometrical relationships to each other. The pattern forms a network called a *crystal lattice* or *space lattice*, which consists of *structural series* and *structural planes* (Fig. 4). The grouping of atoms occupying the individual nodal points in the structure is determined by the chemical composition of the mineral. The arrangement of the atoms in the structure may vary even in substances with the same chemical composition; for example, diamond and graphite, the two crystalline forms of carbon (C), have different internal structures — in diamond the atoms are closely packed in the lattice, in graphite they have a more loose arrangement (Figs 5, 6). As a result diamond and graphite have different crystal forms and different physical properties. This is called *polymorphism*. Diamond and graphite are *dimorphous* forms of carbon, calcite and aragonite are

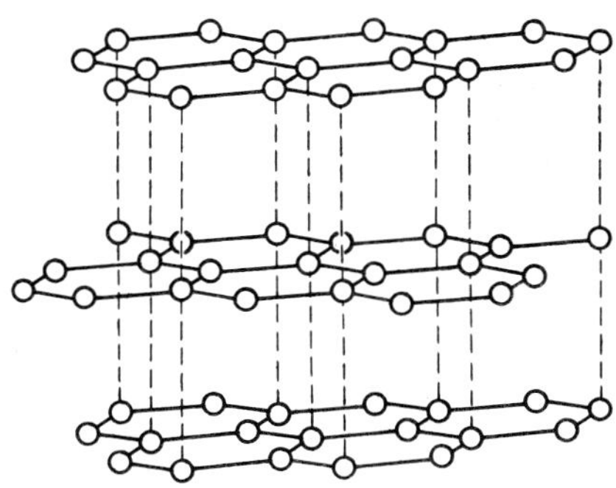

Fig. 5 Structural space lattice of graphite.

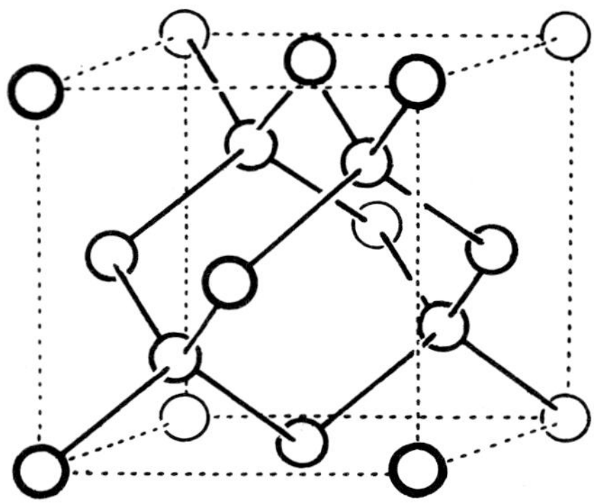

Fig. 6 Structural space lattice of diamond.

dimorphous forms of calcium carbonate, and pyrite and marcasite are dimorphous forms of iron disulphide. Titanium dioxide (TiO_2) is *trimorphous:* it occurs in three forms — anatase, brookite and rutile. There are several crystalline forms of silica (SiO_2), the commonest being quartz, tridymite and cristobalite. The individual crystal types in which polymorphic minerals occur are called *modifications.*

The ordered internal structure of a crystal gives it a geometry or *symmetry,* which can be highly complex as we shall see. In a simplified form this internal symmetry is expressed externally by the relationship of the crystal faces to each other.

Crystal symmetry

There are three basic *elements of symmetry:* the centre of symmetry, the plane of symmetry and the axis of symmetry (Fig. 7).

The *centre of symmetry* is an imaginary mirroring point at the centre of the crystal: that is, each crystal face must have its mirror counterpart as regards location and size; the same applies to edges and angles.

The *plane of symmetry* divides the crystal into two symmetrical halves — mirror images — that correspond point for point, angle for angle and face for face. For this reason, it is often called the mirror plane.

The *axis of symmetry* is an imaginary line passing through the centre of the crystal about which a crystal, when rotated, returns two, three, four or six times to its original position in space during a complete revolution. The axes of symmetry are thus described as *twofold* (diad, digonal), *threefold* (triad, trigonal), *fourfold* (tetrad, tetragonal) and *sixfold* (hexad, hexagonal), according to the number of times an identical face is displayed when the crystal is rotated through 360°. In other words, a crystal that shows two identical faces (each at 180°) during the rotation is called a diad; one that shows three identical faces (at 120°) a triad, and so on. For instance, a cube has a fourfold axis of symmetry passing at right angles through the centre of symmetry of any of its faces. If rotated, it appears the same four times in each complete rotation. But a rectangular block has only a twofold axis of symmetry passing at right angles through the centre of any face and if rotated the same faces occur only twice in a revolution. There are also more complex symmetries derived from combinations of the basic elements which you will find described in detail in textbooks of crystallography and mineralogy. Crystals in the cubic system have the highest symmetry, those in the triclinic system the least symmetry (see below). Some crystals in the triclinic system are entirely asymmetric.

The symmetry of a crystal can sometimes be determined directly from the crystal's appearance, but in most cases it can be identified with certainty only with the help of a special instrument called a *goniometer,* which measures interfacial angles.

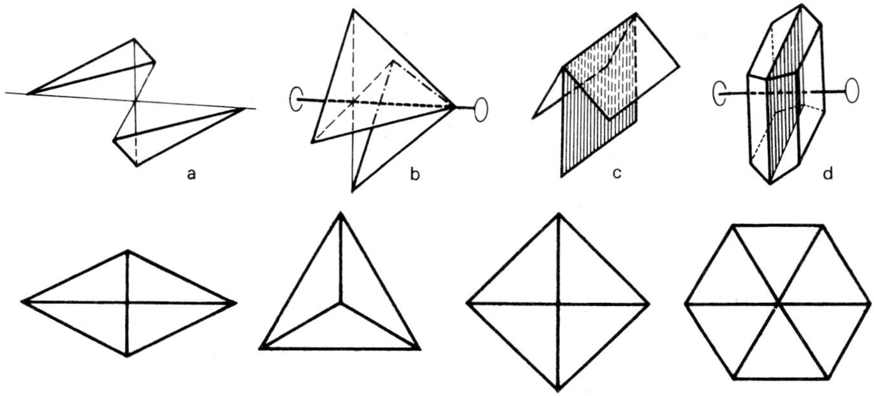

Fig. 7 Top: (a) centre of symmetry, (b) bifold axis of symmetry, (c) plane of symmetry, (d) crystal of gypsum with plane and bifold axis of symmetry. Bottom: (left to right) plots of pyramids symmetrical according to bifold, threefold, fourfold and sixfold axes.

Crystal form

In ideal conditions a mineral crystallizes into well-developed geometrical *forms* bounded by smooth plane surfaces (faces) which have the same chemical and physical properties and the same angular relationship to the elements of symmetry for that particular substance. It is, however, rare to find a perfectly developed crystal. Usually the crystal faces develop in a distorted fashion (see Fig. 12 a). This happens, for example, when there is a one-way or irregular transport of building particles while the crystal is growing in the melt. Or the growing crystals may interfere with each other so they are poorly developed. Thus a fluorite cube may develop into a prism-like form with a square or even a rectangular base. The faces, however, remain at right angles to each other. The prismatic faces of quartz may be of different sizes but they will always intersect at angles of 60°.

It was the Danish scientist Niels Stensen (Nicolaus Steno) who discovered, in 1669, that the angles between faces are constant in all crystals of an individual mineral, irrespective of the size or uneven development of the crystal. His *Law of Constancy of Interfacial Angles* states that the angle of the edges formed by adjacent or corresponding faces are constant for all crystals of the same chemical composition in the same temperature and pressure. This fact should be remembered when crystals are being classified by their form, which may be deceptive at first sight.

Although all crystals of a particular mineral must display the same assemblage of symmetry elements, this does not mean that they all look alike; they may show a range of crystal shapes depending on which crystal forms — singly or in combination — are developed. For example, the cube (six faces), the octahedron (eight faces) and the rhombic dodecahedron (twelve faces) are different forms displayed by crystals with cubic symmetry.

Some crystals (for example, those with cubic symmetry) are bounded by *like* faces — they all have the same properties. Faces with different properties are described as *unlike.* A crystal form made up entirely of like (isometric) faces is termed *simple* (the cube and octahedron). Such forms totally enclose a volume of space and can form solid crystals by themselves — they are described as *closed.* Other forms are described as *open* because they have too few faces to enclose a volume of space and so can form solid crystals only when they combine with other forms, which may be other open forms or closed ones.

Many different names have been given to crystal faces and forms. Some of the

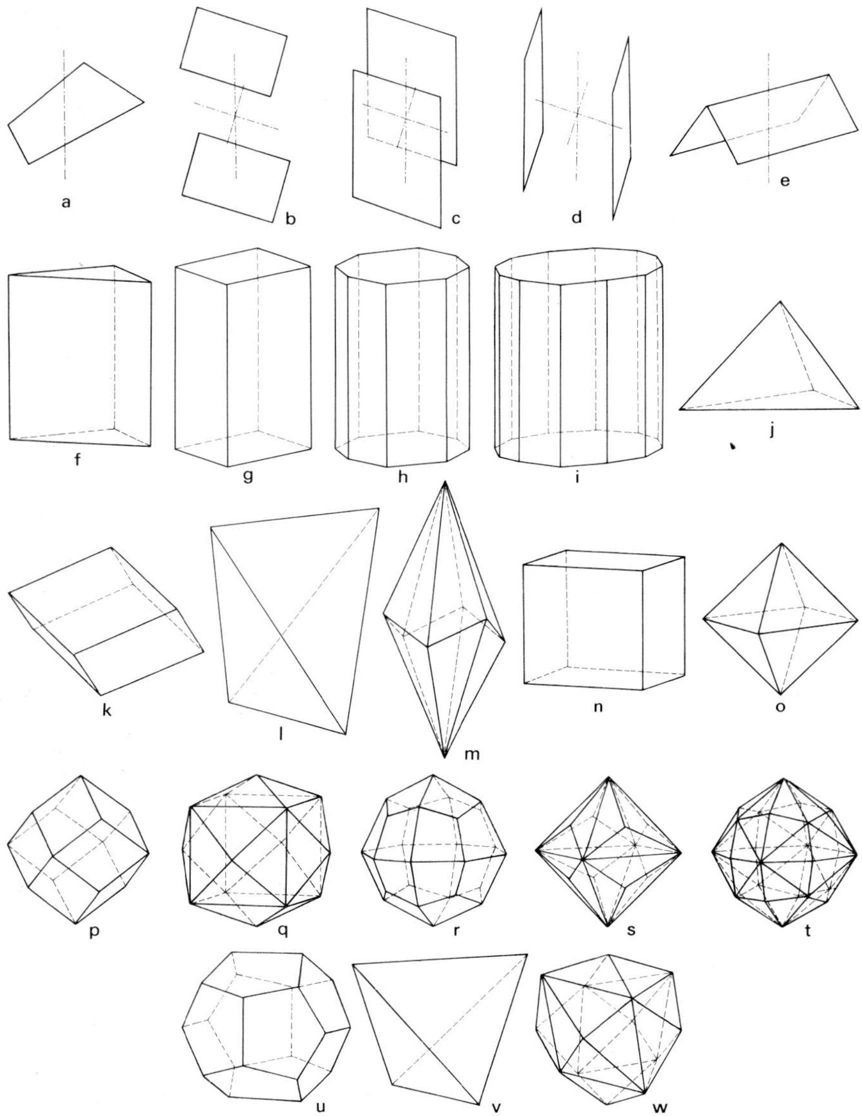

Fig. 8 Some common crystal forms: (a) pedion; (b) basal pinacoid; (c) front-and-back pinacoid; (d) right-and-left pinacoid; (e) dome; (f) trigonal prism; (g) tetragonal prism; (h) ditetragonal prism; (i) dihexagonal prism; (j) trigonal pyramid; (k) rhombohedron; (l) bisphenoid; (m) scalenohedron; (n) cube; (o) octahedron; (p) rhombic dodecahedron; (q) tetrahexahedron; (r) trapezohedron or icositetrahedron; (s) trisoctahedron; (t) hexoctahedron; (u) pentagonal dodecahedron or pyritohedron; (v) tetrahedron; (w) hexatetrahedron.

commonest ones are shown in Fig. 8. Each form in the cubic system is closed and has been given a special name (see below). General names are used for forms in the other crystal systems. The most important of these are:

Pedion A form with only 1 face (Fig. 8a).

Pinacoid A form with 2 parallel, not intersecting faces. This form (and the pedion) may have any orientation with respect to the chosen crystallographic axis (Fig. 8 b, c, d). The faces forming the top and bottom of a crystal are referred to as *basal pinacoids*; these often terminate the faces of a prism.

Dome A form with 2 intersecting faces which cut the vertical axis and one horizontal axis and are parallel to the other horizontal axis (Fig. 8 e).

Prism A form with 3, 4, 6, 8 or 12 intersecting faces which are parallel to the vertical axis and cut the horizontal axes (Fig. 8 f, g, h, i and Fig. 9). This is one of the commonest forms.

Pyramid A form with 3, 4, 6, 8 or 12 nonparallel triangular faces that meet at a point; each face cuts all the axes (Fig. 8 j and Fig. 9).

All the above forms are open. Those below are closed:

Bipyramid A form with 6, 8, 12, 16 or 24 faces consisting of two pyramids on opposite side of the horizontal plane, each half being a mirror image of the other (Fig. 9).

Rhombohedron A set of 3 pyramidal faces above and 3 below which are not mirror images of each other — the intersecting edges are not at right angles (Fig. 8 k). This form is found only on crystals of the trigonal (rhombohedral) system.

Sphenoid A double wedge-shaped form of 2 faces (Fig. 7 b).

Bisphenoid A form with 4 faces consisting of two sphenoids on opposite sides of the horizontal plane, each half being a mirror image of the other (Fig. 8 l).

Scalenohedron A form with 8 (tetragonal) or 12 (hexagonal) faces, each a scalene triangle when perfectly developed; each face cuts the vertical and horizontal axes at unequal distances. The faces are grouped in symmetrical pairs (Fig. 8 m).

Trapezohedron A form with 6, 8 or 12 faces, each a trapezium when perfectly developed; 3, 4 or 6 faces above and the same number below the horizontal plane. (There is also an isometric trapezohedron — see below.)

The special forms, all closed, peculiar to the cubic system, include:

Cube or *hexahedron* A form with 6 square faces which cut one axis and are parallel to the other two (Fig. 8 n).

Octahedron A form with 8 faces, each an equilateral triangle; each face cuts all three axes at equal distances (Fig. 8 o).

Dodecahedron or *rhombic dodecahedron* A form with 12 faces, each rhomb- or lozenge-shaped; each face cuts two axes at equal distances and is parallel to the third (Fig. 8 p).

Tetrahexahedron or *four-faced cube* A form with 24 faces, each an isosceles triangle; each face is parallel to one axis and cuts the other two at unequal distances (Fig. 8 q).

Trapezohedron or *icositetrahedron* A form with 24 faces, each a trapezoid; each face cuts two axes at equal distances and the third at a smaller distance (Fig. 8 r).

Trisoctahedron A form with 24 faces, each an isosceles triangle; each face cuts two axes at an equal distance, and the third at a greater distance (Fig. 8 s).

Hexoctahedron A form with 48 faces, each a scalene triangle; each face cuts the three axes at unequal distances (Fig. 8 t).

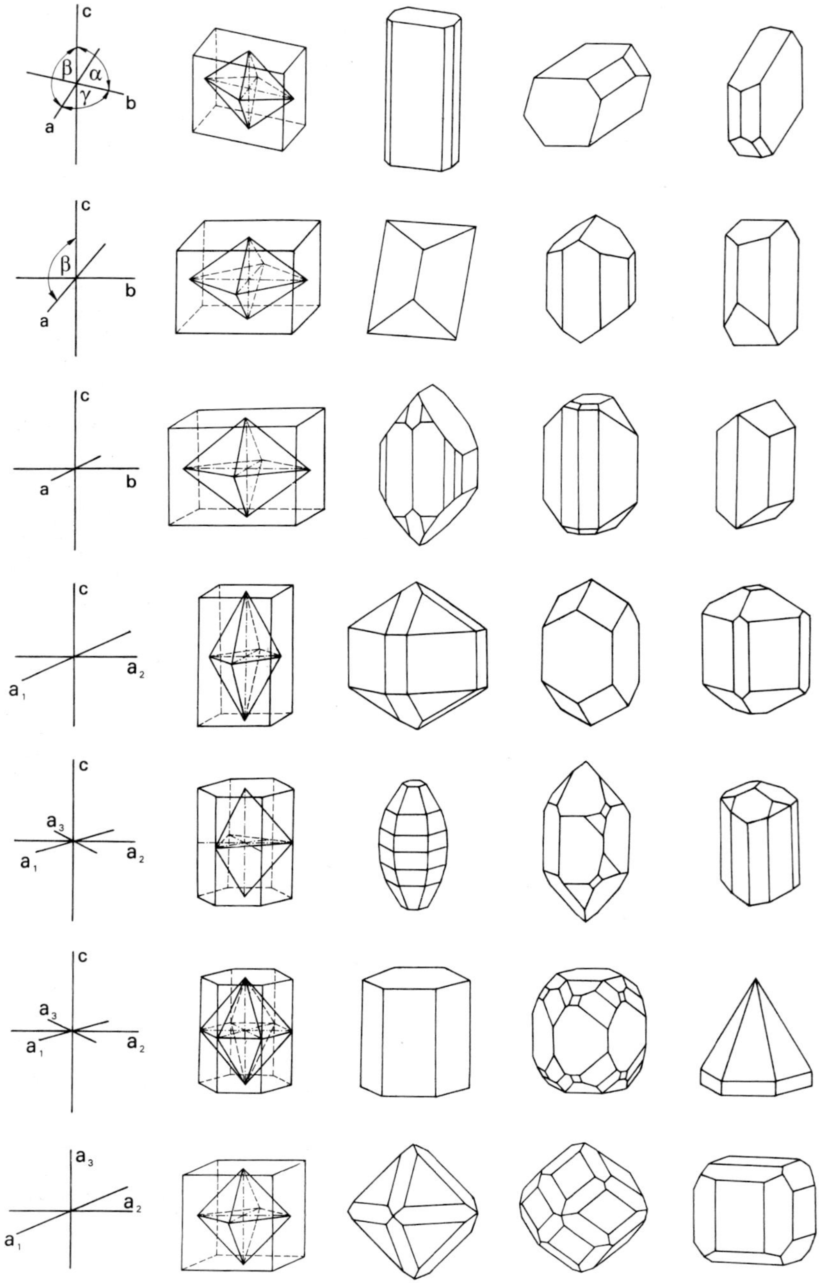
c
β
α
γ
b
a
c
β
b
a
c
a
b
c
a_2
a_1
c
a_3
a_1
a_2
c
a_3
a_1
a_2
a_3
a_2
a_1

Pentagonal dodecahedron or *pyritohedron* A form with 12 pentagonal faces; each face cuts two axes at different distances and is parallel to the third (Fig. 8 u).

Tetrahedron A form with 4 faces, each an equilateral triangle; each face cuts the axes at equal distances (Fig. 8 v).

Tristetrahedron A form with 12 faces which correspond to half of those of a trapezohedron.

Hexatetrahedron A form with 24 faces which correspond to half of those of the hexoctahedron (Fig. 8 w).

The crystal systems

According to the possible combinations of the elements of symmetry, crystals are divided into 32 *crystal classes:* classes with similar symmetry are grouped into seven *crystal systems.* Crystals are also classified in terms of three or four auxiliary and imaginary lines of reference called *crystallographic axes,* which pass through the centre of the crystal. Generally the crystallographic axes are parallel to the main edges of the crystal and mostly they correspond to the directions of the main axes of symmetry. Crystals are allocated to the systems according to the number of these axes, their length and the angles between them (Fig. 9).

There is a conventional notation for the lettering and order of the crystallographic axes. In the most general case (triclinic crystals) — where all three axes are of unequal length and none of the axes is at right angles to any other — the crystallographic axis which is taken as the vertical axis is called *c,* that running from right to left is *b,* and that running from front to back is *a.* One end of each axis is positive and the other end negative. The angle between $+a$ and $+b$ is called γ, that between $+b$ and $+c$ is called α, and that between $+c$ and $+a$ is called β. If the two (or three) horizontal axes are equal in length they are called *a* and the third (vertical) axis is *c.* If all the axes are equal in length — they are interchangeable — they are all called *a.*

Only the most characteristic crystallographic elements are used in the following description of the seven crystal systems.

1. **Triclinic system.** Crystals have either only a centre of symmetry or are entirely asymmetric. There are no axes or planes of symmetry. There are three crystallographic axes (*a, b, c*) of unequal length, all at oblique angles to each other. The angles between the axes are called α, β and γ. Crystal forms include the pinacoid (2 faces) and pedion (1 asymmetric face only).
Examples: albite and other plagioclase feldspars, axinite, kyanite, microcline, rhodonite, turquoise.

Fig. 9 Crystallographic axes, pinacoidal, prismatic and pyramidal (cubic and octahedral) forms, and representative minerals of the seven crystal systems.
Triclinic system: kyanite (five pinacoids); axinite (five pinacoids); albite (six pinacoids).
Monoclinic system: titanite (two pinacoids, one prism); augite (two pinacoids, two prisms); orthoclase feldspar (three pinacoids, one prism).
Orthorhombic system: olivine (five prisms, one pinacoid, one bipyramid); topaz (one bipyramid, three prisms, basal pinacoid); aragonite (two prisms, one pinacoid).
Tetragonal system: cassiterite (two bipyramids, two prisms); zircon (one bipyramid, one prism); vesuvianite (one bipyramid, two prisms, basal pinacoid).
Trigonal system: corundum (three bipyramids, basal pinacoid); quartz (one hexagonal prism, two rhombohedrons, one trigonal bipyramid, one trapezohedron; right); tourmaline (two prisms, two upper trigonal pyramids; two lower trigonal pyramids; not seen in Fig).
Hexagonal system: beryl (one prism, basal pinacoid); apatite (four bipyramids, one prism, basal pinacoid); zincite (one pyramid, one prism, one pedion; not seen in Fig.).
Cubic system: spinel (octahedron, rhombic dodecahedron); garnet (rhombic dodecahedron, icositetrahedron); pyrite (cube, pentagonal dodecahedron).

2. **Monoclinic system.** Crystals are symmetric about one plane of symmetry, or about one twofold axis, or a combination of both; in the last case, the twofold axis is always at right angles to the plane of symmetry and is orientated in the right-to-left direction (Fig. 7d). There are three crystallographic axes (*a, b, c*) of unequal length, two of which intersect at an oblique angle (β); the third (*b*) is at right angles to the other two. Crystal forms include the prism (4 faces), pinacoid (2 faces), dome and sphenoid (2 faces) and pedion.
Examples: augite, azurite, brazilianite, euclase, gypsum, jadeite, lazulite, nephrite, orthoclase feldspars, serpentine, spodumene, titanite.

3. **Orthorhombic system.** Crystals have combinations of three planes of symmetry, which are at right angles to each other, and three twofold axes placed at the point of intersection of the planes, or they are symmetric about two unequal planes of symmetry with one twofold axis at intersection of both or three twofold axes which are at right angles to each other. There are three crystallographic axes (*a, b, c*) of unequal lengths at right angles to each other. Crystal forms can include the rhombic bipyramid (8 faces), prism (4 faces), rhombic pyramid (4 faces), bisphenoid (4 faces), dome, pinacoid and pedion according to possible combinations of the elements of symmetry.
Examples: andalusite, aragonite, chrysoberyl, cordierite, danburite, kornerupine, marcasite, natrolite, olivine, prehnite, sillimanite, staurolite, thomsonite, topaz, variscite, zoisite.

4. **Tetragonal system.** Crystals have one fourfold axis of symmetry which corresponds to the vertical crystallographic axis *c* (without or with the other possible combinations of the elements of symmetry — plane of symmetry, twofold axis and centre of symmetry). There are two horizontal crystallographic axes (a_1, a_2) of equal length at right angles to each other, and a third (principal) vertical axis (*c*), which is either shorter or longer than the other two and is at right angles to them. Crystal forms include the ditetragonal bipyramid (16 faces), tetragonal bipyramid (8 faces), ditetragonal prism (8 faces parallel to *c* axis), tetragonal prism (4 faces parallel to axis *c*), basal pinacoid and some other rare forms.
Examples: cassiterite, rutile, vesuvianite, wardite, zircon.

5. **Trigonal (rhombohedral) system.** There are four crystallographic axes (a_1, a_2, a_3, *c*) arranged as in the hexagonal system, but the symmetry of crystals in the trigonal system is lower than that of hexagonal crystals, the principal *c* axis having only a threefold (not sixfold) symmetry. There are also combinations with other elements of symmetry — plane of symmetry, twofold axis and centre of symmetry. The commonest crystal form is the rhombohedron (6 faces) which looks like a cube that has been compressed along one of the diagonal threefold axes. Other forms include the prism, pyramid and bipyramid, trigonal trapezohedron (6 faces), ditrigonal scalenohedron (12 faces), basal pinacoid and pedion (in some cases).
Examples: benitoite, calcite (Iceland spar), corundum, dioptase, haematite, phenakite, quartz, rhodochrosite, smithsonite, tourmaline.

6. **Hexagonal system.** Crystals have a sixfold axis of symmetry which corresponds to the vertical crystallographic axis *c* and other possible combinations of the elements of symmetry — plane of symmetry, twofold axis and centre of symmetry. There are four crystallographic axes (a_1, a_2, a_3, *c*), three of which are of equal length, are horizontal and intersect at 60° ; the fourth (principal) axis is at right angles to the others and may be either longer or shorter than them. Common forms include the hexagonal and dihexagonal prisms (6 and 12 faces parallel to *c* axis), pyramids (6 and 12 faces) and bipyramids (12 and 24 faces), hexagonal trapezohedron (12 faces), basal pinacoid or pedion (in some cases).
Examples: apatite, beryl, zincite.

7. **Cubic (isometric) system.** Crystals have characteristic four threefold axes of symmetry and other possible combinations of the elements of symmetry. There are three

Fig. 10 Characteristic striation of (a) pyrite, (b) quartz and (c) tourmaline.

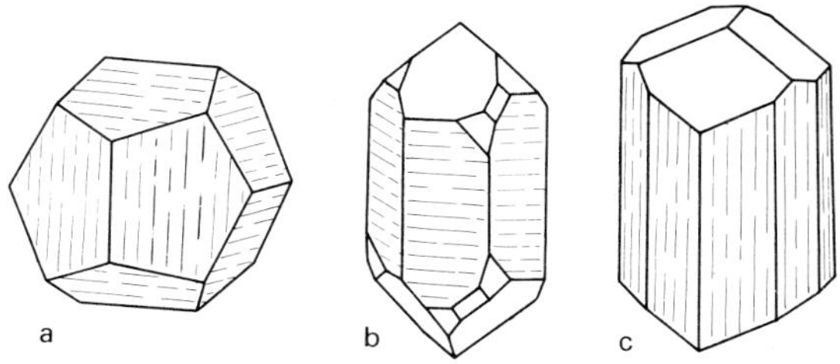

crystallographic axes (a_1, a_2, a_3) of equal length which intersect at right angles. Common forms include the cube (6 faces), octahedron (8 faces), rhombic dodecahedron (12 faces), icositetrahedron or cubic trapezohedron, trisoctahedron and tetrahexahedron (each with 24 faces), the hexoctahedron (48 faces) and some others, for example, pentagonal dodecahedron or pyritohedron (12 faces), tetrahedron (4 faces) and hexatetrahedron (24 faces).
Examples: cuprite, diamond, fluorite, garnet, lazurite, sphalerite, spinel.

The thread-like growth lines or *striations* on like faces can help to establish the orientation of a misshapen crystal and may also aid in identification (Fig. 10). The striations of pyrite, tourmaline, quartz and topaz are very characteristic: the prismatic faces of topaz are vertically striated, those of quartz are horizontally striated. In a true cube all six faces should show the same markings. Sometimes during rapid crystallization skeletal crystals are formed. The crystal grows more rapidly on the edges than in the middle of the faces and the faces thus become step-like, as can be seen, for example, in some fluorite varieties and garnets.

Crystal habit

The relative width, length and the number of faces determine a crystal's overall shape or *habit*. This can be affected, as we have seen, by the conditions of crystallization and also by the presence of impurities in the solidifying melt. A particular habit may thus be characteristic of crystals from a certain locality.

Many terms — mostly self-explanatory — are used to describe a crystal's habit. A crystal is described as *prismatic* if it is markedly longer in one direction than in the other two. More specifically such a habit is termed:

Acicular — needle-like (the crystal inclusions in rutilated quartz or Venus'hair stone)

Barrel-shaped (Corundum)

Bladed — with thin edges (actinolite)

Columnar (beryl, tourmaline)

Fibrous — fine strand-like (serpentine)

The *lamellar* habit refers to a crystal that is much shorter in one direction than in the other two. Such crystals can be called:

Tabular — thick crystals (kyanite, zoisite)

Platy — thin crystals (some haematite varieties)

Micaceous — sheet-like crystals that easily split apart (micas)

Foliated — the thin sheets or lamellae may be folded and distorted,

In crystals belonging to the cubic system all the faces are equally developed — they are *isometric*.

Fig. 11 Amethyst crystals in an agate geode (Brazil). 100 × 75 mm.

Growths and twin crystals

Crystals of the same mineral often grow associated in groups. These growths may be irregular groupings of crystals of one mineral growing from a common base. Even when joined at the base, the crystals are otherwise perfectly bounded by faces. When grouped in clusters, such crystals are called *druses*. A special type of druse is the *geode* (Fig. 11), the crystal-lined cavities found in amygdaloidal rocks. More regular associations of crystals of the same mineral are seen as *parallel growths*. In these growths, the edges and faces of the crystals have the same parallel orientations.

When two or more crystals grow together symmetrically — in other words, they share some crystallographic direction or plane but other parts are in a reversed position — they are *twins*. Usually twin crystals differ from single crystals in having re-entrant angles (interior angles greater than 180°) at some edges, but there are twins with no re-entrant angles as, for example, in quartz (Fig. 12 b). Twins have either their symmetrical parts in contact (*contact twins*) or the parts grow out of one another — they twin about an axis instead of a plane (*interpenetrant twins*). An example of the latter is the cross-shaped twins of staurolite and interpenetrated cubes of fluorite (Fig. 13). Repeated twinning can lead to *trillings, fourlings, sixlings*, and so on. If the repeated twinning is in a parallel plane it is described as *polysynthetic*, or *lamellar*, because it has the appearance of thin plates. When the twin-plane is not parallel, the growth becomes curved. This type of repeated twinning is called *cyclic*.

The above types of growths are made up of crystals of the same mineral, and they are therefore described as *homogeneous*. Growths of crystals of two or more minerals are termed *heterogeneous*. The regular growth of two minerals, which may even belong

Fig. 12(a) Distorted (misshapen) quartz crystals. (b) Left-handed and right-handed quartz distinguished according to the position of the trigonal trapezohedron (dotted faces). (c) Quartz twinnings (left to right: Dauphiné twin, Brazil twin and Japan twin) with typical striation on the prism faces.

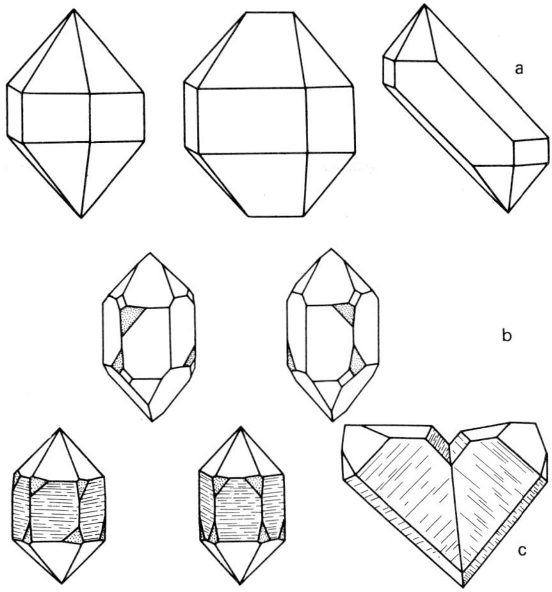

to different crystal systems, is called *epitaxis*. Such epitaxial growths are oriented along structural planes that have similar linear and angular dimensions in both minerals. Epitaxial growths of quartz and feldspars are quite common; those of kyanite and staurolite, topaz and garnet, and rutile and haematite are rarer.

Aggregates

If many crystals grow simultaneously in a confined space, the result is a clump or *crystalline aggregate* of interlocked crystal grains without crystal forms. The appearance of these aggregates is very variable and many terms are used to describe them. Their texture may be *granular* (fine-, medium- or coarse-grained), *earthy, compact* or *massive* (the individual crystal grains cannot be seen with the naked eye), *columnar* (Fig. 14), *fibrous, lamellar,* and so on. Then the arrangement of the crystal individuals within the aggregate may be *banded, cockscomb* (fan-like), *reticulated* (net-like), *radially divergent* (the crystals are arranged round a central point — Fig. 15). The overall

Fig. 13 Twin crystals: (a) fluorite (interpenetrant twin), (b) gypsum, (c) cassiterite (contact twin).

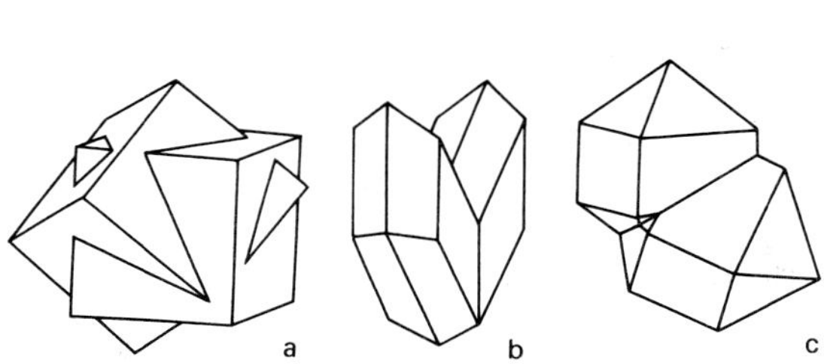

Fig. 14 A columnar aggregate of topaz, also known as pycnite (Altenberg, GDR). 120 × 80 mm.

Fig. 15 Star quartz, an example of a radially concentric aggregate (Peřimov, Czechoslovakia). 80 × 80 mm.

shape of the crystalline aggregate can be *reniform* (kidney-shaped) or *botryoidal* (resembling a bunch of grapes). When minerals are found in detached masses they are described as *concretionary* or *nodular*. Their shape may be spherical (as in spheroids), ellipsoidal or irregular. The typical shape is very often *stalactitic*. *Mammillary* is the term applied to large spheroids intersecting one another to give a gently rounded shape to the aggregate. *Spherulites* (or spherules) are rounded aggregates of very fine crystals radiating from a common centre. They may also be concentrically banded or layered. Small spherulitic growths resembling fish roe are described as *oolitic*; aggregates with larger spherulites are called *pisolitic* (pea-like).

In rock fissures one finds *stellate* (star-like) and *dendritic* (tree-like or moss-like) aggregates of crystals. The term dendritic is also often applied to inclusions of iron and manganese oxides and hydroxides in, for example, agate.

Remember that any grain of an aggregate, whether developed irregularly in shape and size or a mere chip, splinter or fragment, still remains a crystal with a homogeneous internal structure.

Cryptocrystalline and amorphous minerals

A few materials, such as natural volcanic glass (obsidian), natural silica glass (lechatelierite), opal and amber, have neither a regular structural arrangement nor characteristic shape, and their properties are the same in all directions. They are *amorphous*. They have an internal structure of sorts, but their atoms and molecules are not arranged in space lattices. For instance, silica glass and some opals contain silicon tetrahedra $(SiO_4)^{4-}$; these coordination groups of four oxygens around each silicon atom are linked irregularly. If the growth of amorphous minerals is unhindered they become spherical or reniform in shape; their habit is described as *massive*.

Amorphous minerals are not in a state of equilibrium and most will crystallize in time. This 'ageing' process is usually slow, but there may be a spontaneous transformation into the so-called *cryptocrystalline* state and then into a *microcrystalline*, finely fibrous, layered or radially divergent aggregate. Chalcedony is usually cryptocrystalline — it outwardly resembles an amorphous substance, yet retains an inner crystalline structure. Some obsidians also contain extremely small crystals called *crystallites*, which form submicroscopic clusters and are the cause of the silky chatoyancy of the stone.

Cryptocrystalline substances are slightly porous, which means that minerals such as agates and chalcedony can easily be stained.

Inclusions in crystals

Inclusions are macroscopic and microscopic imperfections of the crystal homogeneity (Fig. 16). They may be either of a single (*phase*) kind — a solid, liquid or gas — or mixed (*twophase* inclusions). Inclusions are usually remnants of the melt in which the crystal formed. Twophase (gas-liquid) inclusions are quite common in smoky quartz and rock crystal, and in many other minerals. The cavities are usually spherical or oval-shaped. Cloudiness in amber is caused by microscopic air bubbles.

Crystals may also contain inclusions of other minerals that crystallized earlier and were imperfectly absorbed by the melt, or they are epitaxial intergrowths. Thus, zircon crystals are found in some cordierites and pyropes, rutile in olivine and garnet, and spinel may occur in diamond. These ingrowths are usually typical for certain localities and are important aids in identification.

Pseudomorphs

Some minerals assume a crystal form that is not their own — they 'copy' the form of

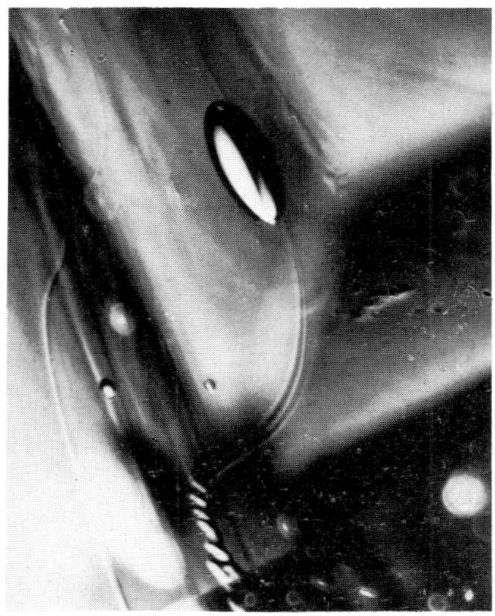

Fig. 16 Inclusions: (left) zircon crystal in almandine garnet, (right) gaseous inclusion in moldavite. × 80.

another mineral. Such 'crystals' — called *pseudomorphs* — have either partially or totally replaced the original mineral. There are several types of pseudomorph. There can be chemical alterations of one mineral to another, but the original form is retained. For example, pyrite may alter into limonite or goethite, olivine often alters into serpentine and azurite into malachite. Then the crystals of one mineral may form a coating or incrustation on the crystals of another. Later the first mineral is removed, leaving behind a mould or *negative pseudomorph.* This in turn may be filled by another mineral unrelated to the first one. Of more interest to the gemmologist is the conversion of one mineral polymorph to another. There is a change in crystal structure but not in the crystal form or chemical composition; for example, graphite can 'take after' diamond, and calcite after aragonite. These pseudomorphs are called *paramorphs.*

Optical properties of gemstones

Some optical properties of gemstones are discernible by the unaided eye but others can be determined only with the help of various instruments. The optical properties of minerals stem from the manner in which the mineral affects the light that falls on it and is transmitted by it. Those light rays that are reflected back determine the lustre and the colour of the mineral in reflected light; the rays that pass through the mineral determine the degree of transparency. Optical properties of minerals are a great help in identification and some can even be determined in stones set in jewellery without any danger of damage to the stone.

Colour and streak

Thousands of years ago the blue colour of turquoise and lapis lazuli attracted the attention of prehistoric people and set gemstones apart from other minerals. For many gemstones colour is still their most striking property (Table 1). The rich colours of ruby, sapphire and emerald, for example, are particularly distinctive. But care must be taken in using colour for identification purposes. For one thing, the colours of minerals come in every conceivable hue; for another, some minerals (for example, quartz) come in many different coloured varieties. Even the same crystal of a mineral may show different colours if viewed in different directions.

Optically the colour of a mineral is not a single colour but a complex of individual components of the spectrum that are not absorbed by the stone but are transmitted by it. A colourless transparent mineral does not absorb any light as it passes through the stone. A mineral appears yellow if it absorbs the wavelengths at the violet end of the spectrum but transmits the other components. The colours of two minerals may appear identical to the naked eye, but are really composed of different wavelengths because the stones have absorbed different components; the transmitted 'mix' of wavelengths produces the same colour. This absorption of some wavelengths of white light is called *selective absorption.* The phenomenon can be studied with an instrument called a spectroscope, in which the wavelengths of light absorbed by a stone appear as dark bands. These bands, known as an *absorption spectrum,* are characteristic for each mineral and so can be used to distinguish gems of the same colour and synthetic stones from natural ones. The technique is discussed in more detail in the section on mineral identification (pp. 58-60).

Several factors contribute to the way a mineral absorbs and transmits the components of light and acquires its colour. A mineral's *true colour* depends on the stone's chemical composition; for example, malachite (copper carbonate) is coloured green by containing copper in its composition; rhodonite (manganese silicate) is given its pinky-red colour (when pure) by manganese. Minerals containing aluminium, potassium or calcium tend to be white or light-coloured; for example, aragonite (a form of calcium carbonate) is a white or grey stone. Complex minerals, such as spinel (magnesium

Table 1 Colours of the principal gemstones

Colourless Corundum (leucosapphire), danburite, diamond, diopside, euclase, feldspar (orthoclase), fluorite, natrolite, opal (hyalite), phenakite, quartz (rock crystal), rutile (synthetic), spinel (synthetic), spodumene, strontium titanate, topaz, tourmaline (achroite), yttroaluminate (YAG), zircon, Zirconia

White Aragonite, calcite (marble), chalcedony, gypsum (alabaster), ivory, opal, pearl, quartz, sepiolite, thomsonite

Yellow to orange Amber, apatite, aragonite, axinite, beryl (heliodor), brazilianite, calcite (marble), cassiterite, chalcedony, chrysoberyl, diamond, feldspar (orthoclase), fluorite, garnet (hessonite), jadeite, marcasite (brass yellow), opal, phenakite, pyrite (brass yellow), quartz (citrine), rutile (synthetic), smithsonite, spessartite, sphalerite, spinel, spodumene, titanite, topaz, yttroaluminate (YAG), vesuvianite, zircon

Pink and red Amber, andalusite, beryl (morganite), calcite (marble), cassiterite, coral, corundum (ruby, pink sapphire), cuprite, diamond, fluorite, garnet (pyrope, almandine), haematite, jasper, opal (fire opal), pearl, phenakite, quartz (rose quartz), rhodochrosite, rhodonite, rutile, smithsonite, spinel, spodumene, staurolite, topaz, tourmaline (rubellite), zircon, zoisite (thulite)

Violet Apatite, axinite, beryl, calcite (marble), charoite, corundum, dumortierite, fluorite, garnet (almandine), lepidolite, quartz (amethyst), spinel, spodumene, tourmaline, zircon

Blue Azurite, benitoite, beryl (aquamarine), chalcedony, cordierite, corundum (sapphire), diamond, euclase, fluorite, kyanite, lapis lazuli, lazulite, pearl, sillimanite, smithsonite, sodalite, spinel, topaz, tourmaline (indicolite), turquoise, vesuvianite, wardite, zircon, zoisite (tanzanite)

Green Agalmatolite, andalusite, apatite, beryl (emerald), calcite (marble), chalcedony (chrysoprase), chrysoberyl (alexandrite), chrysocolla, diamond, dioptase, diopside, feldspar (amazonite), fluorite, garnet (demantoid, uvarovite), jadeite, kornerupine, malachite, moldavite, nephrite, olivine (peridot), prehnite, serpentine, sillimanite, smithsonite, spodumene, titanite, topaz, tourmaline (verdelite), turquoise, variscite, vesuvianite, wardite, zircon

Brown Amber, andalusite, aragonite, axinite, calcite (marble), cassiterite, chalcedony, garnet (hessonite, spessartite), jasper, moldavite, obsidian, quartz (smoky quartz), rutile, sphalerite, staurolite, titanite, topaz, tourmaline (dravite), vesuvianite, zircon

Grey Calcite (marble), chalcedony, cordierite, diamond, feldspar (labradorite), obsidian, sillimanite

Black Agate (onyx), amber, calcite (marble), cannel, coral, diamond, garnet (andradite, melanite), haematite, jet, obsidian, opal, pearl, quartz (morion), tourmaline (schorl)

Multicoloured Agate (onyx), chrysoberyl (cymophane or cat's eye), crocidolite, feldspar (labradorite, sunstone), jasper, opal (moss opal, precious opal), quartz (cat's eye, tiger's eye), tourmaline aluminium oxide), are coloured by the main constituent in the admixture of elements.

Impurities in a mineral can also affect its colour. For example, carnelian is a translucent chalcedony tinted a reddish-brown colour by inclusions of the iron-rich mineral haematite. Another factor influencing colour is the bonding of the mineral's atoms in the crystal structure — different types of packing of the carbon atoms are responsible for the colourless nature of diamond and the black opacity of graphite. Some naturally coloured diamonds owe their colour to defects inside the crystal structure. In natural blue diamonds, for example, these colour-producing defects are caused by the presence of boron atoms in place of some of the carbon atoms. Distortion of the crystal structure can also cause a colour change in a mineral; for example, if heated, violet amethyst becomes yellow citrine and, if irradiated, rock crystal changes into smoky quartz. Several gemstones are in fact treated commercially in this way to improve or change their colour. (Some of the consequences of exposing gemstones to excessive temperatures are dealt with later in the book; see pp. 55-56.)

Note that a few minerals will change colour naturally in daylight; in time, the finest of emeralds may turn cloudy if exposed too much. Some minerals change their colour as illumination changes; alexandrite, for example, changes from a moss green to an emerald green in daylight and from a red to mauve in artificial light. Other ways that gemstones change colour are discussed under 'Sheen' and 'Pleochroism' (pp. 36 and 45).

On the basis of their colour minerals are described as idiochromatic, colourless or allochromatic:

1. *Idiochromatic* minerals always have the same colour or the colour varies only in shades; the colour is the intrinsic property of the mineral's chemical composition (malachite is always green, azurite and lazurite are always blue).

2. *Colourless* minerals in their chemically purest form lack colour altogether (diamond, rock crystal, leucosapphire).

3. *Allochromatic* minerals are basically colourless but are coloured by various impurities, such as mineral inclusions or traces of other elements. These chemicals, usually oxides of certain metals, are often scattered through the stone as minute impurities in such small amounts that they are not included in the chemical formula (some coloured varieties of quartz).

Idiochromatic minerals can be distinguished from allochromatic ones by the colour of their *streak* — the colour the specimen leaves behind when rubbed on a piece of roughened glass or unglazed porcelain, called a *streak-plate.* It is in fact the colour of finely pulverized mineral. The streak of a mineral is constant irrespective of colour variations. As a rule, idiochromatic minerals produce a coloured streak slightly lighter than the true colour of the stone. Allochromatic minerals generally produce one that is either white or greyish white, or possibly very slightly tinged.

Some minerals produce a streak quite different from the colour of their mass. This is particularly the case in minerals with a metallic lustre: for instance, yellow pyrite produces a yellowish black streak; black or brown cassiterite has a white or grey streak; and black haematite gives a red streak.

Sheen

Some minerals show special colour effects which are produced by the reflection of light rays from inner parts of the stone.

Chatoyancy, for example, is the 'cat's eye' effect caused by the reflection of light from parallel groups of mineral fibres or fibrous cavities inside a stone. This effect is seen in such stones as quartz tiger's eye and especially in the cymophane (cat's eye) variety of chrysoberyl as a wavy band of light at right angles to the direction of the fibres.

Asterism, or the star effect — rays of light extend in a starlike fashion across the rounded surface of a stone cut into the cabochon form — is caused by the reflection of light from fine particles arranged in certain crystallographic directions in some stones. Where there are three sets of such particles (for example, fibres) crossing at angles of

60° a six-pointed star is seen (some rubies and sapphires); where two sets intersect at 90° a four-pointed star is displayed (some garnets).

The beautiful play of rainbow colours — *iridescence* — seen in precious opal and the feldspar labradorite is produced by interference between light rays reflected from the surface and from within the stone. The two rays are parallel, but because one has travelled further it may be out of step, or out of phase with the other one. This can cause extinction of a particular wavelength, and the remaining components combine together to form a complementary colour, as in selective absorption.

If the rays are 'in phase' (crest corresponding to crest), there is reinforcement of a particular wavelength and this colour will be the predominant one in the reflected light. The phenomenon is seen especially well in precious opal. In this stone, the colours are caused by interference of light reflected from millions of closely packed microscopic spheres of amorphous silica. These spheres are all of the same size and are arranged in ordered rows. The rainbow effects are produced by a combination of interference and diffraction of light.

In common ('potch') opal the spheres vary in size and this lack of symmetry in their arrangement means that there is no diffraction or reinforcement of colour. The result is a milky-white sheen, with little or no play of colour. This subdued colour effect is sometimes called *opalescence,* but the term is also applied to the pearly iridescence seen in precious opal.

Labradorite displays a particular type of colour play, which is sometimes called *labradorescence.* It is a blue and green iridescence caused by the interference of light reflected from this plates of feldspar beneath the stone's surface.

The *schiller effect,* an almost metallic shimmering lustre seen in moonstone, is another form of iridescence, which is again caused by interference of light from thin plates of two sorts of feldspar, orthoclase and albite, arranged in parallel planes inside the stone.

Stones showing one or other of these different effects are usually cut in cabochon style to show the colour play to full advantage.

Transparency

The term transparency is used to describe the amount of light transmitted through a substance. A mineral is more transparent the more light passes through it. It is rarely a stable property; in most minerals it varies greatly according to colour, thickness of the stone, the presence of flaws and impurities, and so on.

A mineral is transparent if an object can be seen through it, as through glass (diamond, rock crystal). It is *semitransparent* if the outline of the object is blurred but still recognizable (moonstone). Impurities and inclusions can cause transparent minerals to lose some of their transparency and to become *translucent.* A translucent stone allows some light to pass through, but an object cannot be seen through it (chalcedony, jadeite). *Semitranslucent* stones transmit light only through the edges (turquoise). Translucent and semitranslucent stones may become transparent in thin section. The term *nontransparent* (or *nontranslucent*) is used as the next step to *opaque* minerals (pyrites), which allow no light to pass through, not even in thin section. A mineral that is both colourless and transparent is described as *lucid.*

Lustre

The characteristic brilliancy or *lustre* of transparent gemstones is produced by the reflection of incident light from the mineral's surface. The smoother the surface, the greater the intensity of the lustre. The property can thus be improved by cutting and polishing and because a higher degree of polishing can be achieved with hard stones, it follows that the intensity of lustre can be correlated with the degree of hardness of a mineral. Lustre is also affected by refractive index: minerals with high refractive indices (diamond, zircon and rutile) display the most intensive lustre known as *ada-*

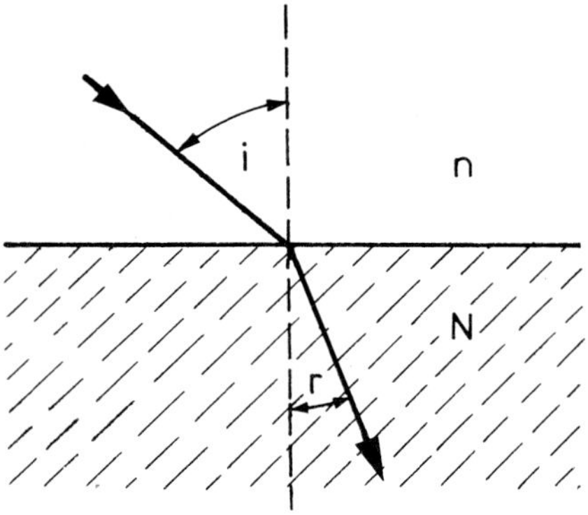

Fig. 17 Reflection of a light beam at the boundary of two optically different media. The angle *i* is the angle of incidence; *r* is the angle of refraction.

mantine (diamond-like). A few opaque gem materials (pyrite, haematite) have the high-intensity *metallic* lustre associated with metals such as gold and silver, but most gemstones have what is called a *vitreous* or glassy lustre. This type of lustre is found in transparent, semitransparent, translucent and opaque minerals. Its intensity varies from mineral to mineral; for example, the vitreous lustre of topaz is more intensive than that of quartz.

The weak types of lustre known as *resinous* (amber), *greasy* (serpentine) and *waxy* (turquoise) occur only rarely among gemstones. Some minerals display a *pearly* lustre on cleavage faces (rhodonite). Fibrous minerals, such as the quartz variety called tiger's eye, have a characteristic *silky* lustre. If there is little or no lustre the gem is described as *dull*.

Refractive index

A mineral acquires its lustre, as we have just seen, from light reflected off its surface. However, the greater part of the light ray passes into the stone. In this denser medium light travels more slowly than in air and it changes direction, or bends, so that the path it follows is closer to the *normal* (perpendicular) to the interface between air and the

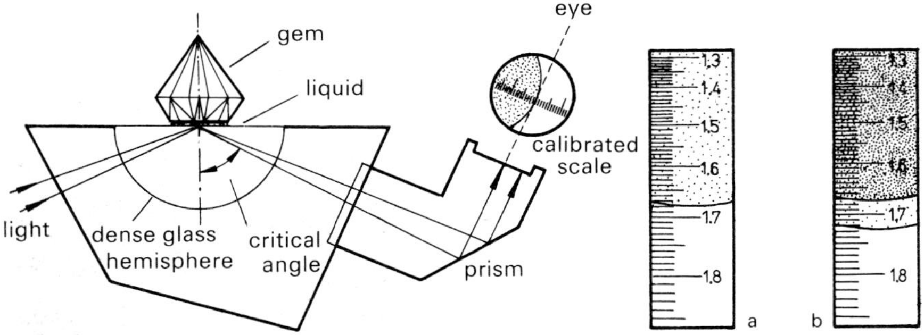

Fig. 18 Section through a refractometer with (a) a singly refractive gem and (b) a doubly refractive gem of the scale.

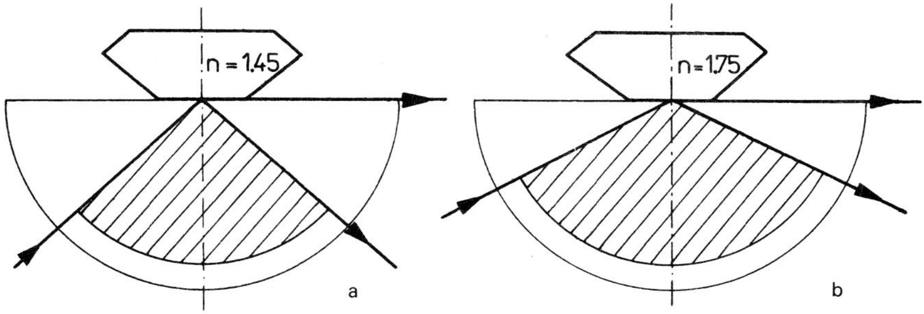

Fig. 19 Total reflection and critical angle in (a) opal, (b) spinel.

stone. The magnitude of this bending or *refraction* of light on entering the stone depends on the medium's refracting ability or *refractive index* (*n*). Most gemstones have a characteristic refractive index that can be measured with accuracy to three decimal places or more and for this reason it is a very important property for identification purposes.

The refractive index of a substance can be defined as a constant of the ratio of the sine of the angle of incidence (the angle between the incident ray and the normal) and the sine of the angle of refraction (the angle between the refracted ray and the normal) of light at the boundary between air and the substance under investigation (Fig. 17). This law of refraction, which the Dutch mathematician Willebrord Snell devised in 1621, is based on the transition of light from air into a medium of higher optical density. Since the speed of light in both media is different, the refractive index can also be expressed as the velocity of light in air divided by the velocity of light in the medium. Refractive indices are always equal to or greater than 1.00; for air $n = 1.00029$ (in this case related to vacuum); for opal $n = 1.45$; for zircon $n = 1.93$-1.99; and for diamond $n = 2.42$.

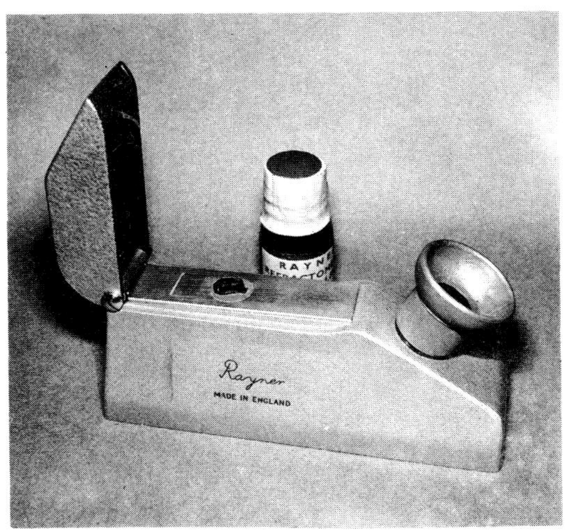

Fig. 20 The Rayner refractometer.

Amorphous minerals (such as obsidian and opal) and those that crystallize in the cubic system (diamond) produce only one refracted ray because light passes through them at the same speed in all directions (the symmetry of cubic crystals is of such a high order that the individual crystallographic directions are optically identical). These minerals thus have only one refractive index and are termed *isotropic*. But in minerals of the other six crystal systems, rays travel through the stone at different speeds in different directions. These *anisotropic* minerals thus have different refractive indices.

If all that needs to be known is whether a mineral is isotropic or anisotropic, this can be found with a polarizing microscope or *polariscope*. There are several methods for determining refractive indices. For direct measurements calibrated instruments called *refractometers* are used (Fig. 18). The principle is based on the total reflection of light from the contact area between the dense glass of known refractive index in the refractometer and the cut stone (Fig. 19). Between the two media is a contact fluid, again of known refractive index, which must be higher than the refractive index of the gem being studied and lower than the refractive index of the refractometer glass.

For cut stones there is a special gemmological refractometer available (Fig. 20), but this can be used only for perfectly smooth surfaces. The gem being tested is placed with one of its facets against the refractometer lens, which is a heavy glass prism or hemisphere. A drop of some refractive immersive liquid (oil) is put between them to exclude air and bring them into optical contact. Light from an external source, either natural or artificial, is directed by a mirror through the refractometer lens and against the flat facet of the stone. The portion of light that strikes at more than the critical angle is totally reflected and produces a band of light, the edge of which is read on a graduated scale and corresponds to the refractive index of the gem. For the most accurate measurement of refractive indices it is best to illuminate the refractometer with monochromatic light (light in one wavelength only, as distinct from daylight which is polychromatic), preferably a yellow sodium light source (wavelength 589.3 nm).

The standard refractometers are limited by the upper refractive index value of the refractometer glass, the highest reading possible being 1.8-1.9. Thus they cannot be used for four important gemstones — diamond, zircon, sphene and andradite garnet. Their brilliancy is too high and their critical angle too small for a reading and so for them a special lens of higher refractive index is used.

An indirect means of determining the refractive index of a gemstone is the immersion or dipping method. The stone under investigation is immersed in a liquid of known refractive index and the refractive indices of the mineral and liquid are compared. If the stone's refractive index approximates that of the liquid, the outline of the mineral is very indistinct, even under a microscope. Sets of immersion liquids are sold. They include:

(Water	1.33)	Iodobenzene	1.62
Acetone	1.36	Monobromonaphthalene	1.66
Carbon tetrachloride	1.46	Methylene iodide	1.74
Toluene	1.50	Methylene iodide saturated with sulphur*	1.78
Ethylene dibromide	1.54	Phenyldi-iodoarsine*	1.85
Clove oil	1.54	West's solution*	2.06
Bromoform	1.59		

(Caution: *Most of these chemicals should not be bought or used without advice from a qualified gemmologist.* Avoid skin contact and inhalation of vapour. On no account should any be swallowed. Those marked with an asterisk are expensive to buy and unpleasant to handle; they should be used only by experienced workers. In particular, phenyldi-iodoarsine causes blistering of the skin; it is very poisonous.)

If necessary, the immersion liquids can be mixed until the refractive indices of the stone and the fluid mixture are identical. The refractive index of the mixture is then measured with a refractometer. This is a useful method for determining the refractive

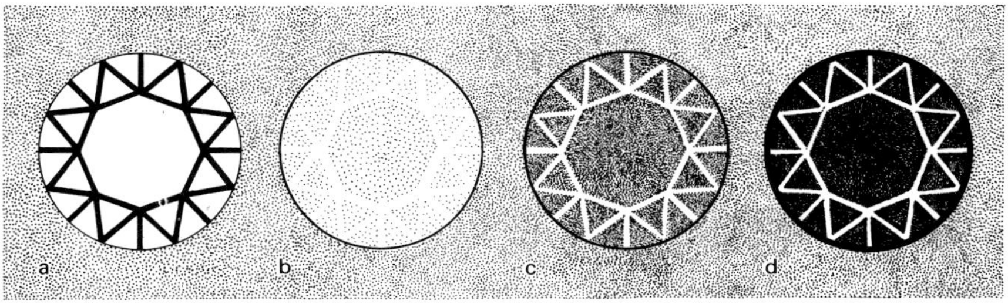

Fig. 21 Macroscopic immersion method for testing refractive index: (a) shadow image of a cut gemstone with a refractive index lower than that of the immersion fluid; (b) shadow image of a cut stone with refractive index almost equal to that of the immersion liquid; (c), (d) shadow images of cut stones with refractive indices higher than that of the immersion liquid.

indices of uncut or carved stones or several small stones set in a brooch. It should not, of course, be used for gemstones that are porous, such as opal and turquoise, or for those that might be soluble in the testing liquid.

Another technique especially suitable for determining the refractive index of cut gemstones is the immersion method with *shadow projection* (Fig. 21). A glass vessel filled with an immersion fluid of known refractive index is placed on a sheet of white paper. The stone is immersed, table facet down, in the liquid and it is then illuminated from above with intense light from a single overhead lamp. The shadow image is then observed. The general rule is that if the stone has a refractive index higher than that of the liquid, it will cast a dark-rimmed shadow on the paper below and the projected facet edges appear light. Stones with a refractive index lower than that of the immersion liquid show a bright outline and the facet edges appear as dark lines. When the refractive indices of the mineral and the immersion medium are identical or almost so, the inside facet edges disappear from the shadow image altogether and the outline proper becomes almost invisible.

Table 2 shows the range of refractive indices possessed by gemstones.

Double refraction (birefringence)

One of the manifestations of optical anisotropy is the phenomenon of *double refraction* or *birefringence,* which is particularly pronounced in a variety of calcite called Iceland spar, but it occurs to varying extents in all anisotropic minerals. (Singly refractive (isotropic) minerals — amorphous substances and those that crystallize in the cubic system — do not, of course, show the phenomenon.)

We have seen how in anisotropic substances light rays travel through the stone at different speeds in different crystal directions. When a beam of light enters an anisotropic mineral it splits into two refracted rays that pass through the stone at different speeds and are polarized — the waves of the refracted light vibrate at right angles to each other (Fig. 22). These two rays are called the *ordinary ray* and the *extraordinary ray.* Because they travel at different speeds the two rays are refracted differently so that an object or writing viewed through such a mineral is seen twice (Fig. 23).

These minerals are, however, not doubly refracting in all directions. There is either one (*uniaxial*) direction or two (*biaxial*) directions along which no double refraction occurs. These directions of single refraction (or isotropy) are called *optical axes* (Fig. 24). In uniaxial crystals, such as calcite, the ordinary ray travels with a constant

Table 2 Range of refractive indices of the principal gemstones

1.433	Fluorite	1.644-1.723	Dioptase
1.43-1.46	Opal	1.65-1.68	Sillimanite
1.48	Sodalite	1.655-1.909	Malachite
1.48-1.49	Natrolite	1.651-1.681	Spodumene
1.48-1.53	Obsidian	1.652-1.671	Euclase
1.488-1.503	Moldavite	1.654-1.667	Jadeite
1.5 (mean)	Chrysocolla, lapis lazuli	1.654-1.670	Phenakite
1.52-1.53	Gypsum (alabaster)	1.66 (mean)	Jet
1.52-1.66	Pearls	1.662-1.699	Olivine (peridot)
1.522-1.527	Orthoclase	1.665-1.682	Kornerupine
1.52-1.54	Thomsonite	1.674-1.699	Axinite
1.522-1.573	Cordierite	1.686-1.723	Dumortierite
1.53 (mean)	Agate, microcline, sepiolite	1.691-1.700	Zoisite
1.530-1.685	Aragonite	1.700-1.752	Vesuvianite
1.54 (mean)	Chalcedony	1.713-1.732	Kyanite
1.542 (mean)	Amber	1.713-1.760	Pyrope
1.542-1.549	Oligoclase	1.715-1.720	Spinel
1.544-1.553	Quartz	1.715-1.747	Rhodonite
1.55 (mean)	Lepidolite	1.730-1.838	Azurite
1.56 (mean)	Serpentine	1.738-1.745	Grossular
1.550-1.559	Charoite	1.739-1.792	Staurolite
1.55-1.59	Variscite	1.746-1.756	Chrysoberyl
1.56-1.57	Labradorite	1.757-1.804	Benitoite
1.57 (mean)	Agalmatolite	1.76-1.81	Almandine
	Beryl:		Corundum:
1.570-1.575	Aquamarine	1.760-1.768	Sapphire
1.579-1.585	Emerald	1.764-1.772	Ruby
1.580-1.590	Morganite	1.78-1.84	Zircon (low — metamict)
1.590-1.599	Wardite	1.79-1.81	Spessartite
1.599-1.641	Nephrite	1.83-1.87	Yttroaluminate (YAG)
1.600-1.820	Rhodochrosite	1.843-2.093	Titanite (sphene)
1.602-1.623	Brazilianite	1.85-1.89	Andradite
1.606-1.638	Topaz	1.87 (mean)	Uvarovite
1.61-1.64	Prehnite	1.923-2.015	Zircon
1.61-1.65	Turquoise	1.997-2.093	Cassiterite
1.612-1.638	Amblygonite	2.20	Cubic zirconium oxide (Zirconia)
1.615-1.654	Lazulite	2.368-2.371	Sphalerite
1.616-1.652	Tourmaline	2.41 (mean)	Strontium titanate (Fabulite)
1.621-1.849	Smithsonite	2.418 (mean)	Diamond
1.629-1.647	Andalusite	2.493-2.554	Anatase
1.630-1.636	Danburite	2.62-2.90	Rutile
1.634-1.640	Apatite	2.85 (mean)	Cuprite
		3.0 (mean)	Haematite

velocity regardless of this direction. It therefore has a fixed refractive index. However, the speed of the extraordinary ray varies according to the crystal direction. Its refractive index therefore varies. Along the optical axis, the extraordinary ray has the same speed as the ordinary ray, but at right angles to the optical axis its speed is faster or slower than that of the ordinary ray. Furthermore, the ordinary ray vibrates at right angles to the optical axis and the extraordinary ray vibrates in the same plane as the optical axis and at right angles to the direction of vibration of the ordinary ray. Tetra-

Fig. 22 Birefringence and polarization of light in an anisotropic crystal. A beam of parallel light rays falls on a crystal's face and, on entering the crystal, refracts into two polarized rays that vibrate at right angles to each other (e = extraordinary ray, o = ordinary ray).

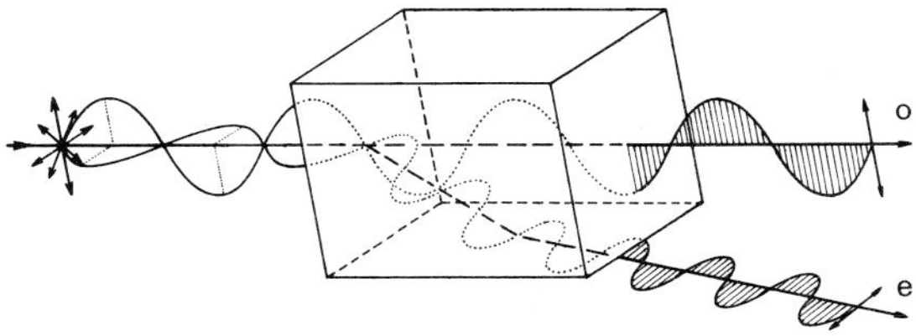

gonal, hexagonal and trigonal crystals are all uniaxial in having just these two directions of vibration. Their two refractive indices are designated ω for the ordinary (horizontally vibrating) ray and ε for the extraordinary (vertically vibrating) ray.

Biaxial minerals on the other hand have three refractive indices. The refractive indices of the two (extraordinary) refracted rays vary as the directions of the incident ray is changed. There are fast and slow directions of vibration at right angles and also a third direction, at right angles to the other two, along which the vibrations have an intermediate speed. These three directions of vibration, all at right angles to each other, give members of the remaining mineral groups — orthorhombic, monoclinic and triclinic crystals — three indices of refraction identified as α (fast), β (intermediate) and γ (slow).

When a doubly refractive gem is tested in a refractometer, the band of light produced ends in two parallel lines. These may move a little on the scale as the stone is turned; their extreme high and low readings correspond to the maximum and minimum values of the refractive index. The most strongly birefringent gems show, of course, the widest separation of the terminal lines.

The amount of birefringence shown by a gem can then be obtained simply by subtracting the lowest refractive index from the highest. This value is useful for identification purposes because some minerals show a characteristic high amount of birefringence (for example, zircon, sphene and rutile).

Special gemmological laboratories have instruments for the direct measurement of birefringence on orientated sections of crystals. Approximate values can be obtained with a polarizing microscope.

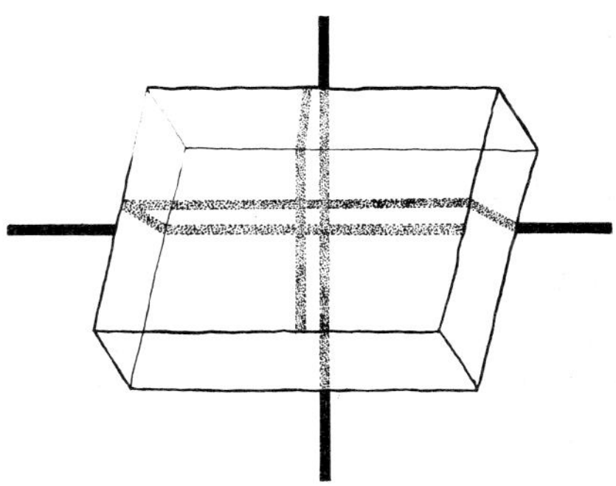

Fig. 23 Double image of a cross seen through a calcite rhombohedron.

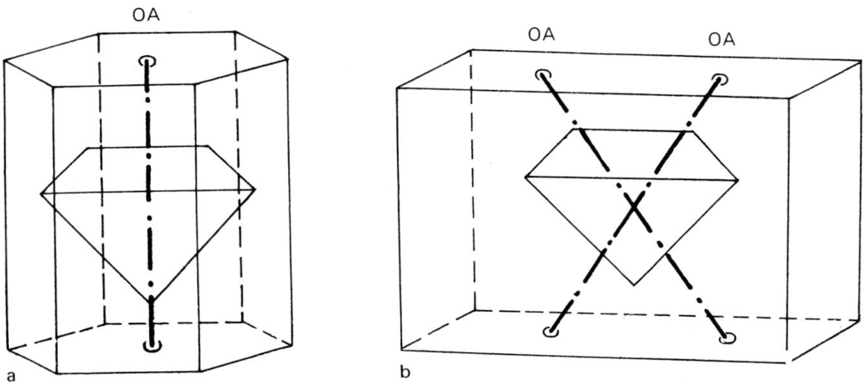

Fig. 24 Uniaxial (a) and biaxial (b) crystals. OA = optical axis.

Dispersion

The separation of white light into its component colours proves not only that light bends upon entering a crystal or cut stone, but also that each colour of the light spectrum is refracted by a different amount, as is shown in Fig. 25. This spread of colours is called *dispersion.*

The phenomenon is best illustrated by observing what happens when light enters a prism and splits into its spectral colours. It is also shown well on the edges of certain cut stones as rainbow-coloured flashes of colour called 'fire'. The red component in the light – with the longest wavelength – is refracted the least (it is farthest way from the normal) and the violet component – with the smallest wavelength – is refracted the most (it is nearest the normal). The value of the refractive index thus progressively increases from the red to the violet ends of the spectrum.

With a few exceptions dispersion in a mineral increases with the refractive index of the stones concerned. An exact value for dispersion can be obtained by subtracting the gem's refractive index for the red wavelength (the Fraunhofer B line = 686.7 nm) from that for the violet wavelength (G line = 430.8 nm). (The Fraunhofer lines are a series of thin dark vertical bands which can be seen crossing the continuous spectrum of

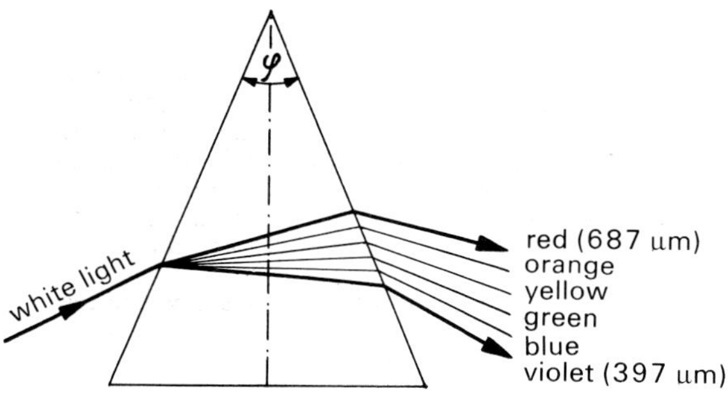

Fig. 25 Dispersion of a beam of white light into its spectral colours by a prism.

white light radiation by the sun. The lines are mainly caused by the absorption of certain wavelengths of light by the vapour of various elements in the chromosphere surrounding the sun. The most conspicuous of the absorption bands bear letters assigned to them by the German physicist J. Fraunhofer (1787-1826) — see Fig. 33.) In practice exact measurements of dispersion are not often used in mineral identification because there are simpler and more reliable methods of distinguishing one stone from another, but the characteristic 'fire' of certain cut stones can be a useful identification feature. The lapidary can enhance the effect by choosing appropriate cuts. Highly dispersive gemstones include sphalerite, sphene, diamond, rutile and zircon; quartz, fluorite, topaz, beryl and pure corundum have a low dispersion (see Table 3).

Table 3 Colour dispersion of the principal gemstones

Rutile	0.28	Olivine (peridot)	0.020
Strontium titanate (Fabulite)	0.20	Vesuvianite	0.019
Sphalerite	0.156	Corundum	0.018
Cassiterite	0.071	Cordierite	0.017
Cubic zirconium oxide		Tourmaline	0.017
(Zirconia)	0.066	Spodumene	0.017
Andradite (demantoid)	0.057	Andalusite	0.016
Titanite (sphene)	0.051	Euclase	0.016
Diamond	0.044	Chrysoberyl	0.015
Benitoite	0.040	Sillimanite	0.015
Zircon (not metamict)	0.039	Phenakite	0.015
Yttroaluminate (YAG)	0.028	Topaz	0.014
Spessartite	0.027	Beryl	0.014
Almandine	0.027	Quartz	0.013
Pyrope	0.022	Apatite	0.013
Dioptase	0.022	Feldspar	0.012
Spinel	0.020	Fluorite	0.007

The values are the differences between the refractive indices of gemstones for the B (red) line (686.7 nm) and the G (blue) line (430.8 nm) of the solar (Fraunhofer) spectrum. The dispersion is in some cases considerably different for the different rays in doubly refractive minerals.

Pleochroism

Pleochroism is the property by which the colour of some minerals varies according to the direction in which the stone is viewed. Minerals change colour in this way because they absorb different wavelengths of light in different crystal directions. When the mineral has two main colours it is described as *dichroid*; when three colours are produced, it is *trichroic*. Only anisotropic (doubly refracting) coloured minerals are *pleochroic* — but not those tinted by mechanical impurities. Thus, no colourless gems are dichroic, nor are singly refractive isotropic stones (amorphous substances and any mineral crystallizing in the cubic system).

The phenomenon of pleochroism is explained in terms of the directions in which the light rays vibrate as they pass through the stone. Dichroism is associated with coloured uniaxial stones in which there is differential absorption of the two polarized (ordinary and extraordinary) rays so the rays differ in colour when they emerge from the stone;

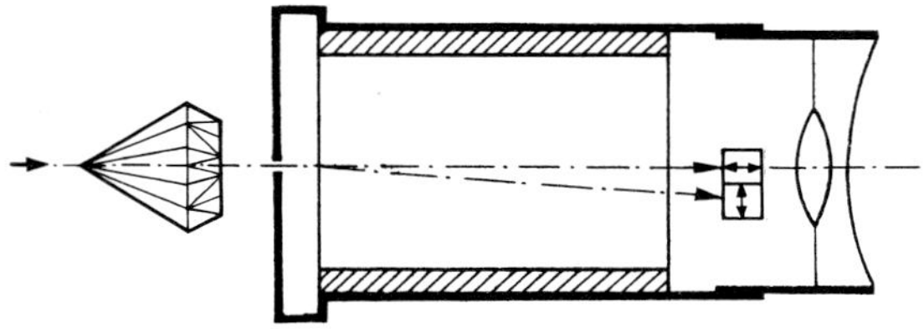

Fig. 26 Section through a dichroscope

trichroism is associated with coloured biaxial stones in which three rays corresponding to the three principal vibration directions are differentially absorbed.

Pleochroism can be a useful identifying feature, but only a few minerals — for example, cordierite, tourmaline, kunzite and some rubies and sapphires — display pleochroism sufficiently strongly for it to be seen with the naked eye when they are turned in various directions. In most cases the property can be observed only with a polarizing microscope or with a special instrument called a *dichroscope* that separates the emerging rays from the stone and enables the two colours (or two of the three colours) to be seen side by side.

The dichroscope (Fig. 26) consists of a short tube with a round opening at one end and a square opening at the other. In the instrument there is a piece (rhomb) of clear calcite (Iceland spar) and a magnifying lens is sometimes added to enlarge the image. Through the round hole the observer looks at a gem held beyond the square aperture. The strong doubly refractive power of the calcite rhomb presents this square to the viewer as if it were two squares side by side and it intensifies the original double refraction of the gem. Each of the two rays emerging from the gem is seen in a separate frame. Comparing the twin colours is thus simplified. The colours should change place slowly if the gem is rotated.

Gemstones are often cut in special ways to take advantage of the attractive quality of pleochroism. Among the more important gems, ruby can be unfailingly identified by its distinct two colours — yellowish red and purplish red — and thus distinguished from the isotropic red spinel, garnet and red glass. Likewise, blue sapphire can easily be distinguished from blue spinel and glass imitations, and emerald from demantoid, the green garnet.

Luminescence

When exposed to invisible ultraviolet light in the dark, some minerals will start emitting visible light of characteristic colour. This *fluorescence*, as the phenomenon is called, may continue after the existing radiation has been stopped. This 'afterglow', shown well by kunzite, is termed *phosphorescence*. Fluorescence is seen well in fluorite after which the phenomenon is named. Some varieties of fluorite have a purplish glow even in daylight. Both fluorescence and phosphorescence are combined under the general term *luminescence*.

Luminescence is caused by the ability of some minerals (and certain chemicals) to transform various kinds of absorbed energy into cold light. According to the kind of energy that excites the atoms, ions or molecules of the mineral into releasing this visible light, various types of luminescence are distinguished: *photoluminescence* is induced by electromagnetic radiations (fluorescence, phosphorescence and thermoluminescence); *triboluminescence* is induced by mechanical rubbing or crushing of crystals; *electroluminescence* is induced by an electric current; and *chemoluminescence* is induced by certain chemicals.

For diagnostic purposes in mineralogy, photoluminescence is the most important (see Table 4). The mineral emits light when irradiated intensively with ultraviolet rays, cathode rays, X-rays or gamma rays. The standard practice is to use ultraviolet light

Table 4 Luminescent properties of the principal gemstones (fluorescence colours under ultraviolet light)

Amber	Powder-blue 'bloom'
Apatite	Yellow, red and green orange
Alexandrite	Deep red
Aragonite	Pink red, yellow and greenish
Chrysoberyl	Yellow green
Diamond	Blue, green and yellow; rarely orange and red, most commonly blue (violet blue or 'lilac')
Emerald	Some are green
Fluorite	Violet, blue and yellow
Gypsum	Green, orange, yellow and blue
Hiddenite	Red yellow and lilac
Kunzite	Orange and yellow red
Opal	Red, bluish, yellowish and yellow green
Pearl	Sky blue
Ruby	Glowing red
Sapphire (blue, yellow)	Orange yellow, yellow, reddish blue and orange red
Spinel (red)	Glowing red
(blue)	Reddish
Topaz (red)	Brown yellow, yellowish and greenish
(yellow)	Orange yellow
Tourmaline (colourless)	Some are green blue
Turquoise	Green
Zircon (red)	Red brown and orange

emitted from a quartz-mercury electric discharge lamp combined with filters producing various wavelengths. For short-wave ultraviolet light the filters transmit wavelengths of between 200 and 300 nm; for long-wave ultraviolet light the emitted wavelengths are between 300 and 400 nm. The radiation emitted by the mineral always has a longer wavelength than that of the applied excitation, which means that visible luminescent effects are produced even if the input radiation has very short wavelengths.

It is important to note that luminescence and its colour are not always the same in an individual mineral. It has been discovered that although pure crystals of a mineral may not luminesce, they will start to do so if they contain inclusions or *activators* (for example, chrome oxide in ruby). The activators that cause luminescence and its colour are usually characteristic for certain localities, so photoluminescence can successfully be used to identify minerals from different localities, and it is a useful technique for distinguishing natural stones from synthetic ones.

Even gems already set in jewellery can be identified by means of this property. Recently the method has been put to good use in the mining industry. For example, all natural diamonds luminesce a chalky blue when exposed to X-rays and this characteristic forms the basis of an important separation technique in diamond mines, as you will see later in the section on gemstone mining.

Other physical properties of gemstones

Specific gravity

The specific gravity of a mineral is its weight compared with the weight of an identical volume of water at a temperature of 4 °C. The difference between specific gravity and density is – for practical purposes – that the first is relative density and is not

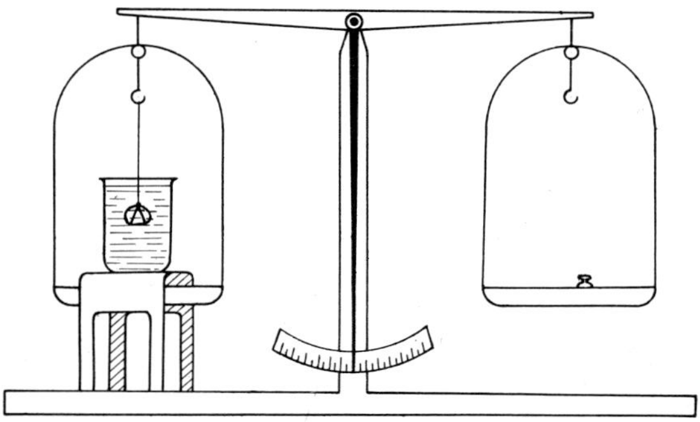

Fig. 27 Hydrostatic balance for measuring specific gravity.

expressed in units, whereas density is given not as a ratio but in terms of units of mass and volume in kilograms per cubic metre (kg per m^3); in practice, smaller units (g per cm^3) are used.

For the determination of specific gravity, a precise *hydrostatic balance* with a sensitivity of ± 0.0002 gram is used. The stone is first weighed in air (a). It is then suspended by a degreased thread or a very fine wire from one arm of the balance and immersed in distilled or boiled water contained in a beaker standing on a simple bridge made from wood or sheet metal placed above the weighpan. Bubbles of air sticking to the stone are removed by a fine paint brush and the stone is then weighed again (b). Neither the bridge nor the beaker must touch the weighpan (Fig. 27). The weight of the water displaced by the mineral ($a - b$) equals the volume of the stone. The specific gravity can then be determined according to the equation $a/(a - b)$.

Jewellers still use *Jolly's spring balance,* a hydrostatic balance which consists of a spring or a rubber band suspended vertically against a scale calibrated in millimetres. Attached to the lower end of the spring are two scale pans, one suspended below the other, the bottom pan always immersed in water up to a certain mark. A reading (a) on the scale at the bottom of the spring is taken; then a small specimen of the mineral is placed in the upper pan and a second reading (b) is obtained. The specimen is then transferred to the lower pan and a third reading (c) is taken. The difference between a and b is the weight of the mineral in air and that between b and c is the loss of weight in water, so the specific gravity = $(b - a)/(b - c)$. Work with this balance is quick and relatively accurate for very small specimens.

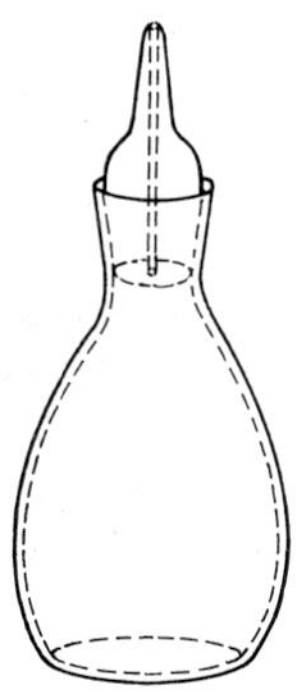

Fig. 28 Pycnometer

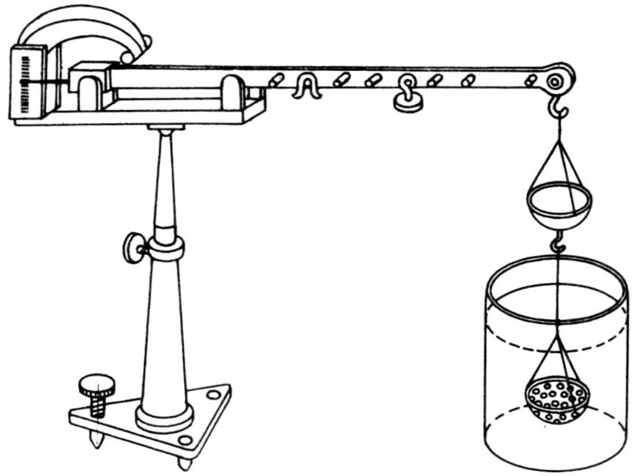

Fig. 29 The Mohr-Westphal balance.

Specific gravity can also be determined with a *pycnometer* or specific gravity bottle, especially for small fragments of minerals providing an average value is sufficient. The pycnometer (Fig. 28) is a thin-walled glass vessel of an exact volume with a narrow neck, which is closed with an elongated ground glass stopper with an internal capillary channel. The mineral is first weighed. The bottle is filled with distilled water. Then it and the mineral are weighed together. The mineral is immersed in the water and the bottle is weighed again. The specific gravity is determined by dividing the weight of the mineral by the weight of the water it displaces.

An alternative (but approximate) way of determining specific gravity involves the use of heavy liquids of known specific gravity, such as:

Bromoform	2.90
Methylene iodide	3.32
Kohlbach's solution (an aqueous solution of barium mercuric iodide)	3.58
Clerici's solution (an aqueous solution of thallium malonate and thallium formate)	4.15

Caution: The same safety precautions need to be applied to these heavy liquids as for those used in the measurement of refractive index – see p. 40. (Clerici's solution is both poisonous and corrosive.)

The mineral is compared with such a set of heavy liquids by immersing it in each liquid in turn. If the mineral sinks to the bottom it is heavier than the liquid; if it rises to the surface it is lighter; and if it remains floating freely, the stone and the liquid have the same specific gravity.

For a more accurate determination of a mineral's specific gravity using these heavy liquids, the immersion liquid is first diluted or concentrated until the mineral neither sinks nor rises but remains suspended. The specific gravity of the liquid is then determined precisely by means of a Mohr-Westphal balance (Fig. 29).

Generally the specific gravity of minerals depends in part on the atomic weight of the constituent elements – the specific gravity rises with the content of heavy metals such as iron and barium – and in part on the compaction of the crystal structure formed by these elements. For example, diamond with close packing of the carbon atoms has a higher specific gravity (3.52) than graphite (2.255), which has a more loose arrangement of the atoms. Most gem minerals have a specific gravity of between 2 and 4 (see Table 5); heavy gemstones include zircon (4.6-4.7), pyrite (4.9-5.2) and the novelty stone Zirconia (5.7). Light gemstones include opal (2.0-2.3) and obsidian (2.3-2.6).

Table 5 Specific gravities (mean values) of the principal gemstones

1.08	Amber	3.28	Axinite
1.25	Jet	3.29	Diopside
1.5	Sepiolite	3.30	Dioptase
1.8	Ivory	3.31	Dumortierite
2.05	Opal	3.32	Kornerupine
2.20	Chrysocolla	3.33	Jadeite
2.25	Natrolite	3.34	Olivine (peridot)
2.3	Gypsum (alabaster), sodalite	3.35	Zoisite (tanzanite)
2.35	Moldavite, pearl (black), thomsonite	3.38	Vesuvianite
2.4	Obsidian	3.4	Grossular (massive)
2.54	Charoite	3.52	Diamond
2.55	Variscite	3.53	Titanite (sphene), topaz (yellow)
2.56	Microcline (amazonite), orthoclase (yellow)	3.56	Topaz (white)
2.57	Orthoclase (moonstone)	3.6	Rhodochrosite, rhodonite, spinel
2.58	Cordierite	3.63	Spinel (synthetic), uvarovite
2.6	Agate, chalcedony, serpentine	3.65	Grossular (hessonite)
2.64	Oligoclase (sunstone)	3.67	Benitoite, kyanite
2.65	Coral, quartz	3.7	Staurolite
2.69	Beryl (aquamarine, heliodor)	3.72	Chrysoberyl
2.70	Labradorite	3.75	Pyrope
2.71	Beryl (emerald), calcite (marble), pearl	3.8	Azurite, malachite
2.8	Agalmatolite, lapis lazuli, turquoise	3.85	Andradite (demantoid)
2.81	Wardite	3.99	Corundum
2.82	Beryllonite	4.00	Zircon (low — metamict)
2.85	Lepidolite	4.07	Almandine
2.9	Prehnite, verdite	4.09	Sphalerite
2.94	Aragonite	4.15	Spessartite
2.96	Nephrite, phenakite	4.25	Rutile
2.99	Brazilianite	4.35	Smithsonite
3.00	Danburite	4.57	Yttroaluminate (YAG)
3.06	Tourmaline	4.69	Zircon (high — not metamict)
3.10	Euclase, lazulite, zoisite (thulite)	4.9	Marcasite, pyrite
3.15	Andalusite	5.10	Haematite
3.18	Fluorite, spodumene	5.13	Strontium titanate (Fabulite)
3.2	Apatite	5.7	Cubic zirconium oxide (Zirconia)
3.25	Sillimanite	6.0	Cuprite
		6.9	Cassiterite

Hardness

Hardness or durability is one of the most characteristic properties of gemstones and it is an important identification feature. For a long time the property formed the basis by which gemstones were classified either as precious or semiprecious stones, the borderline being represented by quartz.

The hardness of a mineral is expressed as the power of that substance to resist scratching when a pointed object or a fragment of another mineral is drawn across it. A comparative hardness scale was devised by the German mineralogist Friedrich Mohs (1773-1839) and it is still used today by mineralogists and gemmologists. The scale is

Table 6 Mohs' hardness scale

Scale	Reference mineral	Note
1	Talc	Scratched with fingernail
2	Gypsum	
3	Calcite	Scratched with a copper coin
4	Fluorite	
5	Apatite	Scratched with a penknife
6	Orthoclase	
7	Quartz	Scratch glass
8	Topaz	
9	Corundum	
10	Diamond	

based on the principle that a harder mineral will scratch one that is softer. Ten minerals were selected (see Table 6), each of which will scratch another mineral with a lower hardness number in the scale and will in turn be scratched by one higher in the scale.

A simple rule must always be observed when a gemstone is tested for hardness; the scale specimens, starting with the lowest grades, are always scratched by the mineral being investigated. Should it be the other way round and the mineral specimen is scratched by the samples, the stone could be damaged and the value of a cut gem drastically reduced.

An accurate determination of hardness by this method is impossible in earthy (sepiolite) and fibrous (serpentine) aggregates because the spaces between the individual grains or fibres are usually lower than the overall hardness. On the other hand, the fibrous nephrite probably gets its unusual hardness and toughness because its microscopic fibres are intertwined. In noncrystalline amorphous minerals, such as obsidian, the hardness is uniform in all directions, but in crystals it can vary, like other physical properties, with the crystal direction. For example, minerals with a distinct cleavage are hardest in the direction perpendicular to the cleavage plane. In kyanite this difference in hardness is very pronounced; it has a hardness of 4-4.5 in the vertical direction and at right angles to this a hardness of up to 7 (Fig. 30).

This directional hardness depends on the way the mineral's structure is arranged. To take once again the example of diamond and graphite, diamond is harder than graphite in which the atomic packing is looser. It is also usually the case that the higher the water content of a mineral the lower the hardness. The angles and edges of a crystal

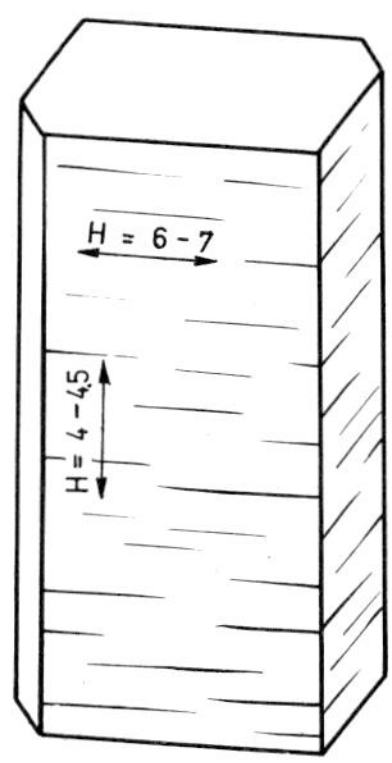

Fig. 30 Hardness of kyanite in different directions.

are sometimes harder than the faces of the same mineral. For instance, the edge of a gypsum crystal will scratch the face of another gypsum crystal.

The Mohs' hardness scale is comparative, not linear, so that the degrees 1 to 10 do not tell us by how much a mineral is harder than talc at the bottom of the scale. There are, however, special instruments called *sclerometers* for determining absolute hardness values. A steel or diamond point is driven into the material being tested and its hardness is determined by weights that impress the point into the mineral. The hardness values can then be determined by the ratio of the force applied (pressure in kilograms) and the area of the impression (expressed in square millimetres).

These absolute hardness values are, of course, totally different from the Mohs numbers. For example, in absolute figures, diamond is more than 4.5 million times harder than talc, corundum 33,000 times, and so on. The smallest difference between the Mohs degrees are between 4 and 5 (fluorite and apatite) and 6 and 7 (orthoclase feldspar and quartz). The greatest differences have been found to lie between the numbers 2 and 3 and 5 and 6. Diamond is about ten times harder than corundum, but corundum is only about 10 per cent harder than topaz.

However, although the Mohs' scale gives only a relative figure of hardness, the property nevertheless remains one of the most useful for the identification of minerals and gemstones (see Table 7).

Table 7 Hardness of the principal gemstones

10	Diamond
9	Corundum
8.5	Chrysoberyl, cubic zirconium oxide (Zirconia)
8	Spinel, topaz, yttroaluminate (YAG)
7.5-8	Beryl, phenakite, zircon
7.5	Andalusite, euclase, garnet (almandine, pyrope, uvarovite), sillimanite
7-7.5	Cordierite, danburite, staurolite, tourmaline
7	Dumortierite, garnet (grossular, spessartite), quartz group
6.5-7	Agate, axinite, chalcedony, garnet (demantoid), jadeite, jasper, kornerupine, olivine (peridot), spodumene, vesuvianite, zoisite (tanzanite)
6-7.5	Sillimanite
6-7	Cassiterite
6-6.5	Benitoite, feldspar (labradorite, microcline), marcasite, nephrite, prehnite, pyrite, rutile, zircon (low — metamict)
6	Amblygonite, charoite, feldspar (orthoclase), haematite, opal, strontium titanate (Fabulite), zoisite (thulite)
5.5-6	Rhodonite, sodalite, turquoise
5-7	Kyanite (varies according to direction)
5-6	Diopside, lazulite
5.5	Brazilianite, moldavite, natrolite, obsidian
5-5.5	Lapis lazuli, thomsonite, titanite (sphene)
5	Apatite, dioptase, smithsonite, wardite
4-5	Variscite
4	Cuprite, fluorite, rhodochrosite
3.5-4	Aragonite, azurite, malachite, pearl, sphalerite
3.5	Coral, lepidolite
3	Calcite
2.5-4	Jet, serpentine
2-4	Chrysocolla, ivory
2-3	Amber
2-2.5	Gypsum (alabaster), sepiolite
1-2.5	Agalmatolite

Cleavage

The splitting or cleavage of many minerals along certain flat planes or directions is related to the form and the internal structure of the crystal. The smooth, flat cleavage surfaces run parallel to some of the crystal faces or forms of the crystal (Fig. 31), and represent planes of weakness in the crystal structure. Some minerals cleave more easily and in more directions than others.

The cleavage planes do not develop at the time of formation of the crystal but usually do secondarily as a result of some kind of mechanical pressure. A mineral in its rough form can sometimes be mechanically cleaved to produce a body bounded on all sides solely by the cleavage planes. Such a body is said to have the cleavage form; for example, calcite cleaves into a rhombohedron, fluorite into an octahedron, diamond into an octahedron and sphalerite into a rhombic dodecahedron.

It is important to distinguish cleavage from fracture (see below), which is irregular and not connected to the crystal structure of the mineral. Amorphous substances do not cleave, they fracture. Crystalline minerals may have both cleavage and fracture, but cleavage tends to predominate over a possible fracture. Emerald is a notable exception as it fractures easily but does not ordinarily cleave.

Cleavage is described according to its quality as: *perfect* or *eminent* if it produces perfect straight and smooth planes (diamond, topaz, gypsum, calcite); *good* (fluorite, pyroxenes); or *imperfect* or *poor* if it produces only uneven planes (garnet, beryl, zircon). Quartz has no cleavage.

The quality of the cleavage is judged by the lustre of the cleavage planes. A pearly

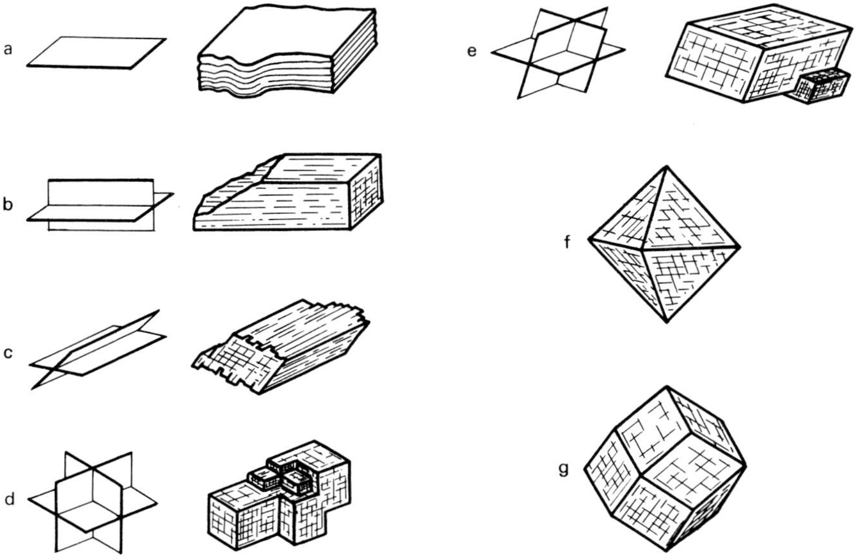

Fig. 31 Cleavage directions in minerals: a, in one direction (mica — lepidolite, topaz); b, in two directions at right angles or almost at right angles to each other (orthoclase feldspar, pyroxene group, rutile); c, in two directions at oblique angles to each other (amphibole group); d, in three directions at right angles to each other (anhydrite ($CaSO_4$), galenite (PbS), halite (NaCl)); e, in three directions at oblique angles to each other (calcite, dioptase); f, in four directions along an octahedron (diamond, fluorite); g, in six directions along a rhombic dodecahedron (sphalerite).

lustre usually implies at least a very good cleavage. In some minerals (topaz) cleavage is manifested by minute, almost indiscernible cracks inside the cut stones. Such cracks may develop when the stone is being polished or may be caused by mechanical damage after the gem has been set, and naturally they reduce the value of the stone. Stones with a poor or no cleavage are therefore preferred for rings and bracelets that are likely to be accidentally knocked.

A good gem cutter selects the type of cut with respect to cleavage. For example, topaz (Fig. 31 a) characteristically cleaves in one direction parallel to the basal face at right angles to the length of the crystal; diamond (Fig. 31 f) splits readily in four directions along the octahedral faces (this property is utilized by the lapidary for splitting the crystal into convenient pieces for cutting — see the section on fashioning and cutting of gemstones (pp. 63-70). Kunzite is exceedingly fragile because of its delicate cleavage in two directions.

The angle formed by the individual cleavage planes is important for the identification of minerals. For instance, amphiboles (Fig. 31 c) can be distinguished from the similarly looking pyroxenes (Fig. 31 b) because in the monoclinic amphiboles the angle of the prismatic cleavage is about 120° whereas in the monoclinic pyroxenes it is about 90°. To complicate matters further, some minerals cleave in two or three different ways.

Fracture

Amorphous substances and some crystalline minerals break or *fracture* in an irregular fashion. The types of fracture of interest to gemmologists are:

Conchoidal: the surface shows a series of concentric arcs that resemble the growth lines on certain shells (quartz, opal, flint, obsidian).

Even: the surface is straight but of small area and irregularly oriented (garnet).

Uneven: the surface has numerous irregularities (pyrite).

Splintery or *hackly*: the mineral breaks into fibrous splinters or in a jagged fashion (serpentine).

Earthy: the type of fracture seen in chalk and sepiolite.

Tenacity

If subjected to pressure or impact, most minerals crumble into small fragments or are reduced to a powder. They are said to be *brittle*. However, a thin leaf of mica can be bent by the fingers and when released it immediately resumes its original shape. In such a case, the material deformation is reversible and the mineral is described as *elastic*. Under pressure nephrite and jadeite are also elastic (see p. 160). Minerals such as talc or gypsum can be bent but they do not spring back to their former position; they are thus said to be *flexible*. *Ductile* or *malleable* minerals, such as the precious metals, can be flattened out into thin sheets.

The brittleness of a mineral is an important factor to be considered in gemstone fashioning (that is, cutting, drilling, polishing and setting — see later).

Properties of magnetism and electricity

Some minerals are attracted in varying degrees to a magnet, especially when they contain a large amount of iron, and the property is used in the separation of important ore minerals. Magnetic iron ore (magnetite) is highly magnetic; haematite is moderately magnetic. Heating may make such minerals more magnetic.

Most minerals are bad conductors of electricity, but a few will pass a current if a voltage is applied to them. Good conductors include native metals and minerals with a metallic lustre, such as many sulphides (for example pyrite). Natural blue diamond, which contains boron, is a semiconductor (its electrical conductivity lies between that of a conductor and an insulator), and this property can be used to distinguish them from diamonds that have been coloured blue artificially. During this test, the natural stones often show electroluminescence. Electrical conductivity is another property used to separate ore minerals.

When heated some minerals develop an electric charge — they become *pyroelectric*. For example, in strong sunlight or artificial heat, a tourmaline crystal becomes negatively charged at its sharp end and positively charged at its blunt end and it will attract tiny particles of dust. Tourmaline is also *piezoelectric* — it becomes electrically charged when stress is applied along certain directions of the crystal. Quartz is the most important piezoelectric mineral and thin plates of it are used as oscillators in electronic circuits. Only crystals belonging to classes lacking a centre of symmetry can be pyroelectric or piezoelectric.

Amber is *triboelectric* — it develops a negative electric charge when rubbed and when it is in this state it attracts tiny fragments to its surface.

Thermal conductivity

If a rock crystal is held in one hand and a piece of amber in the other, the crystal feels colder. This is because the thermal conductivity of the two materials is different. The temperature of the human body is considerably higher than the usual ambient temperature and a stone that is a good conductor of heat and is at the ambient temperature will absorb heat from the skin quickly and will thus feel cold. A poor conductor of heat will feel warmer. In this way, experts can distinguish genuine gems from glass imitations by placing the specimen against the cheek where the skin is most sensitive to changes in temperature. In the case of large stones, the difference in thermal conductivity can be observed when they are breathed upon — the surface of a genuine gemstone will demist more rapidly than that of a glass imitation.

Thermal conductivity must also be taken into consideration when gemstones are cut because certain stones may need cooling during the cutting operation.

Damage to gemstones

Many gemstones are damaged by mechanical impact, by excessive temperatures and by various chemical substances. Although they may be quite hard, gemstones can still be vulnerable to mechanical damage because of their brittleness and cleavage. This applies especially to diamond, topaz, spinel and emerald. Unlike diamond, ruby and sapphire do not cleave and they withstand much higher pressures when cut and set. The resistance properties of the most important gemstones are summarized below.

Resistance to mechanical impact and temperature

Diamond withstands temperatures of up to 720 °C. At higher temperatures in an oxygen atmosphere, it will start burning and its surface becomes covered with a milky tarnish. Excessive heat will incinerate the stone. Some diamonds do not like sharp temperature changes. Diamond has a perfect cleavage so it may split upon accidental impact.

Corundum (ruby and sapphire, both natural and synthetic) withstands very high temperatures without damage although some blue sapphires, if heated excessively, will discolour to paler hues. Since these stones have no cleavage and they possess a relatively high amount of elasticity they are quite resistant to mechanical damage.

Beryl (emerald and aquamarine) is sensitive to great heat and may become discoloured or damaged. Since it often contains fine ingrowths or minute cracks it may splinter when being set in a harder metal. Natural aquamarines usually do not have as many imperfections as emeralds do and the danger of mechanical damage is lower.

Chrysoberyl (alexandrite) and, to some extent, *spinel* withstand soldering temperatures without damage. Their mechanical resistance is about the same as that of corundum.

Topaz, on the other hand, is extremely sensitive to excessive heating, cracks easily and some stones may even change colour when exposed to high temperatures. Extreme care must be taken when the gem is being fashioned because it has an eminent cleavage and even a very slight impact may break it.

Colourless and lightly coloured *tourmalines* easily withstand heat and are quite resistant to pressure and impact, but the red rubellite is somewhat susceptible to splintering.

Of the *garnet* family, only pyrope is not affected by high temperatures; the other varieties become damaged or flawed. Garnets are mechanically quite tough; pyrope is reasonably elastic and is a very good conductor of heat. It is thus fashioned quite easily.

Olivine withstands soldering temperatures relatively well, but is susceptible to mechanical damage when being set.

Of the *quartz* family, amethyst is most susceptible to heat damage. It often happens that when a jewel with a natural amethyst is being repaired carelessly, the high temperature will turn the originally purple stone into a yellow one. Quartz is reasonably elastic and because it has no cleavage it is mechanically tough.

Opals are extremely sensitive to heat and when subjected to excessive temperatures they become dehydrated and lose their opalescence. Opals are also very brittle and may easily crack during setting.

Turquoise will crack in relatively low temperatures and if subjected to intensive heat, it will disintegrate. On the other hand, its considerable toughness makes it mechanically resistant.

Feldspars are sensitive to heat and because they cleave perfectly they may become damaged if handled carelessly.

Stones that look similar can behave quite differently. *Jadeite* is very sensitive to high temperatures and will melt like glass in great heat, but *nephrite* is quite heat resistant. Both minerals are tough so they are considerably resistant to mechanical damage.

Amber, jet, pearls and *corals* must never be exposed to high temperatures. Amber and jet burn; pearls and corals lose their colour and lustre and disintegrate to powder. With the exception of coral, all these materials are very brittle and splinter easily.

The synthetic *novelty stones* usually withstand soldering temperatures quite well although synthetic rutile may change its colour if it is heated in a reducing atmosphere. The colour change is reversible, however, and can be corrected by annealing in an oxygen flame.

Naturally even those gemstones that withstand high temperatures must be heated and cooled slowly when the jewel in which they are set is being repaired, and must not be subjected to thermal shocks. Before repair, the stone should be inspected for foreign inclusions or internal cracks that could cause damage upon heating or impact.

Resistance to chemicals

Although many gemstones are inert to various chemical agents, some are attacked by acids, alkalis, mordants and galvanic baths (see Table 8). Much depends on the concentration of these substances, the temperature, the length of exposure and, naturally, also the chemical composition of the stone.

Acids do not dissolve *diamond,* ruby, sapphire and other coloured varieties of *corundum, beryl* (emerald and aquamarine), *chrysoberyl, spinel, garnet, tourmaline* and *precious opal. Zircon* is also inert to acids, with the exception of sulphuric acid, which will corrode it if left to act for a long time. Similarly *olivine* is also damaged by sulphuric acid if exposed to it for a long time at a high temperature.

Although the entire *quartz* family is inert to acids, with the exception of hydrofluoric acid, the varieties differ in their reaction to alkalis. Crystal varieties, such as rock crystal, amethyst, citrine and smoky quartz, are not attacked by alkaline lyes in low concentrations and at low temperatures. The same applies to the lump varieties, such as jasper, prase or aventurine. However, opals dissolve in lyes easily, and *agate* and *chalcedony* are damaged by them.

Some *feldspars*, such as amazonite, moonstone and labradorite, lose their original lustre if left in acids for a long time.

Carbonates, such as *malachite, azurite, rhodochrosite, calcite* as well as *corals* and *pearls*, effervesce even in very weak acids; malachite is corroded by ammonia.

Lazurite dissolves in more concentrated acids and is corroded by lyes, as is *turquoise*.

Pyrite and *marcasite* are damaged by nitric acid. *Amber* is resistant to diluted acids, but is damaged by concentrated sulphuric acid. It also does not tolerate lyes and cyanide gilding baths, ammonia and alcohol, and is soluble in ether, chloroform and organic solvents.

Table 8 Some chemical tests

Soluble in hydrochloric acid, giving carbon dioxide	*Carbonates*	Aragonite, azurite, coral, malachite, pearl, rhodochrosite, smithsonite
Decomposed by hydrochloric acid	*Sulphides*	Sphalerite
	Oxides	Haematite
	Phosphates	Apatite
	Sulphates	Gypsum
	Silicates	Demantoid (partly), labradorite, natrolite, serpentine, titanite (partly), vesuvianite (partly)
Decomposed by sulphuric acid	*Halides*	Fluorite
	Silicates	Olivine, serpentine, staurolite (partly), titanite, topaz, zircons (some)
Decomposed by nitric acid	*Sulphides*	Marcasite, pyrite, sphalerite
Decomposed by hydrofluoric acid	*Oxides*	Agate, chalcedony, opal, quartz group
	Silicates	All
Decomposed by sodium and potassium hydroxides	*Oxides*	Agate, chalcedony, opal
	Carbonates	Coral
	Silicates	Chrysoberyl, lazurite, turquoise
	Organic comp.	Amber, jet
Soluble in ammonia	*Carbonates*	Azurite, malachite
Soluble in organic solvents	*Organic compounds*	Amber, cannel, jet
Damaged by borax on heating	*Oxides*	Corundum, opal
	Sulphides	Pyrite
	Carbonates	Malachite
	Silicates	Beryl, garnet group, lazurite, olivine, topaz, tourmaline
	Phosphates	Turquoise

Identification of gemstones

Gemstone identification must be based on a careful determination with instruments of all the important properties of the stone. A magnifying glass or a few simple tests will not usually suffice. Not even a gemmologist makes a judgement on the basis of a single glance. The rule is to use only such methods that will not damage the tested stone, especially a cut one. This is also the major difference between gemmological identification methods and those used in mineralogy where a small amount of the mineral may be destroyed during the investigation. With regard to cut gems it often pays to engage a specialist to identify the stone to prevent any damage that could be caused by inexpert hands. There is no exact procedure for identifying a stone — the methods are chosen to suit the specimen being tested. A few simple tests might bring a positive identification; in other cases the testing could be a very complex affair.

Nowadays gemmological laboratories are equipped with instruments that enable a rapid and positive identification without any damage to the stone. Among such instruments are the binocular microscope or stereomicroscope for studying the external and sometimes even internal properties of the specimen and a polarizing or a special gemmological microscope (polariscopes are used only rarely) for determining the optical properties such as anisotropy and pleochroism. Pleochroism can also be investigated with a dichroscope or with a jeweller's microscope.

Gemmologists also need instruments for determining such properties as specific gravity, luminescence and hardness and, of course, a refractometer for measuring the index of refraction. Since minerals are often identified by their crystals, a goniometer is needed to measure the angles of the crystal edges.

Most mineralogical and gemmological laboratories also have instruments for X-ray and spectral analysis. Such analysis always requires professional expertise. Minerals can be identified with certainty on the basis of their absorption of light and there are published tables of the more important gemstone spectra (see Table 9). Then, analytical chemical methods are used to determine the quantitative and qualitative contents. In this way, the chemical formula of a mineral can be determined. Some instrumental methods, for example neutron activation analysis, are nondestructive and are therefore especially suitable for the testing of cut gems. When a minute amount of the material has to be destroyed during testing, it is good practice first to test the material in its rough state in as great a detail as possible and to subject the cut specimen only to a few indispensable tests.

Spectral analysis of the colour of a gemstone is done with an instrument called a *spectroscope*, which uses prisms to break up the light from the gemstone into its spectral colours from the red to the blue/violet bands (see Figs 32 and 33). The method identifies stones of a similar colour and distinguishes genuine gems from imitations. It

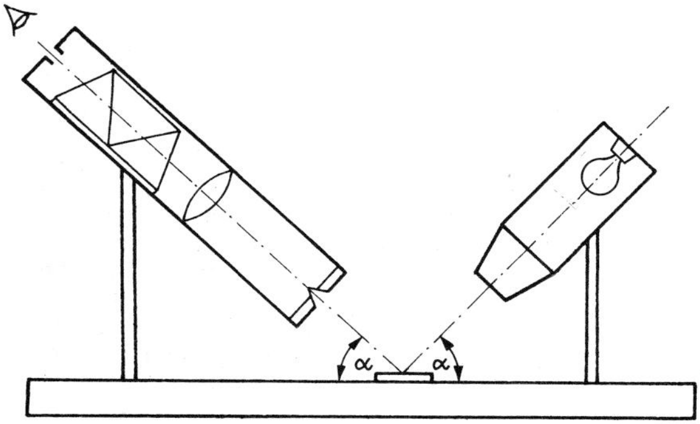

Fig. 32 The principle of the spectroscope.

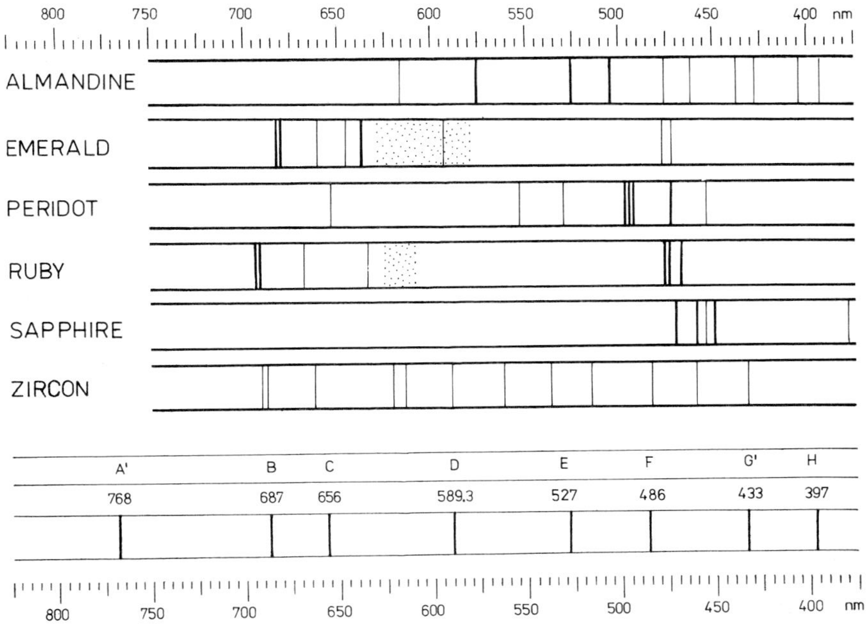

Fig. 33 Absorption spectra of some gemstones with Fraunhofer's spectrum lines (A' = dark red, B = red, C = orange, D = yellow, E = green, F = blue, G' = blue violet, H = deep violet).

can also be used to identify gemstones that have refractive indices too high to be measured by a refractometer.

Absorption spectra were first described by Sir Arthur Church, who published a paper in 1866 on absorption bands in zircon and almandine garnet. The method is still widely used today because it is precise and quick. A spectroscope usually consists of three hollow tubes mounted horizontally on a rotating disk. One of the tubes, the collimater, has an aperture or slit at the outer end and a lens at the inner end that transforms the incoming incident light into a thin beam of parallel rays, that is, a 'pure spectrum' in which there is no overlapping of the component colours. Another tube is the viewing telescope. The third tube contains a calibrated wavelength scale. This is so constructed that the scale is superimposed on the image of the spectrum produced.

At the centre of the disk and between the three tubes is the prism, which disperses the light from the collimater and directs it into the viewing telescope. In some spectroscopes the spectrum is produced not by a prism but by a grating of lines (diffraction grating) spaced very closely together. The slit in the collimater is adjustable so that it can be set to a resolution appropriate to the spectrum being analysed. Focusing can be done by pointing the instrument at daylight and making the necessary adjustments for the best resolution of the Fraunhofer lines (see page 44-45 for an explanation of these). Alternatively the spectroscope is adjusted to the absorption spectrum of the light from an electric light bulb.

When the spectroscope is ready, the gemstone requiring identification is placed on the rotating disk and the dark absorption bands characteristic for that mineral species or coloured variety can be seen in the viewing telescope. Experienced gemmologists can obtain results from a spectroscope in a matter of minutes and there is no doubt that spectral analysis provides a very sure way of identifying not only cut gemstones but also rough crystals and even set gems. The spectroscope also has a very important and sometimes complicated part to play in distinguishing natural from synthetic stones.

Table 9 Absorption spectra of the principal gemstones

Gemstone	Absorption lines (in nm; the most important lines are underlined)
Agate (yellow)	700, 665, 634
Alexandrite	680.5, 678.5, 665, 655, 649, 645, 640-555
Almandine	617, 576, 526, 505, 476, 462, 438, 428, 404, 393
Amethyst	550-520
Aquamarine	537, 456, 427
Chrysoberyl	504, 495, 485, 445
Diamond (colourless to yellow)	478, 465, 451, 435, 423, 415.5, 401.5, 390
Emerald	683.5, 680.6, 662, 646, 637, 594, 630-580, 477.4, 472.5
Fluorite (yellow)	545, 515, 490, 470, 452
Hessonite	547, 490, 454.5, 435
Kyanite	446, 433
Jadeite	691.5, 655, 630, 450, 437.5, 433
Nephrite	689, 509, 490, 460
Olivine (peridot)	653, 553, 529, 497, 495, 493, 473, 453
Opal	700-640, 590-400
Orthoclase	448, 420
Pyrope	687, 685, 671, 650, 620-520, 505
Quartz (synthetic; blue)	645, 585, 540, 500-490
Rubellite	555, 534, 525-461, 456, 451, 428
Ruby	694.2, 692.8, 668, 659.2, 610-500, 476.5, 475, 468.5
Sapphire	471, 460, 455 450, 379
Spessartite	495, 484.5, 481, 475, 462, 457, 455, 440, 435, 432, 424, 412, 406, 394
Spinel (red)	685.5, 684, 675, 665, 656, 650, 642, 632, 595-490 465, 455
Topaz (pink)	682.8
Turquoise	460, 432, 422
Verdelite	497, 461, 415
Zircon	691, 689, 662.5, 660.5, 653.5, 621, 615, 589.5, 562, 537.5, 516, 484, 460, 432.7

Mining of gemstones

The history of the purposeful acquisition of useful minerals and gemstones is tens of thousands of years old. As has been mentioned, nephrite was collected, fashioned and used by Stone Age people. The use of flint and obsidian has a much longer history. Stones were first collected manually from alluvial deposits. Later they were mined from shallow pits and simple shafts or from scoured and underwashed river banks. The broken rock was hauled to the surface in baskets or buckets hoisted by windlasses. This method of mining still survives in some localities. Another method widely used in the past was quarry mining, usually from sedimentary rocks. Gem-rich rocks were first heated by fires, then quickly quenched with water and the gemstones were extracted from the broken rock.

Gem, and especially diamond, mining today is a complex technological industry. Highly productive mining and processing methods enable the exploitation of deposits of a much lower yield than that thought to be profitable in the past. The profitable yield of diamond is usually 0.55 carat per metric ton of parent rock, but it can be as low as 0.15 carat per ton, a ratio of 1:36 million. In South Africa diamond is mined from depths exceeding 1,000 metres. Quarry-mining methods utilize powerful rock breakers and caterpillar excavators. Other methods have been devised for the extraction of diamonds and other precious materials from seabed deposits impossible to reach by conventional means. For these operations special vessels and powerful dredgers have been designed.

Once extracted from the deposit, the material is circulated by water through a system of sieves and the gems are picked out manually. Where there is a huge volume of material the rock is first broken in crushers and then sorted by grain size. The methods for separating the gemstones from the fine waste are usually based on the fact that materials of the same grain size have different specific gravities. In other words, the heavier minerals sink more quickly to the bottom while the lighter ones are more easily carried away by water. This property is the principle behind the age-old method of *placer mining* or *panning* of gems with pans or wicker baskets, screen jigs and the modern gravitational jigs and separation tables of various types. Jigs are usually communicating vessels, one fitted with a screen and the other with a piston. When the piston is pressed down, the water in the other vessel starts rising and floats the minerals to be separated. When the action of the piston is reversed, the water starts falling and carries away the minerals; the rhythmical floating of the minerals separates the heavier and the lighter fractions, yielding the so-called *concentrate.*

The final sorting of the concentrate is done by various methods, which usually differ from place to place according to local mining traditions. One of the oldest methods of separating diamonds from the concentrate is based on the fact that unlike other minerals diamond is largely water repellent and will stick to a layer of grease. The method is still widely used. The concentrate is fed by a stream of water on to vibrating tables or moving belts covered with a layer of grease. The diamond crystals stick to the grease and are subsequently scraped off, cleaned and graded for sale.

A more recent method of diamond separation is based on the principle that all diamonds luminesce blue in X-ray light. The dry concentrate is transported from a hopper and fed by means of a conveyor belt into a *luminescence separator* in total darkness. The concentrate falls down a tube, passing a beam of X-rays en route. If a diamond is in the concentrate, a photomultiplier detects its blue luminescence and sends an impulse via an amplifier to an electromagnetic switch-operated plate that diverts the falling diamond into another tube. The separated diamonds are collected in a trap, while the waste is usually passed through another separator in case any diamonds were missed the first time round. Small portable luminescence separators are based on the same principle and utilize a radioisotope of thulium.

Optical separators of diamond concentrate are based on the fact that diamonds are transparent and strongly reflective whereas the associated minerals are usually non-transparent.

The Sortex-type separators that were developed originally for the sorting of cereal grains are used for the separation of variously coloured gems. A vibrating conveyor belt delivers the concentrate from a hopper to the feeding belt that queues one grain after another. The individual grains fall into a chamber where they are illuminated with diffuse light. The reflected light passes a series of colour filters and activates a photocell of a monochromatic photometer. The instant determination of the colour shade is followed by an impulse sent from the photometer via an amplifier to a high-speed nozzle and the stream of compressed air delivered by the nozzle separates the grains into individual fractions.

Another separation method used for some gemstones is based on the different behaviour of minerals in an electrostatic field. The design of such *electrostatic separators* is very simple. The concentrate travels from a hopper into a negatively charged rotation cylinder and then falls through a chamber with positively charged electrodes. According to their electrical conductivity, the individual minerals are deflected by different amounts by the electrostatic field and the mineral fractions become separated by a series of partitions. The proper operation of these separators is highly dependent on the prevalent climatic conditions, especially the humidity.

For separating several different gemstones, gravitational methods are used. One such method uses the so-called helical separators (incorrectly called the Humphrey spirals). Basically, these are helically shaped troughs in which a combination of the centrifugal force, friction, water pressure and gravitational force separates the fed material into fractions according to specific gravity, size and shape of the grains. The helical separators used by the mining industry are of a simple design and cheap to operate; unlike jigs they have no movable parts and the failure rate is practically nil.

Another advantage of helical separators is that the equipment can be operated either stationary or as a mobile unit mounted on trucks or ships.

Units of weight

As long ago as the classical age, unshaped and cut gemstones were commonly sold by weight, the most precious ones being sold by a special unit of weight called a *carat.* The English word carat (and the German karat) seem to be derived from the Greek *keration,* which in turn may have come from the Arabic word *quirat* for the seeds of the carob or locust tree (*Ceratonia siliqua*), which grows mainly in the Mediterranean area. The pods are generally known as St John's bread. These seeds have traditionally been used for the weighing of gemstones. Carob beans are of a surprisingly uniform size and weigh about 0.2 gram on average.

A carat was originally divided into halves, quarters, eighths, sixteenths, thirty-seconds and sixty-fourths. However, it was not defined precisely and, depending on the country, its value fluctuated between 0.197 and 0.216 gram. This led to great confusion. If somebody, for instance, bought stones by the carat in Florence, the capital of Tuscany, and resold them in the nearby Livorno, they gained 95 carats on 1,000 carats. To add to the difficulties, in France gems were weighed by the ounce, which had a value of 144 carats. In 1907 therefore the so-called *metric carat* was adopted in France, Germany and Italy. It equals precisely 0.2 gram, is divided metrically and can easily be checked because gems can be weighed on standard gram balances.

The metric carat was soon adopted in most other countries, although the old carats are sometimes still encountered, especially in the case of some of the old, famous gems, among them mainly diamonds. Various sources give different weights for these famous gems because the type of carat is not usually known. Thus, we often do not know the exact weight of some of the world's most prized historical gems.

Note that the carats used to express the purity of gold and its alloys are altogether different from the metric carat just discussed. The carat of gold purity represents one twenty-fourth of the total weight of the metal. Thus, 24-carat gold is pure gold and 14-carat gold contains 14 parts of pure gold and 10 parts of other metals, usually copper or silver.

Pearls are weighed either in grams or in *grains* (from the Latin *granum*), the latter being the older unit. One grain is a quarter of a carat, that is 0.05 gram. The traditional Japanese weight called *momme*, used earlier in the pearl trade and equal to 18.75 carats (3.75 grams), has never been common in Europe and for practical purposes it is not used anymore.

Fashioning and cutting of gemstones

Classical writers depicted India as the fairy-tale promised land of inexhaustible richness in gemstones and it can safely be presumed that ancient India was the cradle of the art of gem fashioning. But the ancient methods and processes were not the same as those known and used today. They merely involved making a stone smooth and polished in such a way that as little as possible of the precious material was lost. Cutting as we now know it is a relatively recent method that can be traced to the peak of the Middle Ages when it appeared first in Venice and then spread to Paris, Antwerp, Bruges and later to Germany. The first cuts were naturally of a simple design but although they were gradually perfected during the subsequent centuries, it was not until modern times that fullest use of the physical and optical properties of gems was made.

The art of lapidary is divided into three categories according to the type of stone to be cut — cutting of transparent coloured gems, cutting of diamonds and cutting of nontransparent stones — and for each of the groups special techniques are required. Gem cutting is indeed an art and requires special talent, long experience and an exceptional feeling for the stone.

Before cutting is begun, the cutter must first study the stone thoroughly. The rough stone is placed in an immersion fluid, illuminated and inspected for internal imperfections such as ingrowths, cleavage cracks and inhomogeneities. Recently, ultrasonic inspection methods have been devised for the larger nontransparent stones. A cut is then selected so that all imperfections are removed if at all possible. The orientation of the cut of pleochroic stones must respect the main crystallographical directions to bring out the desired colour shade (see Fig. 34 for orientation of cuts in the dichroic ruby and tourmaline). Similarly, the cut must be suitably oriented for stones showing asterism and similar optical effects.

Large rough stones are then cut with circular saws impregnated with diamond dust into smaller pieces corresponding approximately to the required cut. The rough pieces are fixed to wooden or metal sticks called *dops* or *gemsticks* with heated cutters' cement, a lead-tin solder, or with a mechanical clamping device known as a *chuck*. The rough shaping of the stone or 'blocking out' is done with a rotating carborundum or

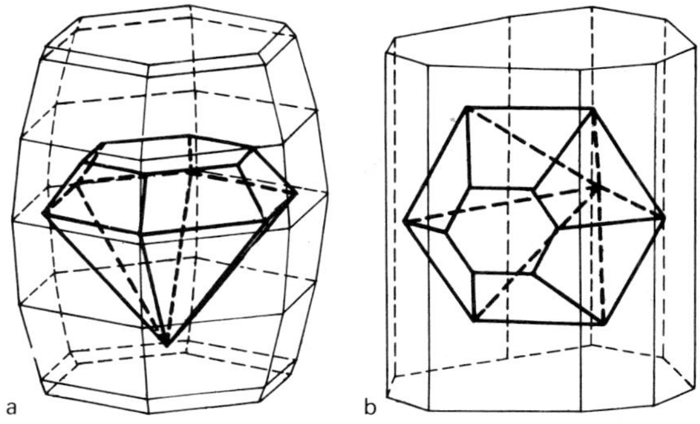

Fig. 34 Optimum orientation of a cut in dichroic crystals: (a) ruby, (b) tourmaline.

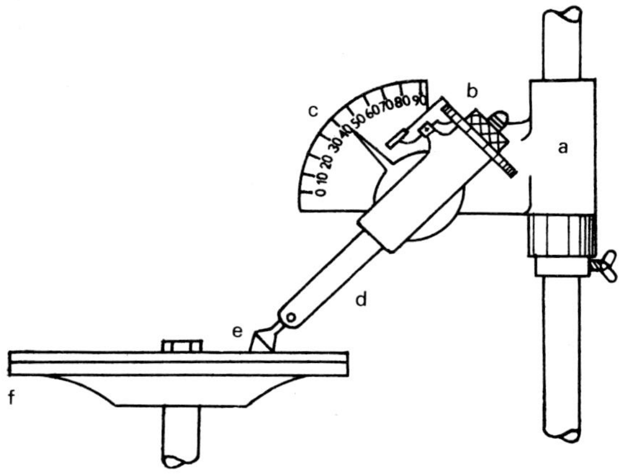

Fig. 35 Dop for gemstone cutting: a, dop body; b, ratchet and pawl; c, scale giving the facet angle; d, dop holder (tang); e, dop with stone; f. skaife (cutting disk or lap).

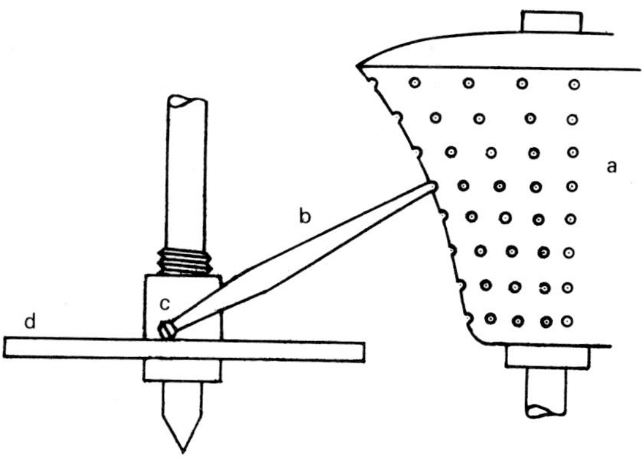

Fig. 36 Jamb peg for free hand-cutting: a, jamb peg with a number of hollowed pits; b, wooden dop; c, cemented stone; d, skaife.

diamond water-cooled disk. The *brutage*, as the rounded stone is called, is first cut on one side, the stone is reset on the dop and then the other side is cut. The rough-cut stone is then removed from the dop, the stone is cleaned and inspected in strong light. If no flaws are found, it is again secured to the dop and the individual facets are cut by bringing the bruted stone into contact with a rotating horizontal lead-alloy disk (*lap*) or *skaife* coated with a mixture of oil and fine carborundum abrasive, with diamond dust or an emery abrasive.

The angle and arrangement of the facets must be selected very carefully with respect to the optical properties of the material, especially the refractive index. The aim of the cutting operations is to give the stone a 'fire and sparkle' after it has been polished.

To keep the dop at the most appropriate facet angle, medieval cutters devised a simple wooden device called a quadrant and this was equipped with a *rachet* and *pawl* to ensure even cutting of the individual facets. The modern high-precision adjustable dops work on the same principle (Fig. 35). The very old method of free hand cutting with the dop is still practised even in modern gem-cutting houses where stones of great value are cut. The dop is fixed with its pointed end resting in one of a series of holes in a wooden holder, either a simple wooden board or a pillar-shaped cylinder, called a *jamb peg* (Fig. 36). Many expert cutters say that cutting by hand gives them a greater feeling for the material, especially when they are dealing with extremely brittle and vulnerable stones.

When one side of the stone has been cut, it is passed to the polisher who adds the final lustre to the facet surfaces. Whereas stones are always cut with materials that are harder, polishing often involves the use of softer materials. The method is similar to that used in cutting, but the polishing laps or skaifes are made of materials such as tin, copper, wood, cast-iron, acrylic resins, wax, textiles or felt. For a better adhesion of the abrasive material, soft polishing disks are usually roughened. The best polishing skaifes are those charged with fine-grained diamond powder. There are several kinds of polishing pastes — suspensions of alumina, powdered haematite (jeweller's rouge), dichromium trioxide, diatomaceous earth (tripoli), diamond pastes and many others. There is no rule concerning the combination of the disk material, speed and abrasive, as each stone requires individual treatment for maximum lustre.

The polishing process is affected by many factors, especially the character of the stone, the grain of the brutage, the disk and lapping paste material, the speed of the disk, the pH and the temperature. When being polished, the layer of the gemstone becomes deformed and starts to flow in a liquid-like manner. Every experienced cutter feels that peculiar surface slip and knows without having to look at the stone that the facet is polished. The lustre also depends on the internal structure of the crystal and stones polish quicker and better in those planes where the atoms are packed together more closely; to achieve the correct surface slip in the cleavage planes takes longer and the surface polishes with more difficulty. Gem cutters thus usually avoid polishing in these planes.

The facets are polished in sequence. First, all the upper facets (*crown*) of the stone are polished, then the *girdle* is polished and, finally, the stone is once again reset in the dop so that the bottom facets (*pavilion*) can be polished.

Diamond cutting involves practically the same procedures as the classical cuts of other gemstones except that diamond is cut and polished only by diamond. Before the brutage stage, diamonds may be cleaved. The stone is first closely examined and the required cleavage directions are marked on the surface with ink. The cutter then

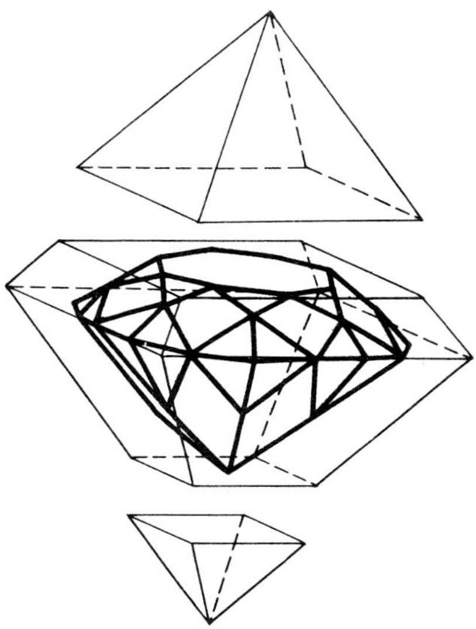

Fig. 37 Octahedral crystal of diamond with truncated apices. The thick line represents the orientation of the intended brilliant cut.

scratches a groove or *kerf* on the surface with a fragment of sharp diamond in line with the cleavage planes. The rough stone is fixed in a dop, a blunt blade is placed in the kerf and this is then given a sharp blow to split the stone into two. This seemingly very simple operation is extremely risky and requires great experience because a single incorrect blow may easily destroy a most prized stone. To minimize the danger a rough stone is sometimes cut with a thin circular diamond saw (Fig. 37 shows how the octahedral diamond crystal is sawed for the brilliant cut).

The bruted diamond is fixed in a traditional-style metal dop or in one of the modern adjustable dops. Because diamonds heat greatly when they are being cut, they are secured in the dop either with a solder or by a special chuck. Cutting and polishing are done on horizontal 12-inch (30-cm) diameter scaifes of porous cast-iron charged with a paste of oil and diamond grit. The skaife is rotated at 2,500-3,000 r.p.m. and the disks must be perfectly balanced. In contrast to other gemstones, diamonds are both cut and polished with one disk. The major diamond-cutting centres today are Amsterdam, Antwerp, London, Paris, New York, Idar-Oberstein in the Federal Republic of Germany, Johannesburg in South Africa and Smolensk in the Soviet Union.

Smaller gemstones are sometimes cut *en gross* into standard cuts on semiautomatic machines similar to those used for glass cutting. *Tumbling* is another method of mass-fashioning of gems. Essentially it involves a simple barrel in which the stones are whirled and tumbled like pebbles into shape. The method is extremely old and primitive but highly effective and its simplicity makes it very suitable for amateur work. Furthermore, in this way even chips and remnants of lower quality can be utilized. The irregularly shaped, polished stones are also very popular in modern jewellery design.

The rough stones are placed in a cylindrical or hexagonal drum (Fig. 38), together with abrasive and water, the drum is covered and then rotated at a speed of 10-30 r.p.m. As the stones wetted with the abrasive solution tumble, roll or slip on each other, they become smooth as pebbles in rivers or the sea. After several days of tumbling the stones are rinsed in water, the drum is filled with the polishing powder (about 15 per

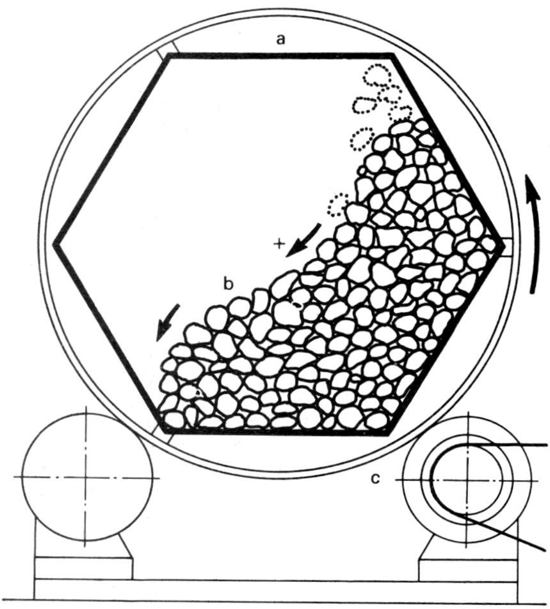

Fig. 38 Tumbling: a, hexagonal tumbler drum; b, charge of stones, abrasive and water; c, rotating equipment.

cent of the weight of the stones) and then rotated until the stones are polished. The duration of the polishing operation is very important because if it is too long, the stones lose their optimum lustre. Tumbler drums are produced and sold in many countries and gemmological magazines advertise many models suitable for amateur lapidary. Amateurs can also build-up their own sawing, cutting and polishing machines from modules sold as hobby kits.

Other, usually nontransparent gems, such as agate, jasper and turquoise, are often hand-cut into rounded facetless shapes called *cabochons*. This type of cut may also be used for stones showing chatoyancy (some rubies and sapphires).

A special branch of lapidary known as *glyptography* (gem engraving) has a very long history, as we saw in the introduction. In prehistoric times engravers carved soft stones, but during the classical period they started using harder gemstones such as agates and jaspers. Carved diamond, however, did not appear until the 16th century. The multicoloured, layered onyx or sardonyx was extremely popular for gemstone carving and the variety of colours was artistically used in the composition. It was from this type of material that the most famous cameos and intaglios were made. The oldest glyptic works — cylinder seals — date back to ancient Mesopotamia, but the art reached its peak in Greek and Roman times.

The carving is done by hand with tiny rotating cutting disks charged with a mixture of oil and an abrasive. In intaglio work, the carving is incised in the gem, in cameos the carving is raised above the surface, forming a relief. Gem carving by hand requires great feeling, extreme patience and exceptional skill. Nowadays carving can be done by machine on a mass scale. A carefully prepared master template is used for the production of series of identical carvings, especially of cheap birthstones.

Types and shapes of cuts

The most common type of cut used for transparent gems, the *brilliant*, has undergone a complex development from the original primitive table cut to the modern standard form. The brilliant cut was invented by the famous French politician and great admirer of gems, Cardinal Mazarin, in 1660. At the end of the 17th century the Genoese cutter Peruzzi greatly improved it by introducing three rows of facets. As facets greatly enhance the brilliance of the cut stone, the number of them grew until the standard brilliant cut was adopted in the early 20th century (Fig. 39).

The brilliant is a type of cut used for any gem, not only for diamond as it is sometimes erroneously thought. It is in fact a bipyramid (or octahedron) with its apex horizontally cut off. The upper part, the crown, is topped with the largest facet called the table. Other, stepped facets in the upper part are of different size and are arranged either in two or in three rows to form a two-row (Fig. 41 d) or three-row brilliant. The thicker lower part, the pavilion, is also symmetrically faceted. At the base of the pavilion is a small facet parallel to the table called the *culet*. The thinner crown and the thicker pavilion meet at a girdle. The girdle is usually smooth but in some modern cuts it is faceted. The thickness of the girdle is usually equal to 1-3 per cent of the stone's diameter.

At first, the brilliant cut was developed only on the basis of experience. Only later were the optimum angles of the facet inclination determined mathematically. With respect to light entering the crystal at right angles and obliquely, the most decisive angles are those formed by the girdle plane and the crown or pavilion. The requirement is that the maximum possible number of light rays falling on the stone at different angles be totally reflected back into the eye of the viewer. Another important feature of the facets is to refract light into the individual colour spectra, which is the cause of the well-known colour play or 'fire' of the brilliant cut (Fig. 40). The standard brilliant has an eightfold symmetry and 58 facets but new types are constantly being developed and the number of facets and the order of the symmetry are increasing. In the 1940s the King Diamond Company of New York developed the so-called *King cut* (Fig. 41 e) with 86 facets and a 12-fold symmetry. The *Princess 144* cut has even more facets.

A recent novelty are the so-called *whirl cuts* used especially for diamonds. The

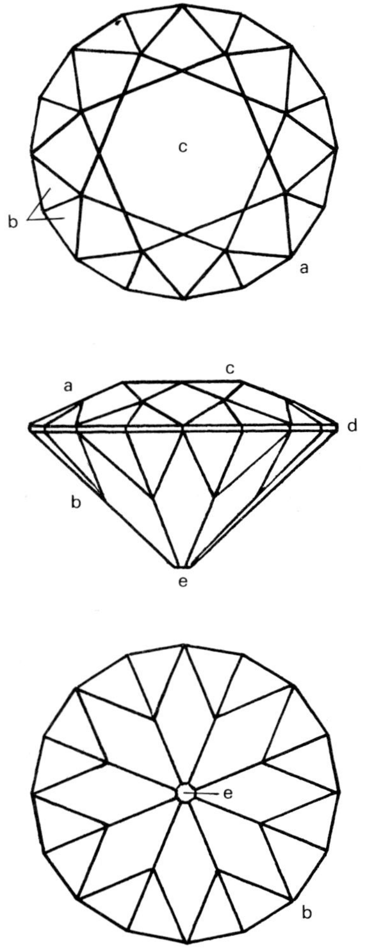

Fig. 39 Standard brilliant cut: a, crown; b, pavilion; c, table; d, girdle; e, culet.

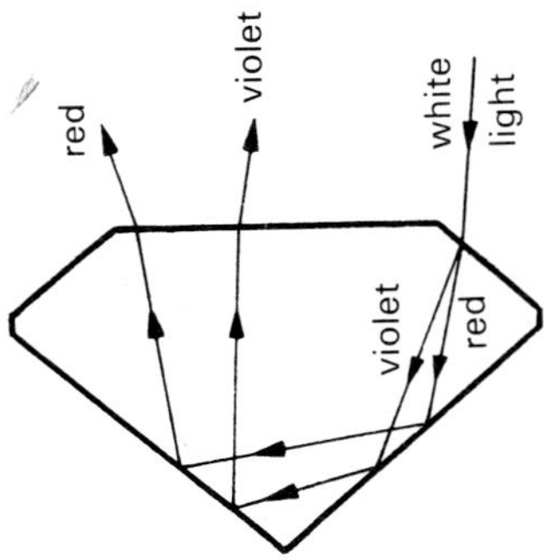

Fig. 40 Passage of a light beam through a brilliant cut.

optical effect is enhanced by the whirling motion of light that falls on and is reflected from the individual facets in more directions than in the classical brilliant cut. The whirl cut replaces the usual straight edges of the crown and the pavilion facets with spiral edges of either constant or variable pitch.

One of the oldest types of gem cuts is the *rose cut* (Fig. 41 g,h). This has only a triangular-faceted crown and a flat base. According to the depth of the gem's colour either a low or a high rose cut is used. Other classical styles are the *table cut* and the *emerald* cut (also known as the *step* or *trap cut,* Fig. 41 a). The crown and the base of table-cut stones are topped with tables of about the same size, and both parts have the same height (Fig. 41 1). Step cuts have several rows of parallel facets between the girdle and the table. The base is terminated in an edge and usually has several rows of facets (Fig. 41 a,k).

There are a great number of other cuts and their combinations (the so-called *novelty cuts*). In 1961 the *Princess cut* was introduced by Arpad Nagy of London in the shape of flat platelets fluted on the underside. A special type is the *fan cut* in the shape of

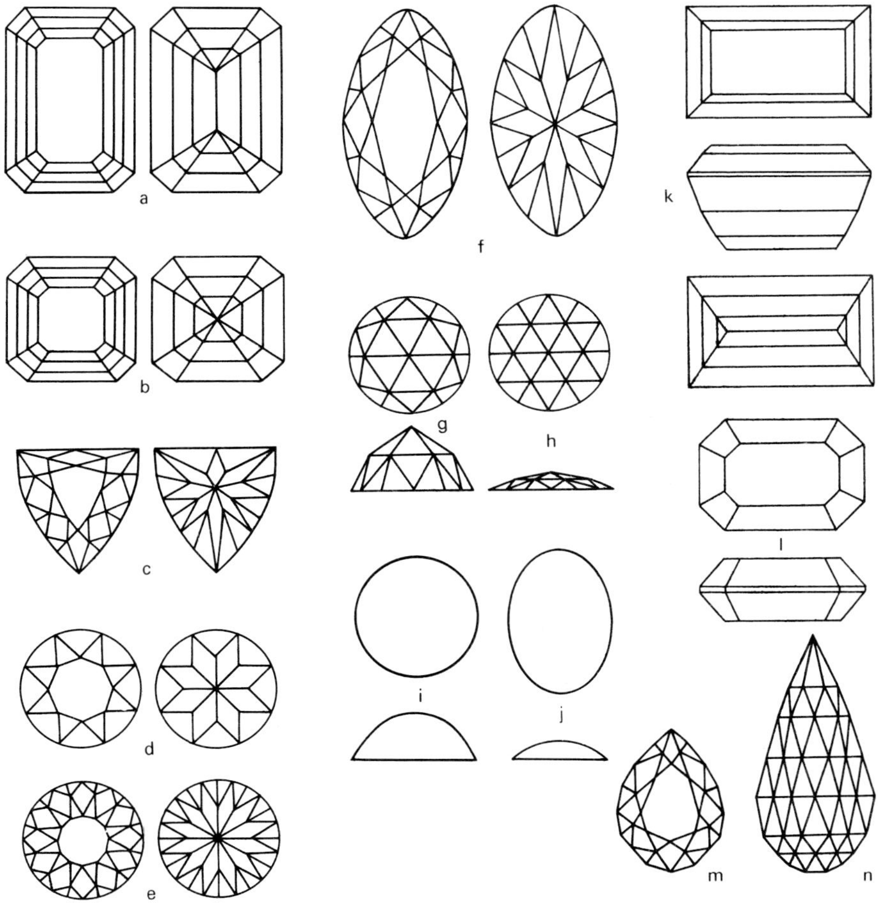

Fig. 41 Various types of gemstone cuts: (a) emerald cut; (b) square trap cut (lozenge); (c) epaulette; (d) two-row brilliant with 34 facets; (e) King brilliant with a 12-fold symmetry and 86 facets; (f) navette or marquise; (g) crowned or Dutch rose; (h) Brabant or Antwerp rose; (i) circular, high-domed simple cabochon; (j) oval, tallow-topped cabochon; (k) step cut; (l) table cut; (m) pendeloque; (n) briolette.

a 12- or 24-faceted tetrahedron or the *parasole* (*girasole*) cut. The outline of the cut usually gives it its name. Some of the most usual cuts are the *baguette* or *baton, octagon, lozenge* (Fig. 41 b), *pentagon, hexagon, wedge, epaulette* (Fig. 41 c), *navette* or *marquise* (Fig. 41 f), *pendeloque* (Fig. 41 m), *briolette* (Fig. 41 n), *mandolette, heart, fan, Swiss, cut-corner triangle, trapeze, keystone, lunette* and *kite.*

Opaque gemstones are usually cut into cabochons. These may be circular in outline (Fig. 41 i), elliptical, oval (Fig. 41 j) or drop-shaped. The dome may be high or low (tallow-topped) and there are double cabochons (with domed bases) and hollow cabochons. Around the circumference a thin girdle is usually cut to improve the setting of stones cut *en cabochon.*

Synthetic gems and imitations

For a long time people have tried to imitate the beauty and rarity of gemstones. Many medieval alchemists attempted to produce artificial gemstones, one of their main objectives being to make the so-called 'philosopher's stone'. In spite of numerous efforts throughout history, the first tiny gem crystals were synthetized only as late as the early 19th century. Larger crystals were made by the difficult process of sintering or fusing together small fragments of natural stones.

The French scientist M. A. Verneuil was one of the first to produce synthetic gemstones and the method he devised for corundum in the 1890s is still in use today. The principle of the *Verneuil* or *flame-fusion process* is based on the melting of very finely pulverized alumina (Al_2O_3) in an oxyhydrogen blowpipe-type burner. The process requires a highly purified alumina and this is prepared by repeated crystallization and subsequent calcination of ammonium alúm, which produces a pure alumina powder with a grain size of approximately 1 micrometre (µm).

The alumina is placed in a container or hopper (Fig. 42) tapped by a mechanically actuated hammer at preselected, adjustable intervals; upon each stroke the alumina is fed through a sieve at the bottom of the hopper. As the powder falls through the oxyhydrogen flame it melts and drops on to a ceramic support rod where it starts to solidify. A typical corundum monocrystal or *boule,* weighing between 200 and 500 carats and with a length of 40-80 mm, grows from a tiny droplet in a few hours. As the boule grows, the support rod is lowered so that the topmost part of the crystal is kept in the hottest part of the flame. The flame and the mushroom-shaped growing crystal are protected from temperature variations by a circular ceramic muffle. The different coloration of the corundum crystals is achieved by adding various metallic oxides to the alum before it is calcined. Today the Verneuil method is used for the production of large synthetic crystals of corundum and spinel and for many other stones not found in nature.

In 1918, E. Czochralski was the first to cultivate monocrystals from a melt (Fig. 43). The source material is first melted in a crucible in an inert-gas atmosphere, then a seed crystal fixed to an artificially cooled rod is dipped in the crucible and slowly raised out of the melt. The molten source material solidifies into a monocrystal as the seed is pulled out of the crucible. The *Czochralski method* is used to grow many garnet-type novelty stones (page 210) and corundums. The cultivated crystals are quite large and are optically very homogeneous.

The *hydrothermal method* is used for the synthesis of rock crystal and is similar in many respects to natural processes of mineral formation. The synthesis takes place in steel tanks or bombs (called autoclaves) under great temperatures and pressures. At the bottom of the autoclave is the source material — crushed quartz in a solution of sodium carbonate. Seed crystals on silver holders (plates) are hung in the solution and the quartz re-crystallizes on them. This method can also be used for the cultivation of stones such as ruby and emerald.

For a long time, all attempts at producing emeralds synthetically were totally unsuccessful. The first attempts date back to the mid-19th century, but good-quality specimens were not obtained until 1935. Even then the process remained a closely guarded secret and it was only in 1960 that a description of the method was published by H. Espig. The method — known as the *flux-fusion process* — is based on the crystallization of emerald from a foreign melt. The source material — a mixture of beryllium and aluminium oxides, plus chromium salt as a colouring agent — is dissolved in a lithium molybdate solvent in a large platinum crucible. Floating on the surface of the melt are slabs of silica glass, below which is a wide-mesh platinum sieve attached to a tube running down the centre of the crucible. The beryllium and aluminium oxides react with the silica to form a solution of beryllium aluminium silicate (beryl). Seed crystals of synthetic or natural beryl are lowered on to the sieve and as the beryl solution becomes supersaturated perfect emerald crystals precipitate out of it and grow on the seeds. The whole equipment is kept at a constant melting temperature of about 800 °C for many months while the crystals grow. More of the source material can be added down the tube.

Small synthetic diamonds for industrial use have been produced under extreme pressures and temperatures in special furnaces since the 1950s. The hexagonal form of graphite is transformed into the cubic diamond in the presence of nickel or other metal catalysts. The conversion takes place in a pressure of about 10 GPa and temperature of about 3,000 °C. Synthetic diamond grit is now produced in this way in many countries. In 1970, the General Electric Company of America succeeded in synthesizing gem-quality diamonds of up to 1 carat in size, but the stones are very expensive to produce and are not yet competitors of natural stones. The possible substitutes for diamond are listed in Table 10.

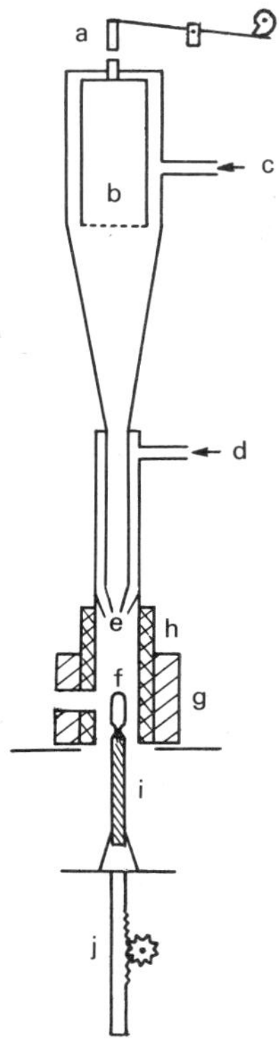

Fig. 42 Diagram of the Verneuil furnace: a, hammer; b, hopper; c, oxygen inlet line; d, hydrogen inlet line; e, blowpipe nozzle; f, corundum boule; g, muffle; h, corundum lining; i, ceramic support rod (candle); j, vertical feed.

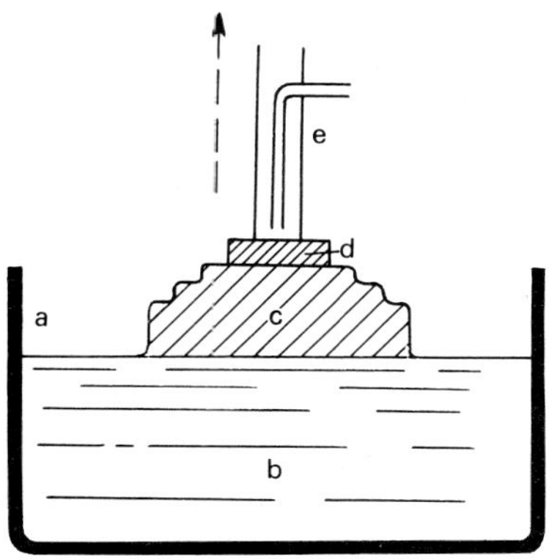

Fig. 43 Principle of the Czochralski method of crystal cultivation: a, crucible; b, melt; c, growing monocrystal; d seed; e, cooled seed holder.

Table 10 Possible substitutes for diamond

Gemstone	Hardness	Specific gravity	Refractive index	Dispersion
Diamond	10.0	3.52	2.418	0.044
Demantoid garnet	6.5	3.85	1.89	0.057
Paste	5.0	3.74	1.64	0.031
Quartz	7.0	2.65	1.54-1.55	0.013
Rutile	6.5	4.25	2.62-2.90	0.28
Sapphire (synthetic)	9.0	3.99	1.76-1.77	0.018
Spinel (synthetic)	8.0	3.63	1.727	0.020
Strontium titanate	6.0	5.13	2.41	0.200
Topaz	8.0	3.56	1.61-1.62	0.014
Yttroaluminate (YAG)	8.0	4.57	1.83-1.87	0.028
Zircon (not metamict)	7.5	4.69	1.923-2.015	0.039
Zirconia	8.5	5.7	2.20	0.066

In the past glass compositions of various colours called *pastes* were widely used to imitate gemstones. The lustre and glitter of the cut-glass 'stones' were improved by metal foil placed on the underside. The glass imitations of the quartz variety aventurine — made by pouring tiny copper flakes into molten glass — were especially good. Unlike natural gemstones, glass imitations are soft and when set they soon lose their original lustre and glitter. Glass also conducts heat less readily than most crystals and it thus feels warmer to the touch.

The so-called *doublets* (Fig. 44) are composite imitation stones made up of two parts cemented together. The parting plane is usually located in the girdle and made invisible by a suitable setting of the stone. Stones composed of three parts are called *triplets*. Doublets can be either genuine, that is composed of two smaller pieces of the same natural stone, or semi-artificial with the top part a natural stone and the bottom made of glass or inferior quality material. For example, doublets can be made of diamond backed with rock crystal, topaz, spinel, and so on. In semi-artificial doublets the top is either a colourless or a coloured stone and the bottom is dark-coloured glass. In this way emeralds are often imitated. There are also hollow doublets with a crown of a colourless natural stone, such as rock crystal, and a cavity cut and polished in the girdle plane filled with a fluid of the desired colour. The pavilion is of either the same natural material or of glass. In triplets a thin plate of coloured glass or another material is sandwiched between two genuine but colourless stones, to give the stone the required hue.

Distinguishing natural from synthetic gemstones

Unless set in a jewel it is not usually difficult to distinguish a glass imitation from a genuine gem, but distinguishing synthetic stones is much more difficult because they have the same physical and chemical properties as their natural counterparts. If the synthetic stone has been produced by the Verneuil method it can be identified by a microscopic observation of the inclusions and growth layers. In natural rubies and sapphires, for example, the growth layers are flat, in synthetic crystals they are slightly curved.

The inclusions and ingrowths in natural stones (Fig. 16) are often characteristic for a particular locality or variety and can be useful identification features. In synthetic stones manufactured by the Verneuil process, the inclusions often take the form of cloud-like clusters of tiny gas bubbles that lack any crystallographical arrangement

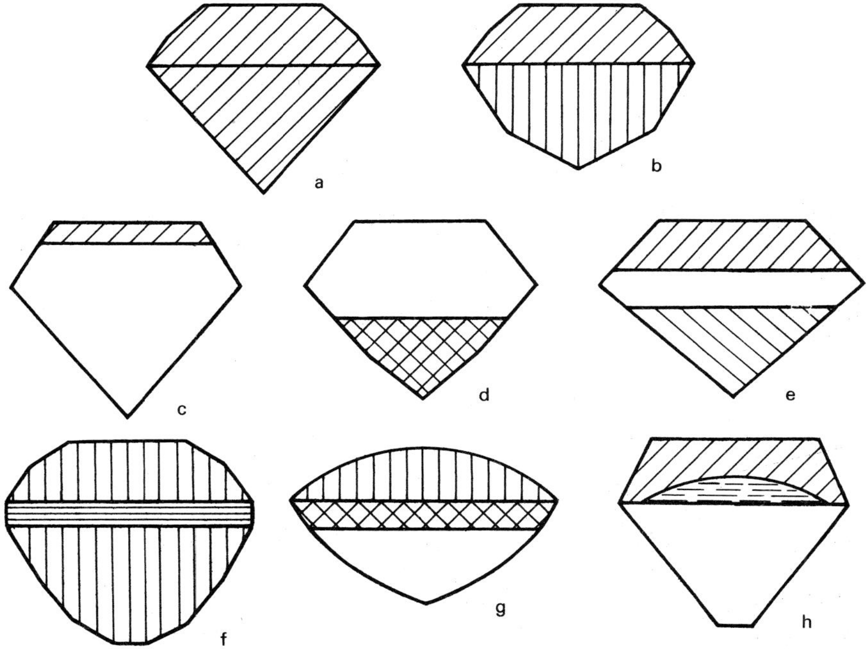

Fig. 44 Various doublets and triplets: (a) A genuine doublet — two pieces of the same natural stone (e.g. ruby) cemented together. (b) A semi-artificial doublet — the top part is a natural stone (e.g. diamond); the bottom part is made of inferior material (e.g. rock crystal). (c) A semi-artificial doublet — the top part is a natural stone (e.g. ruby); the bottom part is made of glass. (d) An artificial doublet — the top part is made of glass; the bottom part is a gemstone simulant (e.g. synthetic rutile). (e) A triplet — a thin plate of colourless glass is sandwiched between two genuine stones. (g) An opal triplet — a cabochon of rock crystal covers a thin plate of precious opal; the bottom part is made of black glass. (h) A hollow triplet — the top part is rock crystal with a cavity filled with a fluid of the desired colour; the bottom part is made of glass.

(seen, for example, in synthetic rutile). However, in crystals cultivated by other methods the orientation of the inclusions is the same as in natural stones, and in such cases spectroscopic tests may be necessary. The identification of synthetic spinels is relatively easy because the synthetic stone has a different chemical constitution from that of the natural stone. Synthetic diamonds can be recognized by characteristic inclusions that are unknown in natural stones.

A frequent question met in the jewellery business is whether pearls are natural or cultivated. If drilled, the pearls can be tested with an instrument called an *endoscope* developed in 1925 in France by C. Chilowsky and E. Perrin (Fig. 45). A hollow needle fitted at the tip with two tiny mirrors oriented at an angle of 45° is inserted into the pearl and illuminated with strong light. The telltale mark of the pearl's origin is the different internal structure: natural pearls have a concentric structure whereas culti-

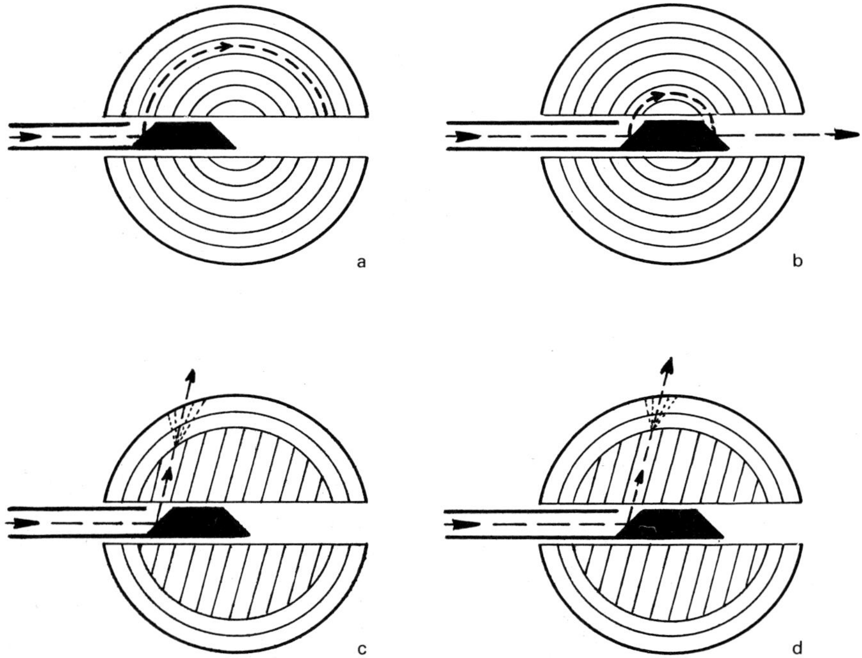

Fig. 45 Principle of the endoscope for testing pearls: (a), (b) passage of a light beam in natural pearl; (c), (d) passage of a light beam in cultivated pearl.

vated pearls are composed of parallel layers of nacre upon the mother-of-pearl nucleus. In natural pearls, a beam of light (from the hole in the needle) reflected by the first mirror passes round the layers by means of inner reflections and can be observed under a microscope in the second mirror. When the needle is inserted approximately to the centre of the pearl, a greater intensity of light will be observed in the mirror. With cultivated pearls, however, there is no flash of light in any position of the needle and the lighter circle appears only on the surface. Undrilled pearls have to be tested with X-ray equipment or magnetic methods.

Collecting, handling and storing of gemstones

If you wish to start collecting gemstones first decide what you are going to collect, and then how your collection is to be arranged. Start by collecting the common minerals occurring locally. In the beginning you will probably want to pick up all the mineral specimens within your reach, but before you do this make yourself familiar with the geological conditions of your local collecting area. A good geological map, some specialized literature and the advice of experienced collectors will all be helpful. Little by little your collecting area can be enlarged and the collection expanded through exchange or purchase until you finally possess a so-called systematic collection which will include samples of all attainable mineral types. Apart from the fact that a mineral collection is never complete, it also takes up much space in the house. So it is best to establish only a 'mini-collection' of small but carefully selected specimens; alternatively a very attractive collection can be made up of individual crystals.

In the course of time, you will want to replace some of the original pieces with better specimens, and you will become more aware of the aesthetic aspects of the collection. The value of a well-organized mineral collection increases. Sometimes an amateur collector possesses better specimens than does a museum. It is a good idea to arrange the minerals of gemstone quality in a separate collection or you could begin with collecting polished and cut stones. This is the beginning of a gemstone collection.

Where are gemstones to be found? They occur, of course, in the same places as minerals, as most gemstones are just high-quality minerals. It requires patience to find them, but it is this seeking and finding that brings the greatest pleasure to collectors.

A large number of interesting minerals and gemstones can be found in mines or on mine heaps. Stone quarries can be also interesting. Do not forget, however, to ask the right authorities for permission to search. Always proceed very cautiously and carefully. *Never* enter abandoned shafts or caves alone! This is very dangerous even for an experienced collector. Also the danger of falling stones should not be underestimated in the excitement of the moment. Sometimes a favourable opportunity for finding good minerals arises during the construction of roads, retaining dams and tunnels or in the sinking of a well or digging of a hole for construction purposes. Many minerals, especially gemstones, can also be collected along the banks of rivers and brooks in alluvia or in gravel and sand pits.

For mineral collecting the most useful tool is a good geological hammer made of hard steel. Pointed hammers and those with sharp edges diagonal to the handle are very useful. The handle is best 30 cm long; the weight of the hammer should be about 900 grams. To crush large stones a heavier, short hammer is used. For gemmological purposes a set of small hammers will also be needed. Different chisels, pointed as well as flat, are also useful. They should be made of hard steel too. The ideal length is 20 cm.

Specimens are usually carried in a knapsack or in small cardboard boxes. For wrapping the specimens to prevent damage, use newspaper, soft paper or cotton-wool. Each sample should be provided with a small label (say 4×6 cm) indicating where it was found. Numbered labels, adhesive tapes, a notebook, pencils and some cards should always be carried. Never place the label directly on the specimen, because it could be dislodged during transport. The wrapping should be as tight as possible to prevent the specimens from moving and tearing the paper cover. Finally close the package by means of adhesive tape. Exposed crystals should first be covered with a layer of crumpled soft paper or cotton-wool, and then wrapped up in paper. Delicate gemstone specimens should be embedded in cotton-wool and placed in cardboard or plastic boxes. It might be necessary to fasten some samples with a piece of thread or a fine wire to the bottom of a box before transporting them.

The number of individual locality labels should tally with the number in your notebook. Apart from the number the label should bear the date, the locality and the presumed mineral variety. The description of the locality should be more detailed in the notebook — for example, walls of a quarry — so that one could find the place again if need be.

An indispensable aid in fieldwork as well as at home is a pocket lens. An ideal lens for mineral and gemstone testing is one magnifying eight to ten times which will enable most of the important features to be seen. A $\times 20$ lens may occasionally be useful, but the field of view is limited and the focus critical. A good pocket lens is so important that it is well worth buying an anastigmatic lens (one made by Zeiss or some other high-class optical firm).

After you have carefully unpacked the specimens at home, dust and clean them. Less-delicate specimens can be brushed in soap and water. Finer samples are better cleaned with a fine brush. Pyrite and marcasite should be cleaned with spirit and not with water, as this may cause them to decompose later. Unmounted cut gems can be cleaned by a quick rub over with a handkerchief. Mounted stones may have gathered a considerable quantity of dirt, particularly on the rear facets which are less accessible. A small pot of water containing a few drops of liquid detergent and a small soft toothbrush are sufficient for cleaning purposes. Gemstones — and all other minerals — should never be exposed to direct sunlight to dry. The stone will dry quite easily if left on clean blotting-paper under the warmth of a desk lamp for a few minutes. You will be amazed by the difference in appearance of the stone after cleaning.

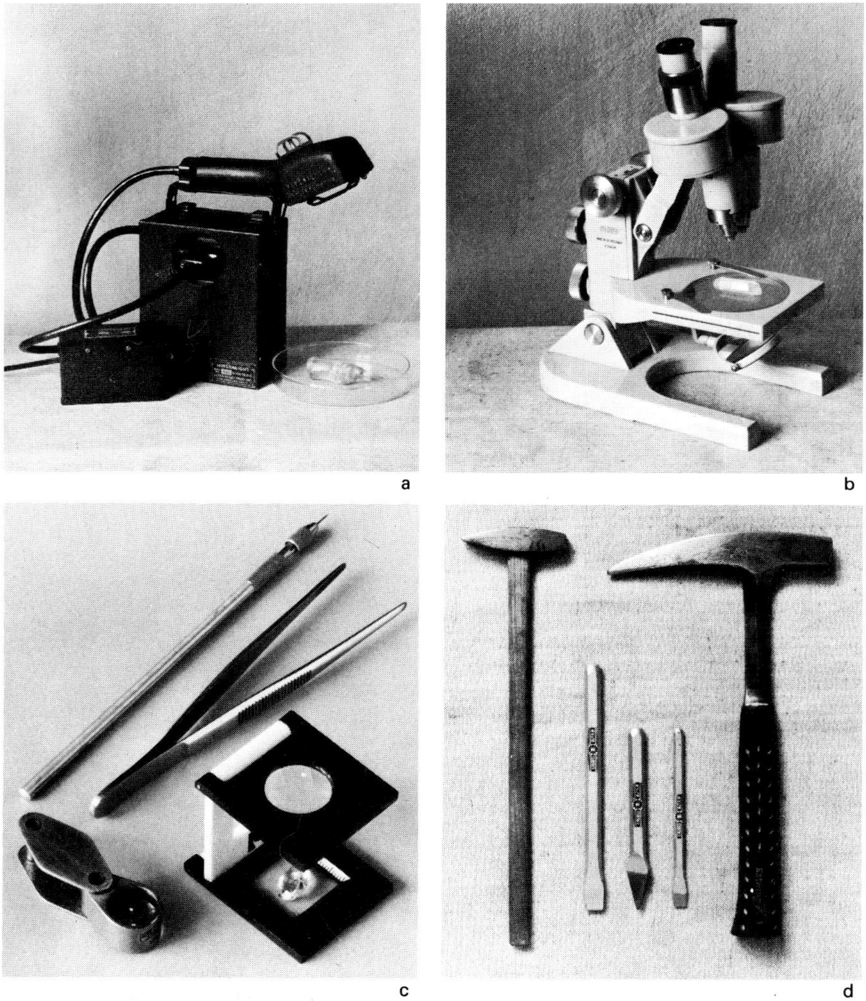

Fig. 46 Equipment for collecting and testing of gemstones: (a) lamp for ultraviolet analysis; (b) stereo microscope; (c) magnifying lenses, tweezers and preparative needle; (d) geological hammers and hand-chisels.

For gemstone examination you will need certain other instruments: (1) a pair of pincers for breaking off small pieces; (2) various tweezers (tongs); (3) a small streak plate of rough hard porcelain; (4) a Mohs' Scale of Hardness; (5) a piece of thick glass; (6) a steel-tipped knife; (7) a magnet or magnetic needle; (8) a steel preparative needle; (9) a piece of copper wire or a copper coin; (10) a good file; (11) a scoop; (12) a hermetically sealed bottle with diluted hydrochloric acid; and (13) a drop pipette. An ultraviolet lamp unit for testing gemstones in ultraviolet light and a stereoscopic microscope for mineral identification and preparatory work are also very useful (Fig. 46).

Gemstones, especially cut stones, are best examined on a cloth-topped desk. Always use tongs when handling stones to prevent them from being soiled. The tongs should not be too sharp or too strongly sprung. Stainless-steel tongs with blunt, rounded tips, scored inside to prevent the stone slipping, and with a mild spring, are very convenient. Tongs with a slide which hold the grip on a stone are also available. They are useful for tilting a stone in different orientations, for example under the microscope. Special spring tongs with strongly grooved lips can be bought for holding gems securely while they are being examined or for sorting and counting stones on a desk and for handling pearls. A small shovel or scoop is useful for transferring the stones or pearls from a desk to pocket speedily and safely.

Identify your minerals by labelling them with a number affixed to the reverse side where it is least obtrusive or the stone can be painted on the reverse side with white enamel and the number written in black Indian ink upon it. Very small crystals or gemstones are best placed in glass tubes with their number fastened to the cork or in folded stone-papers. Special glass-topped wooden or aluminium boxes with labels for marking the minerals can be bought. Such boxes have a number of round or oval depressions in which cut stones can rest. In either case you can press the stones into pads of cotton-wool of sufficient thickness to hold the specimens firmly when the lid is closed. Pure beeswax is an alternative to cotton-wool.

Serious collectors compile a list — a catalogue — of their collections. The catalogue should contain the data on the labels and can be made more complete by including a more detailed description of the locality, references to special literature, conditions of exchange, and purchase or price. For large collections it is advisable to compile a card index of minerals in alphabetical order.

Fine gemstones may, of course, be enormously expensive and very difficult to obtain. Fortunately even inferior or broken stones will show the characteristic properties of their variety. Do not neglect synthetic and imitation stones. You should become familiar with the appearance and properties of these.

Every gemstones collection must be carefully protected from dust and humidity. Excessive dryness and great variations in light and temperature can in some cases be harmful too.

Comparison of gemmological and mineralogical classifications

Gems were separated from the mineralogical system only because they are considered attractive and usable in jewellery and other decorative objects. From a scientific point of view, however, gems do not form a natural order and their classification in the gemmological system is quite arbitrary. In the mineralogical system, as we have seen, minerals are classified solely on the basis of their crystallochemical properties, that is, their chemical composition and crystal symmetry. Properties such as colour that can vary in the same variety according to where the mineral is found are not usually taken into consideration. Colour is, however, one of the most important properties of gemstones and is often the decisive factor with regard to how minerals are used in jewellery. For instance, alumina is classified in the mineralogical system as corundum but the jewellery trade recognizes each of its coloured varieties as a gem on its own and although mineralogically all the varieties are identical, the gemmologist will call them by different names (for example, ruby and sapphire) and the jeweller will regard them as quite different stones. A classification based on colour (see Table 1) is therefore much more important in systematic gemmology than in mineralogy.

Rarity and value are two other criteria used to classify gem minerals. That is why the top position in the gemmological system is occupied by diamond, ruby, sapphire and emerald, and why less noble minerals such as quartz and agate occupy the bottom positions. Pearls, corals, amber and synthetic stones, doublets and imitations are classed separately in the system.

Jewellers' usage of common and incorrect names for gemstones of the same colour regardless of their mineralogical composition has led to frequent mistakes in the past. Modern gemmology therefore tries to respect — if possible — the mineralogical affinities of the individual gems, although other, practical aspects are also taken into consideration. So gemmologists now mainly use the internationally approved classification of jewellery stones following the RAL 560 A5 Directive issued by the German Gemmological Society. This classification, which is outlined below, is the one used in the main pictorial part of this book. The main varieties, enclosed in parentheses, follow the mineral name. Asterisks indicate some of the minor gemstones and ornamental stones that are arranged separately in alphabetical order towards the end of the book after 'Novelty Stones'. Majority of the 'minor' gemstones is not classified here as the stones are only occasionally used for jewellery purposes.

A Gems and jewellery stones

I Not artificially coloured

1. Diamond
2. Corundum (ruby, sapphire, leucosapphire, padparadscha)
3. Chrysoberyl (alexandrite, cymophane or cat's eye)
4. Spinel (pleonaste or ceylonite, chlorospinel)
5. Topaz
6. Phenakite
7. Beryl (emerald, aquamarine, morganite or vorobevite, heliodor)
8. Zircon (hyacinth)
9. Tourmaline (various coloured varieties)
10. Euclase
11. Garnets: almandine, andradite (demantoid, melanite, topazolite), grossular (hessonite, tsavorite), pyrope, rhodolite, spessartite, uvarovite
12. Andalusite (chiastolite)
13. Kyanite or disthene
14. Cordierite, iolite or dichroite (sekaninaite)
15. Olivine (peridot or chrysolite)
16. Quartz (rock crystal, amethyst, prasiolite, citrine, smoky quartz, morion, cat's eye, tiger's eye, falcon's eye, blue or sapphire quartz, rose quartz, aventurine quartz, prase)
17. Chalcedony and jasper (carnelian, plasma, sard, cacholong, chrysoprase, heliotrope)
18. Agate (onyx, sardonyx, moss agate, araukarite)
19. Opal (precious opal, white opal, black opal, harlequin, fire opal, hyalite, prasopal, hydrophane, moss opal, wood opal, cacholong)
20. Pyroxenes — spodumene (hiddenite, kunzite), jadeite
21. Amphiboles — nephrite
22. Vesuvianite or idocrase (californite)
23. Pyrite and marcasite
24. Feldspars: orthoclase (adularia, sanidine, moonstone); microcline (amazonite); plagioclase group — albite, oligoclase (aventurine or sunstone), labradorite (spectrolite), anorthite

25. Haematite (specular iron, kidney ore)
26. Titanite or sphene
27. Sodalite group of feldspathoids: lazurite (lapis lazuli), sodalite
28. Turquoise
29. Brazilianite
30. Rhodonite (fowlerite)
31. Dioptase
32. Obsidian (marekanite)
33. Moldavite and other tektites
34. Smithsonite* and sphalerite*
35. Azurite or chessylite (azurmalachite)
36. Malachite (azurmalachite)
37. Aragonite (onyx marble, erzbergite, sprudelstein, peastone)
38. Rhodochrosite* or dialogite*
39. Fluorite (blue-john or Derbyshire spar)
40. Serpentine (bowenite, williamsite, verd-antique)
41. Chrysocolla*
42. Jet and cannel
43. Agalmatolite* or pagodite*; includes talc (steatite), pyrophyllite and micas.
44. Amber (succinite, rumanite, simetite, burmite, valchovite)

II **Stones that change colour on heating, irradiation, chemical dyeing or staining**

B **Reconstituted stones** (sintered fragments of gem and jewellery stones)

C **Synthetic stones**

D **Doublets**

E **Pearls** (1, natural; 2, cultivated)

F **Corals**

G **Imitations and novelty stones**

Important gem minerals

Diamond

Carbon, C; crystal system: cubic; name derived from the Greek adamas *(= invincible); specific gravity: 3.50-3.52; hardness: 10; cleavage: eminent along octahedral faces; fracture: conchoidal; tenacity: brittle; colour: colourless or white, sometimes yellow, red, green or more rarely blue or black; streak: white; transparency: transparent to translucent; lustre: brilliantly adamantine; refractive index:* n = *2.417-2.419; birefringence and pleochroism: none (isotropic); dispersion: strong, 0.044.*

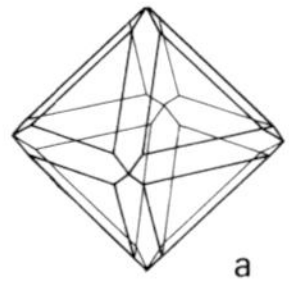
a

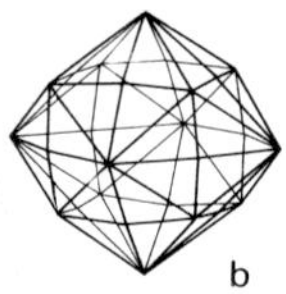
b

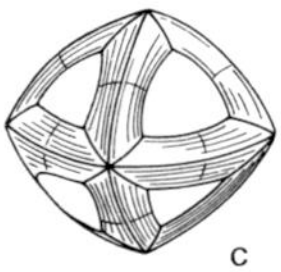
c

The first person to record diamond was probably the Roman naturalist Pliny the Elder. In his days probably only small diamonds were used because it is likely that the Romans did not know how to fashion such a hard gemstone. The stone was thus not very popular in Roman times. It was only much later, during the 16th century, that diamond began to occupy the foremost position among gemstones. For a long time the identity of diamond was not known. Then in 1675 the famous English scientist and mathematician Sir Isaac Newton advanced the hypothesis that diamond is combustible, but the Italians Averani and Targoni were the first to incinerate diamond in 1694. The proof that diamond is basically carbon was demonstrated by the English chemist Humphrey Davy (1778-1829).

It is the perfect crystal form of diamond that makes it so attractive; even the smallest grains show the characteristic trigonal markings. This is because the predominant crystal form is octahedral although rhombic dodecahedral (Fig. a), cubic and trisoctahedral forms are also found. Most characteristic, however, is the so-called diamond form — a hexoctahedron (Fig. b) that attests to the high symmetry of diamond. Many diamonds have curved edges and faces (Fig. c) caused by rapid growth and parallel face growth or twinning of the crystal.

The term adamantine (diamond-like) is used to describe a very high intensity of lustre typical of cut diamonds and cleavage faces of rough crystals. Best prices are fetched by large perfectly transparent specimens. In addition to colourless lucid diamonds, blue, yellow, green, red, brown, grey or black stones occur. Deep-blue diamonds are very rare. Today, diamonds can be coloured artificially by irradiation to desired hues.

On the basis of their physical properties, diamonds are classified into four groups: Ia, Ib, IIa and IIb. Type I diamonds absorb infrared light from 780 nm and transmit ultraviolet light down to 330 nm; type II diamonds do not absorb infrared light at all, but they absorb ultraviolet light down to 220 nm. Type I diamonds contain nitrogen (0.05-0.2 per cent) whereas type II do not. In type Ia the nitrogen atoms are admixtured in layers parallel to the cube faces, whereas in type Ib the nitrogen atoms are dispersed as a result of rapid cooling during crystallization. All synthetic diamonds produced in an argon (an inert gas) atmosphere belong to type Ib.

About 98 per cent of all lucid natural diamonds are of type Ia, the remaining 2 per cent being type II. Although so rare, type II diamonds are among the finest known.

Diamond monstrance. Gilt-silver monstrance with 6,222 diamonds of various cuts (made by M. Stegner and J. Khünischbauer, goldsmiths, Vienna, 1699). The diamonds were originally the property of Countess Eva Ludmila Kolowrat. Height 895 mm, weight 12 kg.

Type IIb diamonds are phosphorescent and possess semiconductive properties lacking in type IIa stones. The four largest stones extracted from the Premier Mine near Pretoria, South Africa, and the Cullinan diamond belong to type IIa; the famous blue Hope diamond belongs to type IIb.

Diamonds were found in environments of high pressures and temperatures deep down in the Earth's crust. They are found either in peridotite rocks known as kimberlites or more commonly as secondary occurrences in riverine and lacustrine alluvial deposits where water has brought them after the parent rock has weathered.

Africa is the richest source of diamonds, with the best fields at Kimberley in South Africa and in Sierra Leone. Well-known diamondiferous alluvia are in Zaire, Angola, Tanzania, Ghana, the Ivory Coast and Guinea. Other famous diamond fields are in the Brazilian state Minas Gerais, Australia, Borneo, Venezuela and Guyana (formerly British Guiana). One of the oldest sources of famous large diamonds used to be India. Recently, diamond fields have been opened up in the USSR on the River Viliuya in the Yakut region, and in the northern Urals.

Perhaps the most famous diamond is the Cullinan which, with an uncut weight of 621.2 grams, is the largest gem diamond ever found. It was found on 26 January 1905 by M. F. Wales, a mining inspector, at the Premier Diamond Mine in Transvaal, South Africa. Jake Asscher of Amsterdam cut it into 105 brilliants, the largest of which weighs 530.2 carats and has 74 facets. This stone — named the Star of Africa — is set in the Royal Sceptre of the British Regalia; the second two largest brilliants decorate the British Imperial State Crown. The Cullinan was originally a mere fragment of a huge octahedron measuring $10 \times 6.5 \times 5$ cm. Another famous South African diamond is the Star of South Africa, or the Dudley, with a cut weight of 47.7 carats. It was discovered in 1869 by a shepherd on the bank of the River Orange who sold the stone to a homesteader for a horse, 10 oxen and 500 sheep. It was the Dudley that provided the impetus for systematic diamond prospecting in southern Africa. In 1974, the stone was sold in Geneva for 1,600,000 Swiss francs.

From the ancient Indian Golconda comes the famous Orloff that is said to have been stolen from the eye of a Hindu idol in a Brahman temple by a French soldier of fortune about 1680. In 1772, Prince Orloff bought the 199.6-carat stone in Amsterdam for £40,000 and presented it to Catherine the Great, the Empress of Russia. The Orloff is mounted in the sceptre of the Romanoffs, which today is kept in the USSR Diamond Fund in Moscow. From the same Indian field also comes the blue Hope diamond which is said to have brought ill luck to all who have owned it. It weighs 44.4 carats and is most probably a part of a 112.5-carat stone found originally in Killur in India, stolen in 1792 and never recovered.

The Oppenheimer from South Africa, a yellow diamond crystal measuring 5.1×5.1 cm and weighing 253.7 carats, can be seen in the Smithsonian Institution in Washington DC. It is the largest known perfectly developed diamond crystal.

Diamond as the hardest of all minerals requires special methods of fashioning. It can be cut only with diamond powder. The principal cut is the brilliant with several facet rows; only smaller and inferior specimens are cut in rosettes. As a rule, cut diamonds are set only in the noblest metals (platinum and gold). In spite of the immense popularity of diamond as a gemstone, most of the world's diamond production is for industrial use.

1 Diamond set (earrings and pendant) in platinum (second half of the 19th century). **2** Brilliant cut of diamond, yellowish in colour (Kimberley, South Africa). 42.9 carats. **3** Diamond in kimberlite (South Africa). 10×10 mm.

1

2

3

Corundum

Aluminium oxide (alumina), Al_2O_3*; crystal system: trigonal; name of Indian origin, derived from the Sanskrit* kuruvinda *or the Hindu* kurund *meaning most probably hard stone; specific gravity: 3.99-4.05; hardness: 9; cleavage: none; fracture: conchoidal to uneven; tenacity: brittle; colour: variable; streak: white; transparency: transparent to translucent; lustre: adamantine to vitreous; refractive indices:* $\varepsilon = 1.765$, $\omega = 1.773$*; birefringence: 0.008; dispersion: weak, 0.018; pleochroism: strong in some varieties; main varieties: ruby, sapphire, leucosapphire and padparadscha.*

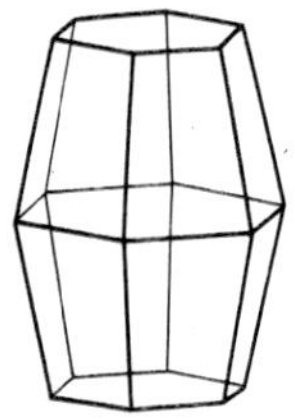

Transparent coloured varieties of corundum — the bright-red rubies and the blue sapphires with their colour resembling cornflowers or bluebottles — rank among the most precious and prized gemstones and their market price often exceeds even that of diamonds. Corundum is one of the gemstones that have been used by man for longest. In classical Greek times a corundum locality was known on the island of Naxos in the Aegean Sea. The oldest written records of ruby mining, at Mogok in Upper Burma, date from the sixth century AD. The name ruby is derived from the Latin *rubeus* (= red); the origin of sapphire's name remains a mystery.

Corundum forms hexahedral, short-to-long columnar crystals of a spindle or barrel-shaped habit (Fig.). Rarer are the low tabular crystals with a large base. Alluvial deposits often contain corundum in the form of rounded grains or pebbles.

With its hardness of 9, corundum is the hardest mineral after diamond. However, its hardness depends on the crystallographic direction: the base of the crystal is harder than the faces of the prismatic zone. Corundum has no natural cleavage, but large crystals may part parallel to the base (so-called false cleavage). It has a high, vitreous lustre, which may be of a pearly character on the bases. It usually withstands heating quite well but when jewels decorated with corundum are repaired, they must be heated and cooled slowly. Some sapphires will change hue if annealed.

Corundum has a worldwide occurrence. It crystallizes in granites and granite pegmatites, in nephelinic syenites, crystalline schists, gneisses, contact-metamorphosed limestones and dolomites. Because corundum is mechanically and chemically resistant, it often occurs secondarily in alluvia. The relatively high specific gravity of the stones permits easy placer mining (panning).

Depending on their origin, natural corundums contain various inclusions and ingrowths of small crystals of other minerals, as well as gaseous and liquid inclusions. These foreign inclusions are usually typical for certain localities and are a better guide to the locality and origin of stones than are hues. A microscopic observation of foreign inclusions is also a useful method for distinguishing natural stones from synthetic ones.

Corundum is found in many colour hues. Some crystals may even be multicoloured and show colour zoning. The most transparent colourless corundum variety is called **leucosapphire**. Unlike the synthetic stones that are always perfectly colourless, natural leucosapphires have a slight tinge. Although leucosapphires are much rarer in nature than rubies or sapphires, they are less valued for jewellery.

1 Ruby in green zoisite (northern Tanzania). 200 × 170 mm. Cross-section of three crystals. Diameter of largest crystal up to 40 mm. **2** Sapphire pebble in conglomerate (Ratnapura, Sri Lanka). 110 × 80 mm. **3** Cross-section of zoned corundum, photographed in transmitted light (Tasmania). Diameter 25 mm. **4** Asteriated sapphires (Tasmania). Diameter of largest specimen 25 mm.

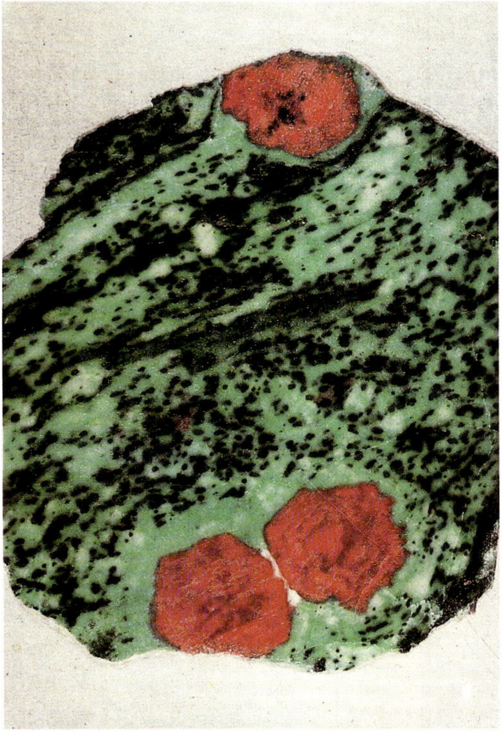

1

2

3

4

The red colour of **ruby** is caused by an admixture of chromium. The content of chromium trioxide in rubies fluctuates between 0.02 and 0.6 per cent, depending on how much aluminium oxide has been replaced in the corundum structure. Rubies occur in various hues ranging from pinkish to full red. Those of the colour of pigeon's blood are rare and valuable and were poetically called 'blood drops from the heart of Mother Earth' in the ancient Orient. Such rubies contain approximately 0.1 per cent of chromium trioxide.

The blue **sapphire** owes its colour to a small admixture of bivalent iron and traces of titanium. The colour of blue sapphires is variable and ranges from pale azure to dark gentian. Most prized are the sapphires of a bluebottle colour. The name sapphire is also applied to yellow, brown, green and violet corundum varieties. The brown and yellow colours are caused by trivalent iron and the green is caused by a mixture of bi- and trivalent iron. The violet varieties contain an admixture of vanadium.

A very rare natural corundum variety is **padparadscha**. The name is originally Indian and is derived from the Sinhalese word *padma-radschen* meaning the colour of a lotus blossom. Padparadscha has a pleasant reddish to orange-yellow colour caused by a small amount of chromium (0.02 per cent), iron (0.04 per cent) and traces of vanadium.

Some coloured varieties of corundum, especially rubies and sapphires, are pleochroic. The change in hue of the transmitted light can easily be observed with the naked eye if the stone is turned in various directions. Pleochroism must be taken into consideration before selecting and orientating the cut. The best hues will be in the direction of the optical axis of the crystal.

When exposed to ultraviolet light, some rubies and sapphires fluoresce intensively. Rubies show a carmine-red fluorescence, but in sapphires the colour of the luminescence depends on the origin of the stones and the wavelength of the illumination.

Some rubies and sapphires possess a distinct optical effect called asterism. In reflected light, the base of such a stone will show a glittering six- or three-pointed star. The effect is caused by the reflection of light from hair-thin rutile crystal ingrowths arranged in six or three directions 60° or 120° apart. Asterism is enhanced if a suitable cabochon cut is selected for the stone. In the past asterism was considered a failproof mark of the natural origin of the stone but asteriated rubies and sapphires are now made synthetically.

The richest and oldest ruby field is at Mogok in Upper Burma. Second in the production league is Thailand where extensive alluvial deposits are worked near the Cambodian border. Beautifully coloured rubies also come from Phailin in Cambodia. Thai rubies are usually dark, and often have a purplish to brownish tint. Alluvial rubies from Ratnapura in Sri Lanka are prized for their intensive vivid lustre. Recently there has been much interest in the full-red nontransparent rubies embedded in green zoisite found in Tanzania. In the USA, corundum varieties are found in North and South Carolina and Montana. The alluvial gravels in Thailand also yield many asteriated dark-coloured sapphires. The most beautiful sapphires of various colours come from Phailin.

1 Rough sapphire with rounded edges (alluvial deposits, Sri Lanka). 12 × 10 mm. **2** Cut ruby (Mogok, Burma). 4.9 carats. **3** Padparadscha corundum. Two step cuts, origin unknown. Weight of the larger stone 2.9 carats. **4** Cut synthetic corundums of various colours.

1

2

3

4

So far the largest rough rubies, weighing up to 80 grams, have come from Burma. A large, asteriated ruby weighing 593.4 carats is known from Sri Lanka. The Bohemian crown of St Wenceslaus is adorned with a large ruby of about 250 carats. The richest collections of large rubies and sapphires are owned by various Indian princes. A 2,000-carat sapphire was used by an American artist for carved heads of Abraham Lincoln, George Washington and General Eisenhower. The American Museum of Natural History in New York is the proud keeper of the Star of India, an asteriated sapphire weighing 535 carats and 4 cm in diameter. The USSR Diamond Fund in Moscow owns a sapphire of Sri Lankan origin that weighs 260 carats. The largest known asteriated sapphire, weighing 63,000 carats, was discovered in Burma in September 1966.

The physical properties of corundums rank them not only among the most valuable gemstones but also among the most prized industrial materials. For example, they are widely used as watch jewels in high-precision timepieces, as bearings in high-precision instruments, as balance blades, needles and hi-fi styli. Rubies are also extensively used in laser technology.

The great demand for corundum and its rare occurrence provided the impetus for the research that ultimately led to its industrial production and since 1902 synthetic corundums of various colours have been produced by the Verneuil process. Very finely pulverized alumina with colouring agents is first melted in an oxyhydrogen flame in special furnaces, where monocrystals of corundum grow without crucibles on fire-clay rods into pear-shaped drops and cylinders called boules. (Further details of the process are given in the introductory part of the book.) Unlike natural stones, synthetic crystals of corundum produced by the Verneuil process contain fine foreign inclusions — mostly microscopic bubbles — oriented in curved planes. Today, large crystals of corundum of any shape are pulled from alumina melt. Corundum cultivated by the hydrothermal method in autoclaves under increased pressure and temperature have their foreign inclusions orientated in planes similarly to those in natural stones, and so it has become difficult to distinguish between natural and synthetic stones. The corundum waste generated in the various processes is used in industry as a high-grade abrasive grit. Two synthetic corundums are marketed under the trade names Alundum and Aloxite.

1 Sapphire set with brilliants, *c.* 1900. **2** Baroque cross with sapphires. Height 70 mm. **3** Crown of Emperor Charles IV, 1346. The crown is decorated with sapphires (largest 52 × 35 × ~12 mm), a ruby (39.5 × 36.5 × 14 mm, one of the largest rubies in the world, located in the centre of the fleur-de-lis on the front side of the crown), spinels (largest 25.5 × 25 × 14 mm, heart-shaped, located on the central petal of the fleur-de-lis, top right of picture), emeralds and pearls. The sapphire located at the top of the crown is unique; it is shaped like a cross and is engraved with a scene of the Crucifixion. Altogether the crown is studded with 96 gems, whose total weight, including the pearls, is 0.75 kg; total weight of the gold is 1.75 kg.

Charles IV dedicated the crown to the Premyslid ruler and patron saint of Bohemia, St Wenceslaus, whom the Emperor worshipped as his personal patron saint, thus stressing his descendance from the Premyslids in the maternal line. The crown is called St Wenceslaus' Crown and Emperor Charles IV was crowned with it on 1 September 1347.

1

2

3

Chrysoberyl

Beryllium aluminium oxide, $BeAl_2O_4$; *crystal system: orthorhombic; name derived from the Greek* chrysos *(= gold); specific gravity: 3.65-3.80; hardness: 8.5; cleavage: marked only in one direction; fracture: conchoidal to uneven; tenacity: brittle; colour: greenish yellow, green or brown; streak: white; transparency: transparent to translucent; lustre: vitreous; refractive indices:* $\alpha = 1.746$, $\beta = 1.748$, $\gamma = 1.756$; *birefringence: 0.01; dispersion: weak, 0.015; pleochroism: strong in deep colours; main varieties: alexandrite and cymophane (cat's eye).*

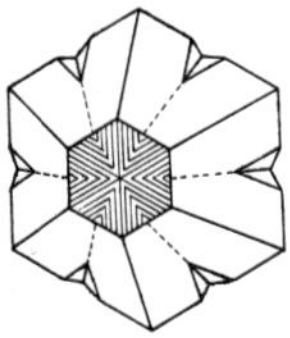

Chrysoberyl forms short columnar or thick tabular crystals. Its heart-shaped contact twins and hexagonal trillings are quite common, especially in the variety alexandrite (Fig.). The faces of the intergrowths show clear feather or plume-like striation.

After diamond and corundum, chrysoberyl is the third hardest gemstone, with good polishing properties. A relatively high refractive index is the cause of the intense brilliance of the mineral. Chrysoberyl comes in various shades of yellowish-green, olive-green, golden-yellow, yellowish-brown and warm tobacco-brown tones. The coloration is caused by admixtures of iron and chromium and by traces of titanium.

In 1830, in the emerald mines on the River Tokovaya in the Urals, a stone was discovered that changes its colour in daylight from a moss green to an emerald green and from a raspberry red to mauve in artificial light. The stone was classified as a variety of chrysoberyl and called **alexandrite** in honour of Czar Alexander II. The colour change is caused by the selective absorption of parts of the spectrum. The stone has a strong absorption band in the yellow part: this, in conjunction with the difference in composition of daylight and artificial light, causes the striking colour change, which is intensified by the strong pleochroism. The stone is now considered to be one of the most valuable gemstones.

Another chrysoberyl variety is **cymophane** (from the Greek *kyma* = wave and *phainein* = to appear), also known as **chrysoberyl cat's eye**. It is a slightly milky stone of a silky lustre and a green, yellow or brown colour. If the stone, especially one cut into cabochons, is moved to and fro, the upper surface will show a chatoyant, milky, bluish and greenish white fluctuating glitter. The glitter is highest in the light silvery band in the centre, which moves as the stone is tilted. The greatest prices are fetched by stones that have a narrow and well-defined band. The chatoyancy is caused by the reflection of light from numerous microscopically fine inclusions oriented parallel to the crystallographic direction. These inclusions also produce the stone's characteristic opalescence.

Chrysoberyl and its varieties are found in granite pegmatites, in metamorphic rocks, gneiss and mica schists, and secondarily in alluvia. The richest chrysoberyl localities are in Sri Lanka where chrysoberyl and sapphires are placer-mined. The largest stone so far found there weighed 16 grams and measured 23 × 17 mm. In Brazil, chrysoberyl is found together with topaz at Minas Novas in the state of Minas Gerais, at São Paulo and Espírito Santo. Other major localities are the USA, Madagascar, Zaire and Zimbabwe. The famous alexandrite localities in the Urals have long since been exhausted.

Chrysoberyl and alexandrite are usually cut into step (trap) cuts or brilliants; cymophane is usually fashioned into circular or oval cabochons.

1 Chrysoberyl embedded in parent rock (Haddam, Connecticut, USA). Crystal 17 × 10 mm. **2** Cut chrysoberyl (Sri Lanka). 27.8 carats. **3** Cyclic intergrowth of alexandrite (Tokovaya, USSR). 50 × 40 mm. **4** Cymophane cabochon (Sri Lanka). Diameter 5 mm.

1

2

3

4

Spinel

Magnesium aluminium oxide, $MgAl_2O_4$*; crystal system: cubic; name derived from the Latin* spina *(= spine, thorn) on account of the most common form of spinel — octahedral crystals with six apices — or the name may be derived from the Greek* spinos *(= spark) because of its sparkling appearance; specific gravity: 3.58-4.06; hardness: 8; cleavage: poor along octahedral faces; fracture: conchoidal to uneven; tenacity: brittle; colour: red, brown or black, sometimes green or blue; streak: white; transparency: transparent; lustre: vitreous; refractive index:* n = *1.715-1.720; birefringence and pleochroism: none (isotropic); dispersion: medium, 0.020; main varieties: pleonaste (ceylonite) and chlorospinel.*

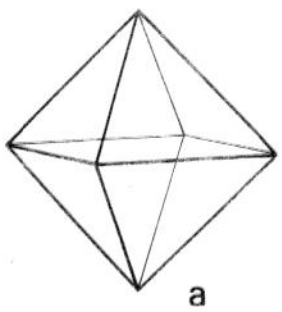
a

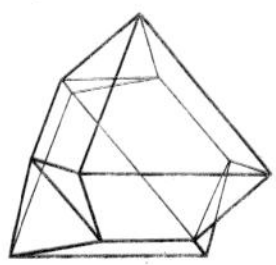
b

Spinel has long been valued as a gemstone. In the past it often used to be mistaken for ruby or sapphire and as such was collected in royal treasuries.

The most common crystal forms of spinel are well-bounded octahedra (Fig. a) that are slightly rounded in larger crystals, or octahedral twins (Fig. b). Alluvia also contain spinel in the form of rounded grains and pebbles. Gem varieties of spinel usually come in delicate shades of red; blue, bluish green, green and violet spinels are rarer. The green variety is called **chlorospinel** and the black non-translucent spinel is known as **pleonaste** or **ceylonite**. In 1955 a great variety was found in Sri Lanka — a black asteriated spinel. The colour variation in spinels is caused by admixtures of iron, chromium, zinc and copper.

Spinels occur as accessory minerals in basic igneous rocks, crystalline schists and contact-metamorphosed limestones and dolomites. Gem varieties also occur secondarily in alluvia and sands. Spinels are usually found associated with rubies and sapphires. The most famous localities are at Ratnapura and Rakwana in Sri Lanka, and Mogok in Upper Burma. The fields in Thailand and India give lower yields.

Like corundum, spinel is produced synthetically in large quantities, usually by the Verneuil process. Synthetic spinels can usually be distinguished from natural spinels and more expensive gemstones by testing the refractive index. An additional identification is the anomalous birefringence of synthetic spinels under a polariscope.

Red spinels may easily be mistaken for rubies, which can be recognized by their birefringence and pleochroism. Red garnets are singly refractive like spinels, and their specific gravity and refractive index may be similar, but they are attracted by strong magnets whereas spinels are not.

Large, gem-quality spinels are very rare. The most famous gem spinel is the Timur-Rubin, a red, polished spinel weighing 352 carats. Its history dates back to the 14th century; today it is a part of the British Crown Jewels. Another famous ruby-red spinel is the oval Black Prince's Ruby, which measures about 5 cm. It decorates the British Imperial State Crown. Especially large and exquisite spinels are set in the Bohemian crown of St Wenceslaus.

Spinels are cut into brilliants, step (trap) cuts and table cuts; rounded cabochons are less frequent.

1 Spinel pebbles (alluvial deposits, Sri Lanka). Length of pebbles about 3 mm. **2** Two cut spinels, green and red (Sri Lanka). Weight of the larger stone 9.8 carats. **3** Spinel cross with brilliants (first half of the 19th century). Cross height 70 mm. **4** Heart-shaped spinel from the central petal of the fleur-de-lis on the St Wenceslaus Crown. The stone was fashioned into an irregular shape to preserve as much as possible of the stone. 25.5 × 25 × 14 mm.

1

2

3

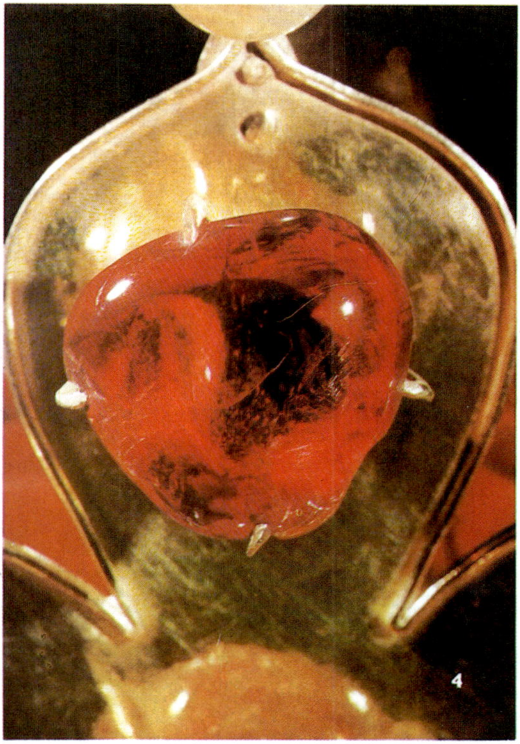

4

Topaz

Hydrous aluminium fluorosilicate, $Al_2[(F, OH)_2|SiO_4]$; *crystal system: orthorhombic; name derived either from the Sanskrit* tapas *(= fire) or from the Greek* topazion, *used to designate gemstones from the island of Topazos; specific gravity: 3.49-3.57; hardness: 8; cleavage: eminent along base; fracture: uneven; tenacity: brittle; colour: variable; streak: white; transparency: transparent; lustre: vitreous; refractive indices:* α *= 1.606-1.629,* β *= 1.609-1.631,* γ *= 1.616-1.638; birefringence: 0.01; dispersion: weak, 0.014; pleochroism: distinct.*

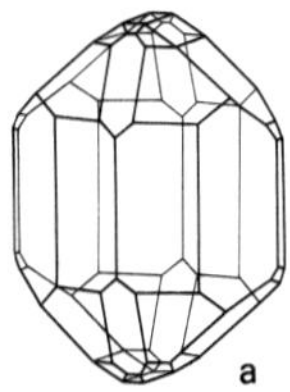
a

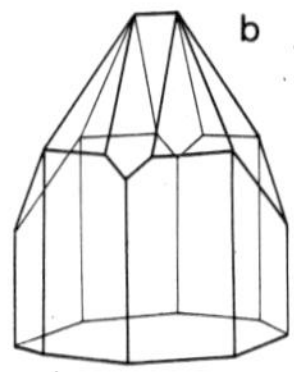
b

For its pleasant, unobtrusive colour, high lustre, great hardness as well as transparency and lucidity, topaz was one of the most valued gemstones as early as Greek and Roman times. Pliny the Elder used the name topaz for a yellowish-green stone from Topazos, but he was most probably mistaken and had chrysolite from St John's Island (now Zebirget) in the Red Sea in mind. During the classical period, the word *topazios* was used to describe most yellow stones known at the time. This incorrect designation of yellow stones has survived till today, and the word topaz supplemented with a qualifier is still used for yellow-coloured stones such as citrine and corundum. From the medieval age until the mid-19th century topaz was a highly prized gemstone that always fetched very good prices on the market. The price dropped only after the rich Brazilian fields had been opened. Although today topaz is no longer considered to be a rare gemstone — its prices are at an all-time low — it still remains very popular. In contrast to other stones, its price depends on colour, not size, and the price differences between topazes of various colours are sometimes astonishing. Today, pink, blue and honey-yellow topazes have the highest value.

In nature, topaz is found in short-to-long columnar crystals with an orthorhombic form, often with multifaced termination (Figs a, b). The crystals may sometimes be quite large. The prismatic faces of topaz crystals are sometimes vertically striated so that topaz can be distinguished from quartz, which is striated horizontally. Topaz occurs as pebbles in alluvia. The lucid, colourless pebbles from the Brazilian placers are known in the trade as *pingos d'agoa* (drops of water).

One of the most distinctive properties of topaz is its eminent cleavage along the base. Sometimes the mere warming of a topaz crystal in one's hand may result in internal cracking. These minute cleavage cracks distinguish topaz from beryl or quartz. The eminent cleavage permits an easy splitting of larger specimens. Topaz requires extremely careful handling while being fashioned because it may split or develop internal cracks when the stone is cut or polished. It should also not be tested for hardness with excessive force. Topaz takes a good polish and the finished stones feels very smooth and even slippery.

1 Topaz crystal (Tonokamiama, Japan). 50 × 50 mm. **2** Perfectly faced topaz crystal (Schneckenstein, GDR). 12 × 8 mm. **3** Blue topaz (Nerchinsk, USSR). 40 × 35 mm. **4** Pink topaz (Minas Gerais, Brazil). 45 × 25 mm.

1

2

3

4

Topaz occurs naturally in a variety of colours. The crystals may be clear, colourless and perfectly transparent or a grey, greenish, wine-yellow, sherry-coloured, reddish, purplish or blue. The colour is never conspicuous but always quite delicate. The coloration is usually even although streaked and mottled stones are not unknown. The property of some topazes to change colour if heated or exposed to radiation is an interesting and commercially useful property. Some honey-yellow and yellowish brown topazes from Brazil will turn red if heated to 300-450 °C. The crystals are placed in coal dust, ashes or sand and then carefully heated and slowly cooled again to prevent cracking. The stone discolours on heating and when it cools down it turns red. Lower annealing temperatures yield salmon-pink hues, and excessive heating produces perfectly colourless stones. If such artificially coloured stones are subsequently exposed to ultraviolet light, they will regain their original colour. Most pink and red topazes sold on the market are heat-treated stones that have changed colour.

Yellow topazes from other than Brazilian localities will only discolour when heated. Blue topazes cannot be heat-treated to change their colour, but a long exposure to sunlight may sometimes change the colour depth of the stone. The dark wine-yellow topazes from Siberia and Japan are especially sensitive in this respect. The different colours of topazes are caused by metallic trace elements, especially chromium and iron.

Topaz is a typical pneumatolytic mineral. It is found in granites, granite pegmatites, quartz porphyry and similar rocks. It crystallizes in paragenesis with tourmaline, beryl, fluorite, cassiterite, apatite, quartz and other minerals. In secondary deposits topaz accumulates in gemmy alluvia. Some topaz colours are characteristic of certain localities and the same applies for ingrowths of microscopic crystals of iron-bearing minerals (for example, ilmenite, haematite or goethite) or for gaseous and liquid inclusions.

In medieval times the most renowned source of topaz was the mining area at Schneckenstein in the Ore Mountains (Erzgebirge) in Saxony where small, wine-yellow stones were found. Many medieval rulers wore jewellery decorated with the 'Saxonian topaz' and the locality is most probably the source of a topaz set in the ring of the Bohemian King Přemysl Otakar (Ottokar) I. Between 1737 and 1800 topaz was extracted at Schneckenstein by regular deep-mining. Today, the locality is a protected natural reservation.

The best-known modern topaz localities are in Brazil and here the stones are mostly honey-yellow, yellowish red, pink-red and purplish, the last being sometimes incorrectly called Brazilian rubies. Much rarer are the blue topazes known as *safiras* and blue-green stones. Some Brazilian topaz crystals are up to a metre long and weigh several hundred kilograms.

1 Pebbles of colourless topaz (alluvial deposits known as *pingos d'agoa*, Minas Gerais, Brazil). Length of pebbles about 5 mm. **2** Brilliant cut of topaz (Brazil). 122.4 carats. **3** Pendant with green topaz cut as a briolette. 98.6 carats. **4** Cut blue topaz. 197 carats.

1

2

3

4

Azure-blue topazes come from Murzinka near Sverdlovsk in the Urals, USSR, where the stones occur in granite cavities in association with other minerals such as smoky quartz, feldspar and lepidolite. Colourless, yellow, pink and violet-blue topazes are placer-mined on the River Sanarka in the southern Urals, and pale blue topazes, similar to aquamarine and often taken for it in the past, come from Nerchinsk in the Trans-Baikal region. The Siberian localities at Adun Chilon yield topazes of various colours. Recently topaz fields have been opened at Podol in the Ukraine and crystals weighing several scores of kilograms have been discovered there.

The well-known placers in Sri Lanka yield topazes that are either colourless, or yellow, yellowish brown or pale green. Superior well-faced crystals also come from Japanese localities such as Takayama and Naegi in Mino Province. The major US localities are Pikes Peak, Colorado, the liparites in the Thomas Range, Utah, and San Diego County, California. In Mexico, topazes are found in San Luis Potosí and in alluvia at Durango where they occur associated with cassiterite. Of minor importance are the occurrences in Africa and Australia.

Unique specimens of beautiful topazes can be seen in many mineralogical collections throughout the world. The American Museum of Natural History in New York has a perfectly bounded topaz crystal measuring 80 × 60 × 60 cm and weighing 300 kg. A museum in Florence exhibits a pink topaz crystal weighing 150 kg. Giant crystals from Murzinka can be seen in collections in Moscow and Leningrad. Perhaps the most famous, although not the biggest cut topaz, is the so-called Braganza, which was found in Ouro Preto, Brazil, in 1740 and was originally thought to be a diamond. The Smithsonian Institution in Washington, DC has some unique Brazilian cut topazes, for example a yellow topaz weighing 7.725 carats, a blue topaz weighing 3.273 carats, and a yellowish green topaz of 1.469 carats. The largest cut topaz in the world is the pale blue Brazilian Princess, which is cut into a regular square and weighs 4,265.5 grams (21,327 carats). It was found at Teofilo Otoni in Brazil.

Colourless topazes are usually cut as circular or oval brilliants whereas coloured stones are mostly sold as step (trap) and table cuts.

The most common imitator of topaz is the rich-yellow citrine obtained by annealing of amethyst and marketed under the trade name Madeira or Spanish Topaz. The so-called Indian or Oriental Topaz is a yellow-coloured corundum. Sometimes even synthetic corundums or spinels are passed off as genuine topazes. On the other hand, the latter can be used to imitate other more valuable gemstones whose price is several times that of topaz.

1 Corroded topaz crystal (Nerchinsk, USSR). Height 92 mm. **2** Cut topazes (Schneckenstein, GDR). Larger stones about 1 carat. **3** Ring of Bohemian King Premysl Otakar I decorated with a topaz cut *en cabochon;* funeral insignia (stone comes from Schneckenstein, GDR). **4** Art Nouveau flacon from Brazilian topaz (Turnov, Bohemia, early 20th century). Height 35 mm.

1

2

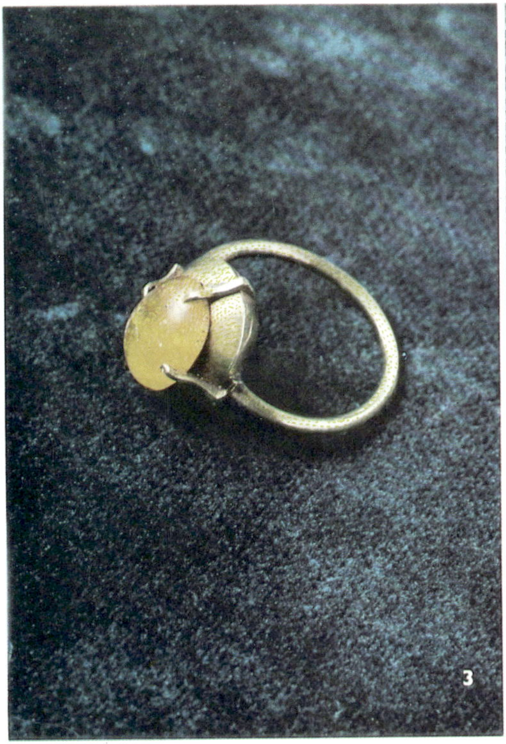
3

4

Phenakite

Beryllium silicate, $Be_2[SiO_4]$*; crystal system: trigonal; name derived from the Greek* phenakos *(= cheater) because it can easily be mistaken for other minerals, especially quartz; specific gravity: 2.93-3.00; hardness: 7.5-8; cleavage: poor; fracture: conchoidal; tenacity: brittle; colour: colourless, yellowish or pale pink; streak: white; transparency: transparent; lustre: highly vitreous; refractive indices:* $\varepsilon = 1.670$*,* $\omega = 1.654$*; birefringence: 0.016; dispersion: weak, 0.015; pleochroism: distinct in coloured stones.*

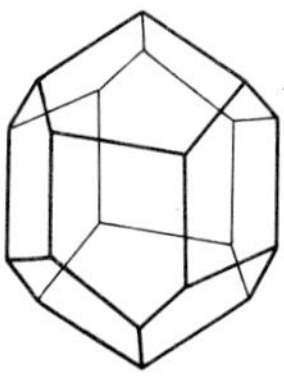

Phenakite occurs relatively rarely in nature and is therefore used only exceptionally as a gemstone. It was first discovered in the early 19th century in the emerald mines on the River Tokovaya in the Urals, near Sverdlovsk. As its transparent colourless crystals and especially their fragments seemed not to differ from rock crystal, phenakite was long thought to be a variety of quartz.

Phenakite forms short or long columnar crystals terminating in rhombohedra (Fig.) or low-profile, lens-shaped crystals with prevailing rhombohedra. Interpenetrate twins, similar to those of quartz, are also common.

Phenakite possesses a highly vitreous lustre that can be enhanced with polishing to a greasy one. When cut, however, phenakite does not display the colourful play of colours that diamond does. Phenakite crystals are chemically very pure, containing only minute traces of impurities and inclusions of other minerals are quite exceptional. Should there be ingrowths of fine acicular crystals, phenakite is translucent and whitish. Stones of this kind can be successfully cut to display an attractive cat's-eye chatoyancy.

Phenakites are often not colour fast: although a crystal may be beautifully coloured when extracted from the parent rock, sunlight may discolour it totally in a matter of months. The coloured varieties show distinct pleochroism. The hues are never deep but pale and delicate.

Phenakite occurs in granites, granite pegmatites, greisen and in Alpine veins. It originates during hydrothermal or pneumatolytic processes and crystallizes either as a primary mineral or originates secondarily as the result of decomposition of beryl. It is often found associated with topaz, beryl (emerald), chrysoberyl, apatite, quartz, microcline feldspar (amazonite), albite and mica.

The classical phenakite occurrences are the emerald mines in the Urals that have already been mentioned, and Miass in the Ilmen Mountains, also in the USSR. The locality of Kragerø, Norway, yields crystals up to several scores of centimetres long. In the USA it is found at Topaz Butte near Pikes Peak, and on Mt Antero in Chaffee County, Colorado. Large colourless crystals occur also at São Miguel di Piracicaba in Minas Gerais, Brazil. Recently phenakite has been discovered in the gem fields in Sri Lanka where a gem of 569 carats has been cut from a colourless crystal fragment.

The most common type of cut used for phenakite is the brilliant. The stone may be mistaken for topaz, beryl, rock crystal, sapphire and diamond.

1 Magnificent columnar crystal of phenakite (Kragerø, Norway). Height 230 mm. **2** Group of phenakite crystals (São Miguel di Piracicaba, Brazil). Diameter of largest crystal about 35 mm. **3** Oblong cut of phenakite (Brazil). 8.3 carats. **4** Step cut of phenakite (unknown locality). 11.8 carats.

1

2

3

4

Beryl

Beryllium aluminium silicate, $Be_3Al_2[Si_6O_{18}]$*; crystal system: hexagonal; name derived from the Greek* beryllos *(whose meaning is not known but it could have been used for any green gemstone), then the Latin* beryllus*; specific gravity: 2.63-2.90; hardness: 7.5-8; cleavage: poor; fracture: uneven; tenacity: brittle; colour: white, yellow, green, blue or, rarely, pink; streak: white; transparency: transparent to translucent; refractive indices:* $\varepsilon = 1.570\text{-}1.588$*,* $\omega = 1.575\text{-}1.591$*; birefringence: 0.005-0.009; dispersion: weak, 0.014; pleochroism: distinct; main varieties: emerald, aquamarine, morganite (vorobevite) and heliodor.*

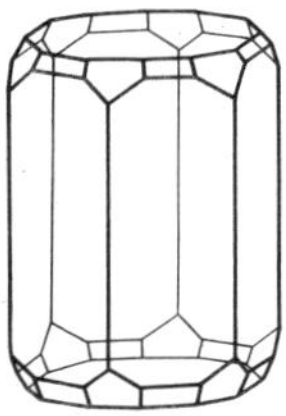

Beryl is one of the oldest known minerals. Its emerald varieties were mined in Upper Egypt south of Koseir as early as 2000 BC. Beryl is mentioned by Theophrastus and by Pliny the Elder. Cleopatra is reputed to have possessed an emerald engraved with her portrait and Nero is said to have used a cut emerald as a monocle to aid his poor sight — this is mentioned first by Pliny. However, the generally poor knowledge of gemstones in ancient times often led to confusions, similar minerals being mistaken for each other. It seems more likely therefore that Nero used not a green variety of beryl (emerald), because it would have been very difficult to obtain the required transparency in the size of stone needed, but an aquamarine. Nevertheless, Pliny's remark is of great historical value because it is the first record of a technical usage of a gemstone. There are more stories like that, usually involving beryl — a common, inconspicuous but indispensable mineral.

Beryl contains beryllium, an element highly valued in metallurgy. Beryllium was named after the mineral because it was first separated from beryl by the French chemist N.L. Vauquelin in 1798.

Beryl is a mineral typical of granite pegmatites where it commonly occurs. Sometimes it is also found in coarse-grained granites, mica schists and in cassiterite deposits in association with such minerals as topaz, tourmaline, fluorite and wolframite. Top-quality emeralds come from limestones at Muzo in Colombia.

Truly gigantic columns of the mineral have been found in pegmatites; for example a crystal 6 metres long and 1 metre thick was discovered in Albany, in the US state of Maine; and beryls extracted from pegmatites in South Dakota have weighed 30-100 metric tons. Beryl crystals are usually simple combinations of a hexagonal prism and basal pinacoid (the figure shows a combination of these forms with two bipyramids). Columnar crystals are also found either singly edged or in druses, sometimes even in lumps ingrown in feldspar or quartz. Some beryls have been found to contain more than 1 per cent alkalis and such crystals have a short columnar form. Beryls containing no alkalis or only minute amounts of them form long columnar crystals.

1 Group of emerald crystals (Tokovaya, USSR). Length of largest crystal about 60 mm. **2** Columnar crystal of emerald (Santa Fé, Bogota, Colombia). 80 × 33 mm. **3** Columnar crystal of aquamarine (Adun Chilon, USSR). 60 × 45 mm. **4** Group of morganite crystals (Pala, California, USA). Diameter of largest crystal about 105 mm.

1

2

3

4

The most valued beryl variety is **emerald**, which may sometimes fetch even greater prices than diamond. The name is derived from an ancient Persian word that appeared later in Greek as *smaragdos,* which in turn gave rise, via Latin, to the Old French *esmaraude,* Middle English *emaraude* and, finally, to *emerald.*

Emerald was being sold on the Babylonian market around 4000 BC and was later symbolically dedicated to Venus, the goddess of love. Emerald is the birthstone for May, the month of love and it is regarded as a symbol of immortality and faithfulness. Its colour of a fresh spring meadow makes it very popular. The colour is caused by an admixture of chromium trioxide. In spite of the deep-green colour, emerald crystals may be perfectly transparent. A great shortcoming, common to all emeralds, is that even an originally perfectly clear and flawless stone will turn cloudy or hazy in time if exposed to air, and may even crack.

Herodotus, the ancient Greek historian, writes of the emerald ring of Polycrates and sings praises of the emerald column in the temple of Hercules in Tyre. There is a story that the wife of the Roman emperor Caligula once came to a feast bejewelled with emeralds and pearls with a value of 40 million sesterces (about 40 tons of silver). In one of the shrines in the Buddha Tooth Temple in Kandy, Sri Lanka, there is an ancient figurine of Buddha carved from a single emerald. The Peruvian Indians used to worship an exquisite emerald of the size of an ostrich egg as a deity. The Spanish conquistadors were much surprised by the magnificent emeralds presented to them as tokens of friendship by the Indians in Colombia where top-quality stones are still mined at Muzo, Cosquez and Somondoco. The mining operations were started there by the conquistadors who 'held the sword in one hand and the pick in the other'. One of the most exquisite jewels of that time is the golden crown of Montezuma decorated with a beautiful emerald druse now kept in the Museum of Natural History in Vienna.

The Muzo deposits have not been depleted and still yield emeralds of great beauty and a rich green colour. The emerald fields on the River Tokovaya in the Urals, near Murzinka are also very rich. The locality was discovered accidentally when a peasant in 1830 stumbled on green stones in a treehole after a violent storm. The largest-known druse of emerald crystals weighing 250 kg, come from the Ural deposits with some prisms measuring 40 × 25.4 cm. A minor European locality is Habachtal near Salzburg in Austria, where emeralds are found embedded in mica schist. Other localities include Emmsville in New South Wales, Australia, Transvaal in South Africa, India, and the US states of North Carolina and Connecticut. The Transvaal fields yield crystals up to 8 cm long and an emerald weighing 11,000 carats is reported to have been found there on 10 October 1956.

In Austria there is an ointment bowl weighing 2,680 carats carved from an emerald by Dionysius Miseroni in the 17th century. The Devonshire Stone weighing 1,386 carats comes from the Muzo district in Colombia and was presented by the Brazilian ruler Don Pedro I to the Earl of Devonshire. Today it is kept in the British Museum (Natural History) in London.

1 Free crystals of heliodor (Nerchinsk, USSR). Length about 22 mm. **2** Cut aquamarines (Brazil). Largest crystal 990.6 carats. **3** Cut morganite (Madagascar). 46.6 carats. **4** Cut green beryl (Sri Lanka). 421.6 carats.

1

2

3

4

Another gem variety of beryl is **aquamarine**. Its colour is pale blue, hence the name which is derived from the Latin *aqua* (= water) and *marina* (= of the sea). Many aquamarines are blue-green. The colourless variety is also known as **goshenite** (after Goshen in Hampshire County, Massachusetts, USA), but the name has not been widely accepted and is often replaced by 'lucid' or 'white' beryl. Aquamarine crystals are frequently corroded by etching. Aquamarine occurs naturally in relatively large amounts and in big crystals. The stone is therefore not so expensive or so rare as emerald. The largest aquamarine crystal known to date was found in 1910 in pegmatite at Marambaio in Brazil. It was 48.5 cm long and 41 cm wide and weighed more than a quintal (520,000 carats). It was split into cut stones with a total weight of about 200,000 carats and for a long time it supplied all cut aquamarines on the world market.

Rich aquamarine deposits are at Adun Chilon in the Baikal region, and Murzinka and Miass in the Urals, USSR. In the 19th century aquamarines used also to be mined in the feldspar quarry called The Picture, near Písek in southern Bohemia. Other aquamarine localities include Madagascar, the US states of Maine, Connecticut, California, Colorado and North Carolina, Burma, India and Zimbabwe. Today, practically all the attractive blue aquamarines used in jewellery are the originally greenish-yellow varieties that have been heated to 400-450 °C; annealing at this temperature produces stones of a beautiful, stable blue colour.

Other varieties of beryl are the extremely rare pink **vorobevite**, also known as **morganite**, and the yellow to yellowish green, golden beryl **heliodor**, which is coloured by caesium oxide. Morganite is named after the famous US magnate and a great admirer of gems, J. Pierpont Morgan, and has a tabular habit with short prisms. It occurs mainly in pegmatites and alluvial deposits in the state of Minas Gerais in Brazil, at Maharitra in Madagascar, and at Pala and Mesa Grande in San Diego County, California.

Heliodor (from the Greek *helios* = sun) is found mainly in Madagascar and Brazil; it also occurs in pegmatites near Písek in Bohemia. A yellowish red variety comes from Santa Maria do Suaçuí in Minas Gerais, Brazil, and from the Roebling Mine, New Mildford in Connecticut. A golden beryl of 2,054 carats, originally from Brazil, is kept in the Smithsonian Institution in Washington, DC.

Little known is the dark-brown asteriated beryl discovered around 1950 in the Governador Valadares region in Minas Gerais, Brazil. Its bronze lustre and weak golden asterism is caused by oriented ingrowths of ilmenite (a titanium iron oxide). The ingrowths are parallel to the base; without the ingrowths the mineral would be a pale-green aquamarine.

All gem varieties of beryl are in great demand for their delicate hues and perfect transparency. They are fashioned into the so-called emerald-cut, that is, elongated oblong trap cuts known as baguettes. Heliodor, morganite and aquamarine are usually cut into brilliants and are often used as centre stones for rings, brooches, pendants and earrings.

1 Cut aquamarines of various shades. **2** Aquamarine cross with brilliants (first half of the 19th century). Cross height 90 mm. **3** Emerald set, with brilliants, in platinum (early 20th century).

1

2

3

Zircon

Zirconium silicate, $Zr[SiO_4]$*; crystal system: tetragonal; name derived from the Persian* zargun *(= golden); specific gravity: 4.6-4.7 and 3.6-4.0 (metamict form); hardness: 7.5 and 6.5 (metamict form); cleavage: poor; fracture: uneven, conchoidal (metamict form); tenacity: brittle; colour: colourless, grey, yellow, green, reddish brown, red or blue; streak: white; transparency: transparent to translucent; lustre: vitreous to adamantine; refractive indices:* $\varepsilon = 1.968\text{-}2.015$, $\omega = 1.923\text{-}1.960$, *metamict form* $n = 1.78\text{-}1.94$*; birefringence (none in metamict form): 0.058; dispersion: strong, 0.039; pleochroism: weak except in blue-coloured stones; main variety: hyacinth.*

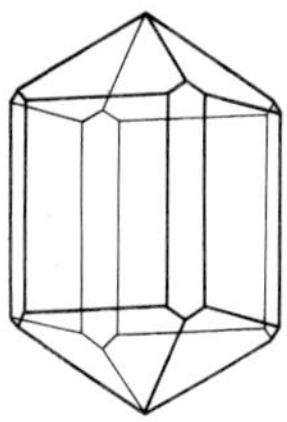

Although zircon has been mined together with other gemstones from alluvia in Sri Lanka for a very long time, it did not become fashionable and popular until the 1920s. Perhaps no other gemstone possesses such variable properties as zircon. For a long time it was regarded as having mystic qualities. Today we know that zircon's mysterious behaviour can easily be explained by its content of radioactive elements.

Zircon crystals form short-to-long columnar prisms that terminate in a bipyramid (Fig.). In alluvia the stone occurs as rounded grains and pebbles. After diamond, zircon has the second highest indices of refraction; it also displays a strong dispersion and intensive lustre. Cut stones have a vivid fire. Birefringence in zircon is so pronounced that when a cut specimen is observed under a magnifying glass, the contours of the rear facets appear double.

One of the major shortcomings of zircon is its considerable brittleness; edges of cut stones are especially susceptible to damage by scratch marks. The minutely damaged edges discernible with a magnifying glass and the marked birefringence can serve as means of positive identification.

Apart from variable contents of hafnium, iron and rare earth elements, certain zircons contain traces of uranium and thorium. Because of the natural decay of these elements the internal structure of zircon is gradually destroyed. At the same time, the physical properties undergo a change: specific gravity and hardness are reduced, birefringence disappears and the colour changes. Crystals transformed in this manner become almost amorphous and are said to be *metamict.* Zircons are thus classed as regular or normal (high), metamict (low) and intermediate types. When heated to 800-1,000 °C some metamict and intermediate zircons transform into normal types, simultaneously undergoing a colour change. The resulting colour depends on whether the stone is heated in a reducing or an oxidizing atmosphere. The gemstone trade highly values the pale-blue 'starlites' and the straw-yellow 'jargoons' or zirconites. Colourless, lucid zircons are sometimes incorrectly called Matura diamonds. However, not all artificially coloured zircons are colourfast in sunlight: some will grow pale in time whereas others will gradually regain their original hue.

Zircon is an accessory mineral in various types of magmatic, sedimentary and metamorphosed rocks. Its gemmy varieties never occur in large sizes; they are placer-mined from secondary sediments, especially in Sri Lanka, Cambodia and Thailand.

Colourless and pale-coloured zircons are cut into brilliants; the reddish-brown **hyacinth** is also fashioned into mixed and step cuts. In earlier times, zircons cut into roses were often passed off as diamonds.

1 Zircon crystal embedded in parent rock (Miass, USSR). Length of crystal 12 mm. **2** Hyacinth pebbles (alluvial deposits, Sri Lanka). Length about 3 mm. **3** Cut zircons (Thailand). Largest stone 4.3 carats. **4** Cut zircons (various localities). Largest stone 5.2 carats.

1

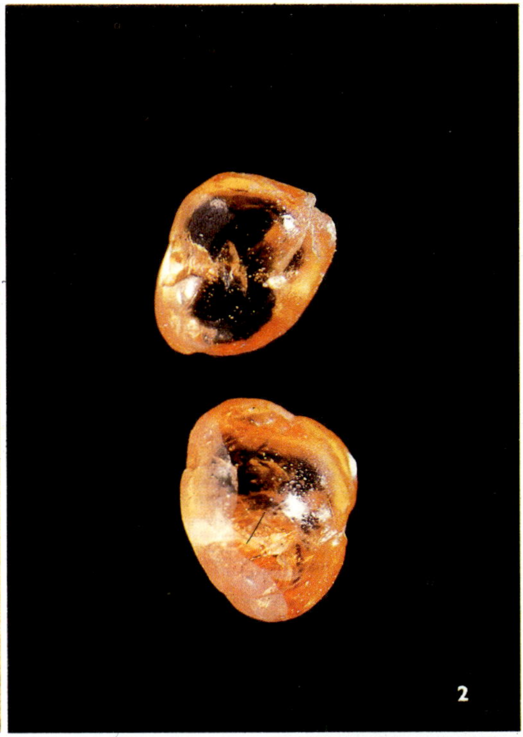
2

3

4

Tourmaline

Complex borosilicate of aluminium and other elements, (Na, Ca) (Li, Mg, Al)$_3$ (Al, Fe, Mn)$_6$ [(OH)$_4$|(BO$_3$)$_3$|Si$_6$O$_{18}$]; *crystal system: trigonal; name derived from the Sinhalese* toramalli *(= cornelian); specific gravity: 3.00-3.25; hardness: 7-7.5; cleavage: none; fracture: uneven to conchoidal; tenacity: brittle; colour: usually black, also blue, green, yellow, brown, red or, rarely, colourless; streak: white; transparency: transparent to translucent; lustre: vitreous; refractive indices:* ε*= 1.616-1.634,* ω*= 1.630-1.652; birefringence: 0.018; dispersion: weak, 0.017; pleochroism: strong; main varieties: achroite, indicolite, schorl, dravite, verdelite, rubellite.*

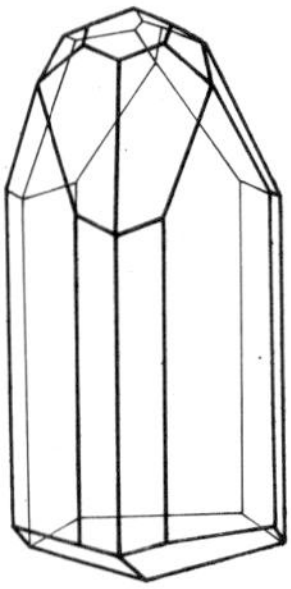

In 1703 the Dutch brought from Ceylon to Europe together with other gemstones a strange red stone called *toramalli* by the Sinhalese. The stone had a special property — on heating it attracted tiny ash particles. Thus the phenomenon of pyroelectricity was first observed in tourmaline. However, one of the black varieties of the stone named schorl had been known long before the discovery of tourmaline but nobody had realized that the black schorl was essentially the same mineral species as the magnificent red, transparent toramalli. Besides red and black varieties, tourmaline also occurs in many other colours that make it permanently popular.

Tourmaline forms short-to-long columnar crystals, usually trihedral (Fig.). Tourmaline crystals are distinctly heteropolar, that is the opposite crystal ends, if developed, are terminated morphologically differently, usually in a combination of various pyramids, or in a basal pinacoid-pedion. The prismatic faces are sometimes longitudinally striated. Apart from having pyroelectric properties, tourmaline crystals are also strongly piezoelectric.

Unlike many other gemstones, tourmaline has no cleavage and only fractures. It takes a good polish and its vitreous lustre is enhanced by cutting. Dispersion is relatively weak. On the other hand tourmaline is strongly pleochroic. This property can be observed with the naked eye even in paler stones and may be used to advantage by the selection of a suitable cut. Stones of deeper colours always have the table parallel to the vertical axis of the crystal. The strong pleochroism also serves as a simple identification test.

The great variety of colours is caused by the highly complex and variable chemical composition. Tourmaline varieties form an isomorphous series of compound crystals. The basic, terminal members of the series include **elbaite** (lithium tourmaline), that can be either colourless or pink or green; the brown or brownish-black **dravite** (magnesium-sodium tourmaline); the ferrous black **schorl**; the red **tsilaisite** (manganate tourmaline); and the dark-brown **uvite** (magnesium-calcium tourmaline). Besides the elements mentioned, tourmalines may also contain admixtures of chromium, vanadium, gallium and titanium. Naturally, the chemical composition alone is not the only factor determining the colour of the crystal, but changes in the chemical composition do affect the optical constants of the mineral, especially the refractive indices. This is also the reason why values of refractive indices given for tourmaline in various tables differ considerably.

Unique crystal of rubellite (Pala, California, USA). Height 121 mm.

In the past, mineralogists and gemmologists differentiated tourmalines by colour into several varieties. **Achroite** is quite rare in nature and, although colourless, it has always a slight pinkish or greenish tinge. **Rubellite** occurs in various shades of red and sometimes resembles ruby in colour. The green **verdelite** is also incorrectly termed Brazilian emerald. **Indicolite** comes in many shades of blue and **dravite** is brown. **Schorl** is a common rock-forming mineral; in the past the stone was used for mourning jewellery. The names of those tourmaline varieties are now not commonly used, the general preference being for the term tourmaline with a colour qualifier (for example green tourmaline).

One of the most unique features of tourmaline is that even a single crystal may sometimes be truly multicoloured, the colour layers being arranged concentrically parallel to the vertical axis of the crystal. Sections of such crystals will show, for instance, a red core surrounded by border zones of different colours. In other cases the crystals may display a longitudinal arrangement of coloured bands. The transitions between the individual colours may be either gradual or sharply defined. One end of the crystal may be green, then the colour may change into a yellow or even a colourless zone, and the other end may be black. Such tourmalines are called **moorheads;** crystals terminating in red are known as **turkheads.** Deeply coloured stones may become paler if heated to 450 °C.

Tourmaline crystals may contain inhomogenities in the form of foreign ingrowths of tiny crystals or minute cavities and capillary passages. The chatoyant sheen of the so-called tourmaline cat's-eye is caused by ingrowths of fine acicular crystals oriented parallel to the vertical axis of the crystal.

Tourmaline occurs most often in granites and granite pegmatites. It is also found as an accessory mineral in some metamorphosed rocks, for example, mica schists, talc and chlorite slates and contact-metamorphosed limestones. Being mechanically and chemically resistant tourmaline also often occurs secondarily in alluvial deposits.

Gem-quality tourmalines are mined in the Brazilian states of Minas Gerais and Bahia, and at Pala and Rincon in San Diego County, California. The popular moorheads come from the island of Elba. Tourmaline is also found in the Urals in the USSR, Sri Lanka, Africa and Madagascar. Rubellite crystals up to 42 cm long are found at Muiiane in Mozambique.

Tourmaline is usually fashioned into oblong step and table cuts, brilliants being less common. The chatoyant sheen of the hazy cat's-eye is displayed most prominently in stones cut into cabochons. Because tourmaline occurs in many colours, it may easily be mistaken for other gemstones.

1 Particoloured tourmaline known as a moorhead (Elba, Italy). Height of crystal 30 mm. **2** Cross-section of a particoloured tourmaline (Sri Lanka). Diameter 105 mm. **3** Cut of particoloured tourmaline (Madagascar). Diameter 12 mm. **4** Cut tourmalines. Top: dravite (Madagascar); centre: verdelites (Brazil); bottom: dark dravite (Sri Lanka).

2

3

Euclase

Beryllium aluminium silicate, $BeAl[(OH)|SiO_4]$; *crystal system: monoclinic; name derived from the Greek* eu *(= good) and* klasis *(= breaking), on account of its easy cleavage; specific gravity: 3.05-3.10; hardness: 7.5; cleavage: eminent in one direction; fracture: minutely conchoidal; tenacity: brittle; colour: colourless to pale blue green; streak: white; transparency: transparent to translucent; lustre: highly vitreous to adamantine; refractive indices:* $\alpha = 1.652$, $\beta = 1.655$, $\gamma = 1.671$; *birefringence: 0.02; dispersion: weak; 0.016; pleochroism: distinct.*

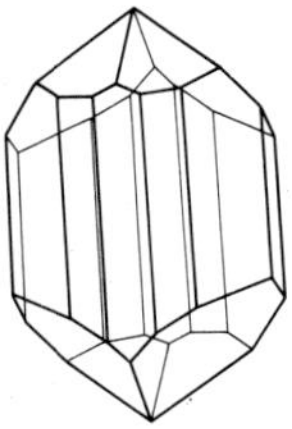

The first euclase crystals were brought to Europe from Peru in 1785. However, no details of the locality were known at the time and it is thought that these first specimens were probably of Brazilian origin. Euclase is a very rare mineral and it is thus used for jewellery only exceptionally; more often it is found in gemmological collections.

Euclase forms columnar crystals elongated along the vertical axis (Fig.), often with a multifaced termination. Twinning has never been observed; vertical striation is quite typical. Euclase splits easily; its cleavage in the direction of the crystal symmetry plane is eminent and it is this property that gave the mineral its name in 1792. The eminent cleavage sometimes causes a pearly lustre of the cleavage faces, and the special, fine internal glitter of the crystals. The easy cleavability renders cutting and polishing quite difficult and the stone must therefore be fashioned with great care. Any fashioning of the natural faces will enhance the live vitreous lustre to an adamantine quality. Transparency is often perfect; foreign impurities occur only rarely.

Euclase is mostly colourless or pale greenish, with a bluish-green or yellowish-green tinge. Sometimes it occurs with an emerald-green tint. Rarer are the vividly greenish blue, azure-blue or indigo-blue crystals; the dark emerald-green varieties are very scarce. Crystals of more intensive hues are pleochroic. However, individual crystals may show different absorption spectra in different crystallographic directions. Coloured stones can be tinted light blue by irradiation but ultraviolet light will discolour them again after some time.

Euclase occurs embedded in granites and pegmatites; in the Alpine paragenesis it is found in the form of small crystals edged on feldspar. Single crystals are extracted from alluvial deposits.

The classical euclase localities are Capão do Lane and Boa Vista in Ouro Preto, Minas Gerais, Brazil. In 1968 a new locality was opened at São Sebastião do Maranhão, Minas Gerais, where crystals exceeding 3 cm in length have been found. The longest crystal (over 7 cm) found to date comes from the gold-bearing alluvia on the River Sanarka in the Urals. In the Hohe Tauern Mountains in Austria euclase crystals ranging in size from a millimetre to a centimetre long can be found on pericline (a variety of albite). Some crystals come from the Morogoro district of Tanzania.

Euclase is usually fashioned into step and table cuts. The best-priced and most sought-after stones are the deep bluish-green crystals. Euclase may easily be mistaken for aquamarine or hiddenite.

1 Crystal of clear euclase (Ouro Preto, Brazil). Height 12 mm. **2** Crystal of coloured euclase (Capão near Villaria, Brazil). Height 37 mm. **3** Step cut of clear euclase (Brazil). 1.4 carats. **4** Cuts of euclase of different colours often confused with stones of the beryl group.

2

3

4

Garnets

Group of binary silicates of various divalent and trivalent elements, the general formula being $A_3^{2+} B_2^{3+}[SiO_4]_3$, *where the* A^{2+} *position may be occupied by the divalent metals calcium, magnesium, ferrous iron, manganese or yttrium, and the* B^{3+} *position may be occupied by the trivalent aluminium, ferric iron, chromium, titanium or vanadium; crystal system: cubic; name derived from the Latin* granum *(= grain) for its frequent occurrence in small rounded grains, or from the Latin* malum granatum *(= pomegranate) resembling in colour the most frequent coloration of garnets; specific gravity: 3.4-4.2; hardness: 6.5-7.5; cleavage: very poor; fracture: conchoidal to hackly; tenacity: brittle; colour: variable; streak: white or slightly tinted; transparency: transparent to translucent; lustre: vitreous to greasy; refractive index:* n = *1.74-1.89; birefringence and pleochroism: none (isotropic); dispersion: strong to medium — 0.057 (demantoid), 0.027 (almandine and spessartite), 0.022 (pyrope); main types (and varieties): almandine, andradite (demantoid, melanite, topazolite), grossular (hessonite, tsavorite), pyrope, rhodolite, spessartite and uvarovite.*

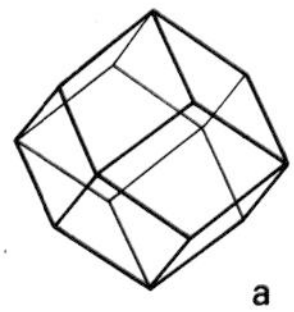

a

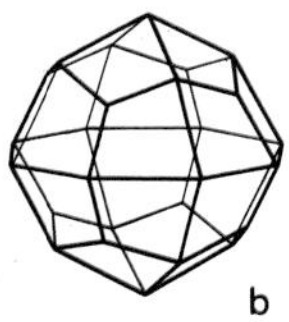

b

Garnets constitute an isomorphous group or family of minerals all with cubic symmetry and basically the same chemical formula. The chemical composition mainly influences the colour and hence, indirectly, also gives garnets their name. Of the entire — and considerably large — garnet family, the jewellery trade mainly uses these six garnet types: **pyrope** (magnesium, aluminium), **almandine** (iron, aluminium), **spessartite** (manganese, aluminium), **grossular** (calcium, aluminium), **andradite** (calcium, iron) and **uvarovite** (calcium, chromium). **Rhodolite** in composition lies intermediate between pyrope and almandine.

A very important characteristic of garnets is the unlimited or partial replacement of the main representatives of the isomorphous series, forming the so-called mixed crystals. According to the prevailing isomorphism garnets are sometimes divided into two groups: pyralspites (pyrope, almandine, spessartite) and ugrandites (uvarovite, grossular, andradite). However, partial substitution of some elements can occur even between the two larger groups. The greatest replacement occurs between almandine and spessartite and between grossular and andradite.

Garnet crystals are usually rhombic dodecahedral (Fig. a) or icositetrahedral (Fig. b) or combinations of these forms. The size of the crystals ranges from a mere millimetre to tens of centimetres. With a cubic symmetry, garnets are normally singly refractive, but some varieties frequently display an anomalous birefringence. Apart from the green grossular, garnets do not luminesce in ultraviolet light.

Garnets are often given incorrect names such as Arizona ruby, Cape ruby or Arizona spinel (pyrope), Adelaide ruby, Ceylon ruby or Alabanda ruby (almandine), Ural emerald or Siberian chrysolite (demantoid) and Ceylon hyacinth (hessonite). Because of these names, garnets may often be mistaken for other gemstones.

1 Andradite crystals in parent rock developed in perfect rhombic dodecahedra (the Urals, USSR). Largest crystal 10 × 10 mm. **2** Demantoids on rock surface (Franscia, Italy). Diameter of largest crystal 5.2 mm. **3** Druse of hessonite crystals (Žulová, Czechoslovakia). Diameter of largest crystal 26 mm. **4** Druse of gem-quality hessonite crystals (Ala, Piedmont, Italy). Diameter of largest crystals about 5 mm.

1

2

3

4

Garnets are fashioned into step and table cuts, brilliants and roses, but apart from faceted cuts and the mixed novelty cuts, low-domed (tallowed) cabochons are also popular. Darker stones are sometimes concavely cut on the underside to enhance the colour, or the cuts are profiled into low domes. For necklaces garnets are cut into small spherical beads or irregular tumbled grains are used.

Pyrope is a magnesium aluminium silicate, $Mg_3Al_2[SiO_4]_3$, with admixtures of chromium and iron. The name is derived from the Greek *pyr* (= fire) and *ops* (= eye) and does justice to the beautiful dark-red colour with which the stone inflames. Its specific gravity is 3.7-3.8 and its hardness is 7-7.5. The colour depends on the content of chromium: as it increases, the colour hue progresses from orange-red (0.5-0.6 per cent Cr_2O_3), blood red (about 1.6 per cent Cr_2O_3) to purple (up to 7 per cent Cr_2O_3). Admixtures of various iron oxides cause a perceptible yellow-brownish hue. The refractive index (n) for pyrope is 1.71-1.76, rising with the percentage of chromium.

Unlike other garnet species pyrope is not always crystallographically bounded and it occurs mainly as rounded grains. The grains range in size from 1 to 10 mm, but pyropes larger than 7 mm are rare. Pyrope often contains impurities in the form of minute crystals of zircon, apatite, chromdiopside, ilmenite, cyanite or pyrite. Pyropes deposited secondarily in geologically older rocks may contain fine channels caused by corrosive action. The parent rocks of pyrope are ultrabasic peridotites, serpentinites and kimberlites. When these rocks weather pyropes are deposited, with zircon, spinel, corundum, ilmenite and diamond, in alluvia.

Pyrope ranks among the most popular of garnets. The first records of pyrope mining and use date from the early Middle Ages. From the 16th century on it was found on the southern slopes of the Bohemian Highlands near Třebenice in northwestern Czechoslovakia. The stone soon became very popular under the name Bohemian garnet. The largest pyrope from this locality, cut into an oval cabochon measuring 35 × 27 × 8 mm and weighing 9.6 grams, ornaments a decoration of the Order of the Golden Fleece now in the Grünes Gewölbe Treasury in Dresden.

The largest pyrope specimen deposited in the Bohemian Garnet Museum at Třebenice is a rose cut with a base 12.3 mm in diameter, a height of 8.6 mm and a weight of 2.64 grams. However, none of the exhibits in the museum surpasses in beauty the famous garnet set of Ulrike von Levetzow with whom Johann Wolfgang Goethe became infatuated at the end of his life. The set is a family heirloom made in 1820 from 448 pyropes.

There is a rich pyrope occurrence in the Kimberley district in South Africa where this garnet is found associated with diamond. Cape rubies, as these pyropes are called, sometimes reach a few centimetres long but they do not have the sparkling blood-red hue of the Bohemian garnets, being more ruby red in colour. Pyropes of various hues are also found in Siberia in the diamond field of the Yakut region, in the US states of Arizona and New Mexico, in Madagascar, Brazil and Tanzania.

Pyrope can be confused with red spinel and almandine. Glass imitations are revealed by different thermal conductivity because pyrope feels more cold to the touch than glass does.

1 Pyropes in parent rock (Central Bohemian Mountains, Czechoslovakia). Diameter of grains about 3 mm. **2** Pyrope grains photographed in transmitted light (alluvial deposits, Třebenice, Czechoslovakia). Diameter of grains about 4 mm. **3** Cut garnets of various colours. Top (left to right): spessartite (Madagascar), almandine (India), demantoid (USSR); bottom: melanite (Mt Vesuvius, Italy).

1

2

3

Almandine is a ferrous iron aluminium silicate, $Fe_3Al_2[SiO_4]_3$. The name is derived most probably from Pliny's coinage *carbunculus alabandicus* based on the original ancient locality near Alabanda in Asia Minor. Almandine has a specific gravity of 3.95-4.20; a hardness of 7.5; a full-red, reddish-brown colour, almost always with a purplish tint; and a refractive index *n* of 1.76-1.81. Some localities are typical with fine acicular rutile forming a densely packed, oriented network within the almandine crystal.

Almandine is one of the most widespread garnets, occurring in perfectly bounded crystals the size of which may reach up to several tens of centimetres. It is found embedded in crystalline schists such as mica schist, gneiss, phyllite, granulite and amphibolite, and it may also occur in granites and pegmatites. Gem varieties are extracted mostly from secondary alluvial deposits.

Almandine was being used as a gemstone in classical times. It was the major representative of the so-called *carbuncles,* a name which was used in medieval literature for a collective designation of all red-coloured stones. The largest known almandine, a cabochon of 175 carats, is in the Smithsonian Institution, Washington DC.

Gem almandines called Ceylon rubies are found mainly in Sri Lanka and India. They also occur in Brazil, Tanzania and Madagascar. Of minor importance are the Austrian localities of Ötztal and Zillertal where the so-called Tirol garnet is found. Almandines are also found at Fort Wrangell, Alaska, and North Creek, New York State, USA, and in Australia.

Rhodolite occupies an intermediate position between pyrope and almandine. The mixed crystals contain about 57 per cent pyrope and 35 per cent almandine constituents. Rhodolite has a pale to deep pinkish-red colour after which it was named in 1898 from the Greek *rhodos* (= pink). Its specific gravity is 3.84 and its refractive index *n* = 1.76. Rhodolite occurs in the US state of North Carolina, in Zambia, Brazil, Madagascar and Sri Lanka.

Spessartite is a manganese aluminium silicate, $Mn_3Al_2[SiO_4]_3$, with an admixture of iron. It is named after the first place of discovery — near Aschaffenburg in the Spessart district, FRG. Its specific gravity ranges between 3.90 and 4.20, its hardness exceeds 7. The colour is yellow, yellow-orange, reddish to reddish brown or brownish red. Its refractive index *n* = 1.79-1.81.

Spessartite occurs in granites and granite pegmatites. It ranks among the more precious gemstones and enjoys a wide popularity for its pleasant colour. Gemmy spessartite occurs in Sri Lanka, Madagascar, Upper Burma, Brazil and Tanzania. Crystals up to 7 cm long have been found in Mexico. The major European occurrences, apart from Spessart, are Ilfeld in the Harz Mountains, GDR, St Marcel in Piedmont, Italy and Elba, Sweden and the Urals.

1 Golden cross with Tirolean almandine garnets (first half of the 19th century). Height of cross 100 mm. **2** Brooch with Bohemian pyrope garnets (Russian work, 19th century). Diameter of largest stone 6.9 mm. **3** Brooch with Bohemian pyrope garnets (19th century). Diameter of brooch 24 mm. **4** Necklace of Indian almandines (larger stones) and pyropes (early 20th century).

1

2

3

4

Grossular is a calcium aluminium silicate, $Ca_3Al_2[SiO_4]_3$, with an admixture of chromium. Its name is derived from the Latin *Ribes grossularia* — the botanical name for gooseberry — because it resembles the berry in colour and shape. Its specific gravity is 3.40-3.68, its hardness 6.5-7.5 and its refractive index $n = 1.738\text{-}1.745$. In contrast to other garnets grossular strongly luminesces in ultraviolet light. It usually forms non-transparent crystals in contact-metamorphosed limestones. Transparent gemmy crystals have recently been found in Tanzania, Pakistan and Zambia, and colourless grossular crystals occur in Quebec in Canada. The lumpy, massive, cryptocrystalline grossular from Buffelfontein in Transvaal resembles jadeite and is called **South African** or **Transvaal jade** because of its green colour.

An iron-containing variety of grossular, called **hessonite**, is a brownish yellow, brownish orange or a rich brownish red colour. The name is derived from the Greek *hesson* (= inferior) because its hardness is inferior to that of the zircon variety hyacinth, which it resembles. It occurs in Mexico, Brazil, Sri Lanka, Canada and the USA. A recently discovered grossular variety is **tsavorite**, found first in 1968 near the River Tsavo at the border between Kenya and Tanzania. It has a pale-to-emerald green colour, a hardness of 7.5, specific gravity of 3.60 and refractive index $n = 1.745$. It also possesses a high dispersion.

Andradite, a calcium iron silicate, $Ca_3Fe_2[SiO_4]_3$, with an admixture of chromium, manganese, magnesium and aluminium, is named after the Portuguese mineralogist J. B. d'Andrada e Silva who described it in 1800. Its specific gravity is 3.7-4.1, its hardness 6.5, its colour green, yellowish green, brown, reddish brown or black, and its refractive index $n = 1.85\text{-}1.89$.

Non-transparent andradite is a common rock-forming mineral; its major gemmy variety is **demantoid**. Demantoid has an emerald-green colour with a yellowish green tint, a high lustre and, in contrast with other garnets, it also has a high dispersion comparable to that of diamond — hence the name. Originally discovered in placers on the River Bobrovka in the Urals, demantoid is one of the most precious garnets. Among other localities are Val Malenco, Italy, and the newly found occurrences in Tanzania and Zaire. A yellow andradite to which the name **topazolite** has been given, is found in small crystals in the Piedmont Valley, Italy and at Zermatt in Switzerland. **Melanite** is a non-translucent to opaque black variety of andradite containing titanium. Its name is derived from the Greek *melas* (= black). Melanite is found in alkaline rocks such as phonolites, mostly in Italy, the Federal Republic of Germany, and at Magnet Cove in Arkansas, USA.

Uvarovite, a calcium chromium silicate $Ca_3Cr_2[SiO_4]_3$, was named in honour of the Russian statesman S. S. Uvarov. Its specific gravity is 3.57-3.70, its hardness 7.5 and refractive index $n = 1.87$. It possesses a beautiful deep emerald-green colour and is one of the rarest gemstones, occurring in chromium ore deposits at Sysert' in the Urals, Outukumpu in Finland and the US states of Texas and California. Recently it has also been found at Oxford in Quebec, Canada.

1 Necklace of Bohemian garnets and seed pearls (Bohemian work, late 19th century). **2** Garnet brooch with pearls (Bohemian work, mid-19th century). Height 80 mm. **3** Garnet set of Ulrike von Levetzow consisting of 448 large Bohemian garnets, probably the most beautiful piece of garnet jewellery ever made (1820).

1

2

3

Andalusite

Aluminium silicate, $Al_2[O|SiO_4]$*; crystal system: orthorhombic; name derived from the Spanish province of Andalusia; specific gravity: 3.1-3.2; hardness: 7-7.5; cleavage: good to indistinct; fracture: uneven, except in the cleavage plane; tenacity: brittle; colour: grey, green, brown or red; streak: white; transparency: translucent to non-transparent; lustre: vitreous to dull; refractive indices:* $\alpha = 1.629\text{-}1.640$*,* $\beta = 1.633\text{-}1.644$*,* $\gamma = 1.639\text{-}1.647$*; birefringence: 0.010; dispersion: weak, 0.016; pleochroism: strong; main variety: chiastolite.*

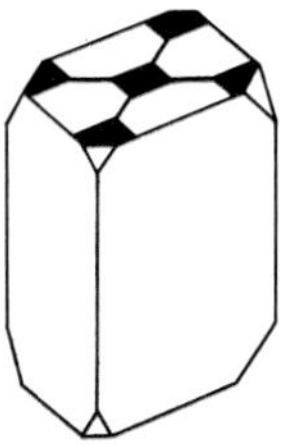

There are three aluminium silicates in nature, two orthorhombic forms — andalusite and the fibrous sillimanite (p. 220) — and the triclinic kyanite (p. 126). Andalusite forms columnar crystals that usually consist of a simple prism terminated by basal faces. It is often non-transparent and somewhat dull on the surface. It occurs in gneiss, contact-metamorphosed slates and in granite pegmatites.

Andalusite is used as a basic raw material for refractory linings and special porcelains. It was first found near Almeria in Spain on the Mediterranean coast. Large andalusite crystals up to 20 cm long and 5 cm thick occur at Lisenz in Austria, where they form almost tetrahedral columns covered as a rule with fine mica flakes. Crystals are often grouped in nicely shaped aggregates such as druses. They also occur singly, but these have no gem value. Andalusite in radial aggregates is found abundantly in pegmatites near Velké Meziříčí in Moravia, Czechoslovakia, where it contains tiny blue sapphire crystals. Other important localities for andalusite include Murzinka in the Urals, Minas Gerais in Brazil and Bimbowrie in Australia.

The dark-green andalusites from gravel alluvia in Sri Lanka and the green andalusite pebbles from Brazil are gems of top quality and are usually cut into brilliants. The Brazilian localities are situated mostly in the states of Espírito Santo and Minas Gerais. Because andalusite is pleochroic, its rich green colour changes into a reddish orange or brown. Gem cutters utilize this property to advantage to produce Brazilian andalusites that usually resemble green tourmalines. They are small, very expensive and quite rare.

A well-known andalusite variety is **chiastolite** (Fig.). Sections of these crystals show a dark, sometimes black cross caused by a graphitic inclusion, and it is because of this feature that the stone was named after the Greek letter *chi*. Longitudinal sections of such chiastolites exhibit an hourglass structure. Chiastolite used to be found abundantly in schists near the Spanish pilgrimage place of Santiago de Compostella where souvenirs decorated with a black cross were the local specialty made from the mineral. They were sold to the pilgrims as the 'cross-stone'. Chiastolite also occurs near Nerchinsk in the Transbaikal region of the USSR, in Brittany and in various US states as well as in Algeria. Large chiastolite crosses (diagonals up to 8 cm) come from Keiva on the Kola Peninsula in the USSR.

1 Columnar crystals of andalusite (Lisenz, Austria). Height 40 mm. **2** Cut andalusites (Brazil). Larger stone 3.2 carats. **3** Chiastolite (Lancashire, England). 60 × 40 × 25 mm. **4** Cross-section of chiastolite (Bimbowrie, Australia). Diameter 25 mm.

1

2

3

4

Kyanite (Disthene)

Aluminium silicate, $Al_2[O|SiO_4]$; *crystal system: triclinic; name derived from the Greek* kyanos *(= dark blue); specific gravity: 3.5-3.68; hardness: 5-7, depending on the direction; cleavage: eminent to good, depending on the direction; fracture: uneven; tenacity: brittle; colour: light blue, green, brown or, rarely, colourless; streak: white; transparency: transparent to translucent; lustre: vitreous, pearly on the cleavage planes; refractive indices:* $\alpha = 1.713\text{-}1.715$, $\beta = 1.721\text{-}1.726$, $\gamma = 1.728\text{-}1.732$; *birefringence: 0.016; dispersion: medium, 0.020; pleochroism: distinct.*

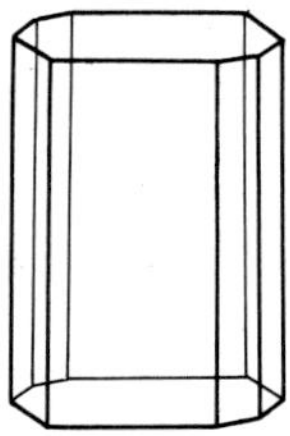

As a rock-forming component of some crystalline schists, kyanite is not a rare mineral in nature but transparent, attractively coloured gem-quality crystals are not often found. Kyanite has never been widely used for jewellery and has not been much valued as a gemstone.

The embedded crystals of kyanite are columnar and broad-bladed (Fig.), often undulated and transversely striated as a result of high slippage and low cohesion. Twinned crystals and parallel intergrowths with staurolite frequently occur. Because the various faces show striking difference in hardness, kyanite was also named **disthene** in 1801. Indeed the dependence of the hardness on the crystallographical direction is perhaps kyanite's most characteristic feature. In the longitudinal direction the pinacoidal faces have a hardness of only 4-5, whereas perpendicular to this direction the hardness is 6.5-7 and the pinacoidal faces have a hardness of 7. Kyanite is brittle and susceptible to splitting because of its low cohesion. These properties require that great care be taken when handling, cutting and polishing the stone.

Kyanite is usually whitish, grey, yellowish grey, bluish, greenish or merely translucent in colour. Totally colourless varieties are rare. The coloration may be uneven in the form of irregular bands or spots. For jewellery purposes, the most valued kyanites are coloured a deep cornflower hue, pale azure blue or bluish green, with perfect transparency. Kyanites of darker hues are pleochroic, with a weak birefringence. The vitreous lustre can be enhanced by polishing; the cleavage faces often exhibit a pearly lustre. Inhomogeneities in the form of inclusions in the crystals may occur. Sometimes kyanite contains admixtures of iron and chromium, and these elements are probably the cause of the interesting magnetic properties of the stone. Blue kyanite crystals suspended on a hair are said to follow the lines of force of the Earth's magnetic field like a compass needle.

Kyanite is mostly found in metamorphic rocks such as gneiss and mica schist, or in pegmatites and secondarily also as pebbles in alluvial deposits. Among its associated minerals are andalusite, corundum and staurolite. Important kyanite localities are in the Alps, for example, Monte Campione in Tessino in the Gotthard Massif. The major US occurrences are in Yancey County, North Carolina, and Madison County, Montana. Kyanite is also extracted from alluvia at Villa Rica in Brazil.

Kyanite is fashioned into elongated table and step cuts or into oval cabochons. It may be mistaken for sapphire and aquamarine.

1 Kyanite crystals embedded with staurolite in parent rock (Pizzo Forno, Switzerland). 80 × 60 mm. **2** Kyanite cabochon (Bečov, Czechoslovakia). 30 × 22 mm. **3** Unique cut of a gem-quality kyanite (India). 14 × 6 mm.

1

2

3

Cordierite (Iolite, Dichroite)

Magnesium aluminium silicate with iron, $(Mg,Fe)_2Al_3[AlSi_5O_{18}]$*; crystal system: orthorhombic; named in honour of the French mineralogist P. L. A. Cordier who described it in detail in 1809; specific gravity: 2.57-2.66; hardness: 7-7.5; cleavage: poor; fracture: conchoidal to uneven; tenacity: brittle; colour: various shades of blue, also greyish; streak: white; transparency: transparent to translucent; lustre: vitreous to greasy; refractive indices:* $\alpha = 1.522\text{-}1.558$, $\beta = 1.532\text{-}1.568$, $\gamma = 1.527\text{-}1.573$*; birefringence: 0,01; dispersion: weak, 0.017; pleochroism: strong; main variety: sekaninaite.*

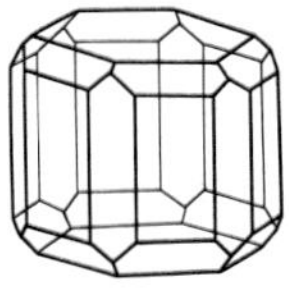

The Vikings are said to have used on their long sea voyages a navigation instrument consisting of a curious blue-violet stone that changed colour according to the direction in which one looked through it. The seafarers were able to tell the cardinal points of the compass with the stone even when the sky was overcast, with partially polarized light. This rather special property of the stone seems to indicate that it must have been cordierite that the Vikings used to get their bearings. In fact, the pleochroism of the stone is so pronounced that it has been called **dichroite** (from the Greek *dichrois* [= of two colours]). Another name given to the stone based on its colour is **iolite** (from the Greek *ion* = violet and *lithos* = stone).

As a part of many metamorphic rocks cordierite is not rare. Its crystals are short-to-long columnar and terminate with a base (Fig.). Pseudohexagonal twinning is quite frequent. Cordierite also occurs in solid lumps or pebbles in alluvia.

The colour of unweathered cordierite is blue violet, grey blue, smoky grey or yellowish; partially weathered cordierite is greenish grey. Because of its orthorhombic symmetry cordierite displays trichroism. Its birefringence is weak; the greasy vitreous lustre becomes more prominent on cut faces. The values of the optical constants vary according to the chemical composition, especially the iron and magnesium contents. The jewellery trade values blue transparent specimens with a violet tint. The cut is selected in such a way as to give the table a deep-blue hue or to show pleochroism when the jewel is worn.

Intergrowths of sillimanite, biotite, zircon and other minerals are frequent. Inclusions of fine haematite crystals give a special reddish tint to the stone.

Cordierite is found in various contact-metamorphosed crystalline schists, gneisses, granite pegmatites and volcanic extrusions. The most attractive gem-quality stones come from Madagascar. Transparent pebbles called water sapphires occur in Sri Lanka. Other famous localities are in Finland, Norway, Sweden, Spain, Murzinka in the Urals, Brazil, North America and Japan. A ferrous cordierite known as **sekaninaite** occurs as large crystals at Dolní Bory in Czechoslovakia. Although sekaninaite crystals can be cut, the stone mostly has a value only to collectors.

Cordierite is used for jewellery only exceptionally because the stone is not much valued. If fashioned, it usually appears in step or table cuts, brilliants or rounded cabochons. It may be mistaken for sapphire.

1 Fragments of rough cordierite (Madagascar). Length about 25 mm. **2** Sekaninaite with distinctive cleavage (Dolní Bory, Czechoslovakia). Detail 70 × 50 mm. **3** Three cordierite plates with different optical orientation characterizing pleochroism (Madagascar). 13 × 8 × 4 mm. **4** Two cut cordierites (Tsilaisina, Madagascar). About 2.8 carats.

1

2

3

4

Olivine

Magnesium iron silicate, $(Mg, Fe)_2[SiO_4]$; *crystal system: orthorhombic; named on account of its olive colour; specific gravity: 3.34; hardness: 6.5-7; cleavage: indistinct; fracture: conchoidal; tenacity: brittle; colour: shades of green, also grey white, yellow, brown or black; streak: white; lustre; vitreous; transparency: transparent; refractive indices:* $\alpha = 1.662$, $\beta = 1.680$, $\gamma = 1.699$; *birefringence: 0.036; dispersion: medium, 0.020; pleochroism: distinct; main variety: peridot or chrysolite.*

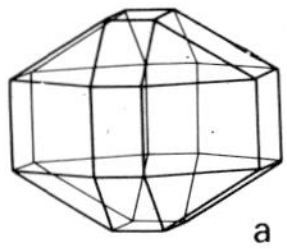

a

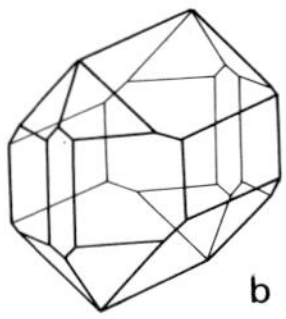

b

The earliest source of beautiful olivines was ancient Egypt. Olivines used to be called *topazios* after the island Topazos in the Red Sea off the Egyptian coast where olivines were mined very intensively. In the course of time this ancient occurrence was forgotten and the Middle Ages remained unaware of its existence. An adequate replacement was found in Bohemian olivines from Kozákov near Turnov.

For a long time Bohemian olivine had no competition, but in 1900 Zebirget (St John's Island) was recognized as the fabled ancient Topazos; the rediscovered mine soon won back its former fame so that today this unique source supplies most of the cut olivines on the market. Zebirget is a volcanic island on which occur much-metamorphosed peridotites with cavities bearing magnificent olive-green to yelowish green, transparent, columnar or tabular crystals of olivine. The largest specimen from Zebirget weighs almost 40 grams. The Smithsonian Institution in Washington DC has a cut olivine weighing 319 carats, and the USSR Diamond Fund in Moscow possesses a Zebirget olivine of 192 carats. The largest olivine from the Kozákov locality has a cut weight of a mere 15.67 carats. At Kozákov specimens of only 5 carats are considered a rare find. A magnificent olivine comes from Pyanggaung in the Mogok gem belt in Upper Burma. Other localities are in the US states of Arizona and New Mexico where olivine freed from the parent rock and deposited in slope clays and sand dunes occur as rolled pebbles and eroded grains. Olivine crystals and rounded pebbles also come from Norway, the Federal Republic of Germany, Brazil, Sri Lanka and other countries. The beach sands in the Hawaiian Islands contain olivine as a heavy mineral. It was deposited in the sand after the volcanic rocks of the island weathered.

Smaller amounts of olivine have been discovered in some meteorites and olivine has been found in basalt rocks on the Moon. In 1772 an expedition headed by the naturalist Peter Pallas discovered that the Tatars in Siberia worshipped a meteorite. Later it was determined that it was meteoritic iron rich in olivine, with some of the grains even cuttable. Following this discovery iron meteorites containing olivine were also found in other parts of the world and called **pallasites.**

1 Chrysolite (peridot) crystals on basalt (Podmoklice, Czechoslovakia). Section width 85 mm. **2** Chrysolite grains (Kozákov, Czechoslovakia). Diameter about 3 mm. **3** Polished section of pallasite, a stony-iron meteorite with olivine (Spring Water, Canada). 45 × 40 mm.

1

2

3

Olivine is an abundant rock-forming constituent of some dark igneous rocks. In basalts it forms small grains or large agglomerates known as olivine balls. These balls are actually a rock called **lherzolite** and probably represent fragments of the Earth's upper mantle. When basalt is quarried, the olivine balls break, and transparent, nicely coloured olivine grains may be retrieved from them. These grains were the source of olivine sold to cutting houses in the past. Together with pyroxene, olivine forms the olivinic rock called peridotite but it is also a major constituent of dunite, gabbro and other rocks. Peridotites are the parent rocks of diamonds in the South African and Siberian diamondiferous belts; peridotites in the Urals bear grains of platinum and chromite. When peridotite is eroded, olivine is deposited in alluvia. Cracked grains disintegrate during transport and only top-quality material remains deposited in the alluvium. If it is of a sufficient size, such olivine is suitable for cutting.

Short columnar or thick tabular olivine crystals are relatively scarce (Figs a and b). The granular, transparent or translucent olivines are much more common. Olivine may often alter into serpentine, talc and iron-bearing minerals such as limonite and haematite. Slightly weathered olivines turn brownish to brown in colour; this is caused by the continuation of oxidation of divalent (ferrous) to trivalent (ferric) iron. From a jeweller's point of view, weathered olivines are not a material of any interest. When peridotites become totally weathered, the originally minute admixtures of nickel in olivine are often separated and eventually form important nickel deposits.

Olivine is softer than quartz and is therefore not suitable for setting in jewellery as the stone is highly susceptible to wear. Its principal attraction is its beautiful yellowish-green colour and its high lustre, which is enhanced by proper cutting. Olivine is usually fashioned into step and table cuts but brilliants, roses or various cabochons are also cut from the stone. Olivine is set in pins, clasps, earrings and pendants. It matches well with Bohemian garnet (pyrope) in jewellery and this attractive combination of gems was a specialty of jewellers in Turnov in Bohemia, where large oval or rounded olivines were surrounded with small garnets.

Olivine — or rather its gem variety **chrysolite** (also known under its older name **peridot**, especially in France) — has never enjoyed a stable popularity and its use has varied as much as its name. The name *chrysolithos* (from the Greek *chrysos* = gold and *lithos* = stone) used by Pliny most probably designated some other gold-coloured stone such as gold topaz, when olivines proper were called *topazios*. Moreover, jewellers used the name chrysolite also for yellow chrysoberyl and other yellow-coloured stones. The name olivine also used to be applied to the green demantoid garnets from the Urals although these stones were always called *khrizoliit* by the local lapidaries. The nomenclature is much confused and it seems that the old French adage remains relevant today: 'If one has two olivines one of the stones is surely something else.'

1 Cut chrysolites (Podmoklice, Czechoslovakia). Largest stone 18 × 12 mm. **2** Step cut of chrysolite (Zebirget, Egypt). 66.4 carats. **3** Brooch with chrysolites and freshwater pearls (second half of the 19th century). **4** Brooch with chrysolite and small pyropes (second half of the 19th century; chrysolite from Kozákov, Czechoslovakia).

1

2

3

4

Quartz

Silicon dioxide (silica), SiO_2*; crystal system: trigonal; name is an old German mining term perhaps derived from* querklufterz, *a word used to describe the milky cross veins in rock; specific gravity: 2.6528; hardness: 7; cleavage: none; fracture: conchoidal, hackly, uneven; tenacity: tough; colour: colourless when pure, often coloured by impurities; streak: white; transparency: gemstone varieties are transparent; lustre: vitreous, on fracture faces even waxy; refractive indices:* $\varepsilon = 1.55336$, $\omega = 1.54425$ *(rock crystal); birefringence: 0.00911 (rock crystal); dispersion: low, 0.03; pleochroism: distinct in deep-coloured varieties; main varieties: rock crystal, amethyst, prasiolite, citrine, smoky quartz, morion, cat's eye, tiger's eye, falcon's eye, blue (sapphire) quartz, rose quartz, aventurine quartz, prase.*

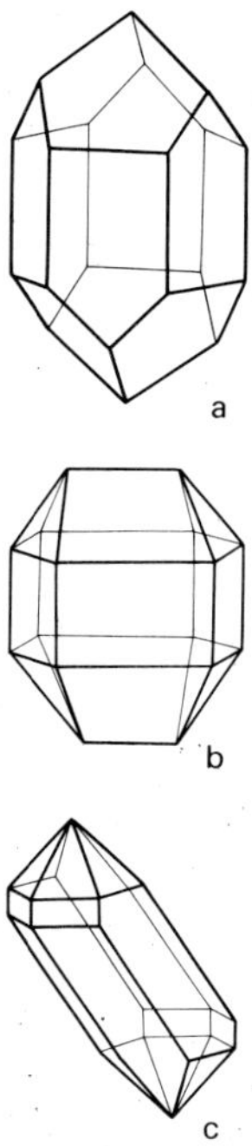
a b c

Quartz is found in crystals, grains and lumps. The crystals are hexagonal prisms terminating in one or two rhombohedra (Fig. a) that may sometimes be equally developed or one predominates. The prismatic faces are usually horizontally striated. Because conditions during the crystallization process may not always be ideal, the crystals may develop in various apparently irregular shapes, the angles between like faces being the same (Figs b, c). If the two terminal rhombohedra are equal, the crystal is a hexagonal bipyramid and the symmetry is hexagonal. Such quartz crystals in some porphyries where the quartz crystallized at temperatures exceeding 573 °C and retained the external development of the higher symmetry quartz even after the temperature had dropped.

The lucid variety of quartz is called **rock crystal**. The name is derived from the Latin *crystallus*, a word now used generally by scientists to designate any geometrical form of crystallized mineral. The Romans thought that the magnificent rock crystal columns from Alpine localities were made of petrified ice, and that the lucid, cool and perfectly developed crystals were so frozen that they would not melt even under the hot Italian sun. Even Pliny the Elder believed this. The ancient Romans were well aware that quartz is a poor conductor of heat because the rich patricians had crystal balls or columns in their houses with which they cooled their hands in hot summers.

Today it is known that quartz originates in many ways in nature. It crystallizes in temperatures ranging from those of the hot volcanic magma deep down in the Earth's crust to those of the cooler surface. Quartz crystals fill cavities in igneous rocks and the mineral occurs abundantly in many ore veins. It may also form quartz veins of its own. Fine crystals, often of gigantic dimensions, are found in pegmatite cavities where conditions were favourable for the crystallization. As a mineral highly resistant to weathering and decomposition quartz is deposited secondarily in screes and alluvial sands and gravels.

1 Group of rock crystals with discernible horizontal striation of the prismatic faces (Dauphiné, France). Height 140 mm. **2** Rock crystal (Ofenhorn, Binnatal, Switzerland). Height 75 mm. **3** Rock crystal reliquary cross of Pope Urban V (mid-14th century). **4** Rock crystal pitcher (11th—12th century, altered in 1348). Height about 400 mm.

1

2

3

4

Giant quartz crystals are known from Madagascar where crystals with circumferences of several metres around the prismatic faces have been found in local pegmatites. One such crystal had a circumference of 7.5 metres and weighed some 40 metric tons. In September 1958 a crystal was found in Kazakhstan in the USSR that was as high as a two-storeyed house. Its estimated weight is 70 metric tons.

Particularly fine examples of rock crystal are extracted from the white marbles in Carrara, Italy. In the Alps, which have been famous for rock crystal since classical times, the quartz veins fill cracks in crystalline schists. In 1719 a rock crystal cellar or vault was discovered at Zinckenstock near Grimsel in the Bernese Alps in Switzerland that yielded more than 100 metric tons of rock crystal of magnificent beauty.

Fine rock crystal also comes from Hot Springs in Arkansas, USA. Some of the largest-known specimens can be seen in the collections of the Urals Geological Museum in Sverdlovsk. Today, the richest rock crystal localities are in Madagascar, Brazil, Central Asia, the Polar Urals, Mount Kimpo in Japan, New South Wales in Australia and Burma. Alluvia in Madagascar have yielded rock crystal boulders weighing up to 50 kg. In Tertiary sandstones and shales of the Carpathian Flysch in the Galicia in the Transcarpathian Ukraine small crystals are often found and passed under the name of Marmarosh diamonds.

In the past large rock crystals were often cut and polished into spherical shapes. This type of fashioning of rock crystal used to be a specialty of Japanese cutters. Today, rock crystal balls with a diameter of 7 cm or more are quite rare. In the US National Museum in Washington, DC, there is a rock crystal ball weighing 48 kg that was cut from a Burmese quartz specimen of 450 kg. Besides the fact that rock crystal balls are cooler than their glass imitations, balls made from genuine rock crystal also possess an interesting optical property associated with the birefringence of quartz. If a letter or a point drawn on a piece of paper is observed through a crystal ball it appears double. There is an exception to this, however, because birefringence is not seen along the optical axis of quartz.

Rock crystals are usually fashioned into brilliants or table cuts. Vases and other vessels are sometimes carved from larger specimens. Rock crystal glyptography was common in Mycenaean and classical Greek times. Exquisite rock crystal engravings are also produced by modern artists.

1 Rock crystal with discernible colour play (Almeria, Spain). 90 × 80 mm. **2** Rock crystal material and necklace from clear bilaterally terminated crystals of the so-called Marmarosh diamonds. **3** Rock crystal cameo after Botticelli (contemporary work of Professor M. Dostrašilová, Turnov, Czechoslovakia). 40 × 25 mm. **4** Engravure in rock crystal with dendritic ingrowths of chlorite (St Gotthard, Switzerland). Sacrifice of Isaac, detail slightly enlarged.

1

2

3

4

Rock crystal sometimes contains inclusions of other minerals. Perhaps the best example is **sagenite (needlestone)** in which bundles of needles of golden-yellow or reddish yellow rutile crisscross in various patterns in the crystal (see also page 218). The mineral is also known as **Venus's hair**, **Cupid's darts** or **flêches d'amour.** Rock crystal may also contain similar needles of black tourmaline or fibres of green actinolite (an amphibole). Crystals of this type are fashioned into cabochons or step cuts. Venus's hair is found in the Alps, New South Wales in Australia and in the Polar Urals.

Fine internal cracks in the crystals sometimes cause a dispersion of light and iridescence. Such rock crystals are cut into cabochons and are called **rainbow** or **iris quartz**.

A very popular variety of quartz is **amethyst.** Its name is derived from the Greek *amethustos* (= nonintoxicated). Formerly it was believed that amethyst protected drinkers from becoming drunk. Worn as an amulet, amethyst was also used as a charm against poisons and for inducing sound sleep. Amethyst owes its violet-to-purple colour to radioactive decay and admixtures of colloidal iron. The saturation of the colour varies according to locality. The colour is generally unstable and some amethysts discolour relatively rapidly in daylight. Crystals are sometimes zoned, with parallel bands of white quartz alternating with coloured amethyst, the bands following the trace of the crystal faces. Such stones are called **amethyst quartz** and are fashioned into irregular-shaped pendants, smoothed cabochons or are carved into bric-à-brac and figurines. The original localities in the Müglitz Valley in Saxony and in Auvergne in France have long been exhausted. Amethyst quartz is sometimes still found near Třebíč in Czechoslovakia; the major occurrences coincide with those of amethyst proper.

In the past the most important sources of deep-coloured amethysts used to be the occurrences near Sverdlovsk and Murzinka in the Urals. Beautiful amethysts are now found in the Primorsk region on the far-eastern seaboard of the USSR. The once famous locality at Idar-Oberstein, FRG, is no longer worked. The richest occurrences are in Brazil at Serra do Mar in the state of Rio Grande do Sul and in Uruguay in the vicinity of Rivera and Artigas where amethyst crystals occur in geodes filling the cavities in amygdaloidal andesite or basalt rocks and form entire amethyst caves. The largest amethyst geode known from Serra do Mar measured 10 × 5 × 3 metres and weighed 35 metric tons. The dark-coloured crystals were as big as a human fist. Deep-coloured amethysts are also exported from Madagascar. In the USA amethyst crystals occur mainly in the states of Montana, North Carolina, California and Maine. Amethyst localities elsewhere include India, Sri Lanka, Burma, Namibia and Japan.

Transparent deep-coloured stones are faceted, but crystals that are merely translucent and of inferior quality are cut into cabochons. Amethyst used to be a gem worn by bishops and other high ecclesiastical officials.

1 Detail of amethyst druse (Brazil). Length of crystals about 50 mm. **2** Top: cut of fortification agate (Schlottwitz, GDR); bottom: cut amethysts and rough amethyst (Brazil). Rough amethyst 30 × 30 × 40 mm. **3** Detail of annulus monstrance with amethysts and rock crystals (Baroque work). **4** Rock crystal with needles of rutile known as sagenite or Cupid's darts (St Gotthard, Switzerland). 50 × 40 × 15 mm.

2

3

4

Amethyst annealed at 500 °C is called **prasiolite**. The first attempts at heat treating amethysts were made in 1950 with stones from Montezuma in Minas Gerais, Brazil. The heated stones changed their colour to a pale green. A new locality yielding amethysts that change their colour on heating has been opened in Arizona. Prasiolites now rank among the most popular gemstones.

The yellow-coloured quartz is called **citrine**. Its hue varies from pale golden yellow to reddish yellow, the tint being most probably caused by admixtures of ferric oxide (Fe_2O_3). Natural citrines are very rare. The most beautiful specimens come from Brazil and the Urals but are sometime also found in Madagascar, Spain and Scotland. For a time citrines were also reported from Pikes Peak, Colorado, USA. Natural citrine displays a distinct dichroism.

Most of the stones marketed today as citrines are in fact heat-treated amethysts or smoky quartzes. They are also commercially known under such names as golden topaz, Spanish topaz (reddish), Madeira topaz (reddish brown) and Palmeira topaz (yellowish brown). When Brazilian amethysts are annealed at 470 °C, they produce pale-yellow citrines, at 550-560 °C they yield citrines of a dark-yellow or red-yellow colour. Some smoky quartzes become a citrine yellow even at 300-400 °C. The name citrine is derived from the word citrus.

Smoky quartz is a variety of quartz with a distinct smoky-brown to brownish black colour. The black, almost nontransparent variety is called **morion**. The coloration is most probably caused by the liberation of silicon atoms from their original position in the crystal structure as a result of radiation. If the mineral is annealed carefully at a temperature of 300-400 °C, the dark colour will disappear. Pale-brown stones heated to 200 °C for one hour will change into pale citrines and dark-hued smoky quartzes, if annealed at 300 °C, may turn almost colourless. However, if such stones are subsequently exposed to strong radiation or X-rays, they will regain their original shade.

The best localities for smoky quartz are the Alps, especially in the vicinity of St Gotthard. A crystal known as the Grandfather from this locality measured 70 cm in length and weighed 130 kg. In 1968 another locality in the canton of Uri yielded about 1.5 metric tons of the crystal. Another large smoky quartz crystal weighing 150 kg and measuring 95 cm was found in the crystal vault on the Tiefengletscher. Finds of large specimens of smoky quartz are also known from the USSR (Murzinka in the Urals, the Volhynia region and Central Asia), Brazil, Madagascar and Pikes Peak in Colorado, USA. Pikes Peak also yields small crystals of exquisite, delicate hues. Gem-quality smoky quartz also comes from the US states of Maine and North Carolina, Japan, Cordoba in Spain and New South Wales in Australia. Pegmatites in West Moravia, Czechoslovakia, have also yielded some large crystals of smoky quartz; one from Kněževes near Velké Meziříčí measured 60 cm and weighed 57 kg. Black morions are found in Brazil, Madagascar and the USSR. A perfectly developed morion from the Volhynia region deposited in the Museum of the Earth at the Lomonosov Moscow State University measures 35 × 10 cm.

1 Druse of citrine crystals (Dauphiné, France). Height 110 mm. **2** Cross with citrines and garnets (first half of the 19th century). Height of cross 75 mm. **3** Brilliant cut of smoky quartz (Switzerland). 746.45 carats. **4** Morion crystal (Swiss Alps). Height 101 mm.

1

2

Fibrous quartz is usually a pseudomorph of crystalline quartz after some other fibrous minerals. Fibrous quartzes include such stones as **cat's eye, falcon's eye** and **tiger's eye**. The greenish grey cat's eye and bluish grey falcon's eye are quartz pseudomorphs after crocidolite — a fibrous variety of alkaline amphibole — with many fibres of the latter still preserved in the stone. They are found in gravels in Sri Lanka and in India: greenish specimens come from the Fichtelgebirge in Bavaria. Tiger's eye from the Doorn Mountain Range in South Africa was also formed as a pseudomorph after crocidolite but the crocidolite fibres have been weathered and contain hydrated ferric oxides and hydroxides. The resulting colour is yellow, alternating with brown. The golden-brown to brown colour and the vitreous lustre, which is improved by cutting, together with the chatoyancy make tiger's eye a very attractive stone. It is cut into cabochons or plates. In spite of its popularity, tiger's eye is not very precious. The best-known localities are in South Africa, but the stone is also found in Western Australia, Burma, India and California, USA.

Also associated with crocidolite or perhaps with rutile fibres is the fine-grained **blue quartz**, a quartz aggregate of a dirty-blue colour, also known as **sapphire quartz**. It is a nontransparent, unevenly coloured stone found in Austria, Scandinavia, South Africa and Brazil.

The most popular lump variety of quartz is **rose quartz**, which has a pleasant pink hue, often with a purplish tint. The colour is caused by small admixture of manganese or titanium oxides and will disappear if the stone is heated to 575 °C. If left exposed to air for a long time, it will turn grey. The most beautiful rose quartzes occur in pegmatite veins. Crystallized rose quartz is so far known only from Brazil. Top-quality material comes from Alto Feio in the state of Rio Grande do Norte and from the Jequitinhonha Valley. Other rich localities are in Madagascar and India.

Aventurine is a rather special variety of lump quartz because it contains spangles of mica flakes — the green fuchsite — or haematite that give it an iridescent sheen. In China the green aventurine known as Imperial Yü stone used to be popular. The mica flakes in aventurine may also be formed by muscovite or biotite, giving the stone a different colour. Aventurine is found in large quantities in the Urals, Siberia, Tibet, India, Brazil and in Steyr in Austria. The green lump variety of quartz is called **prase**. Its green colour is caused by ingrowths of actinolite fibres. It is found at Breitenbrunn in Saxony, GDR, in Finland, Scotland and Salzburg in Austria.

1 Tiger's-eye (Griqualand, South Africa). **2** Falcon's-eye (Doorn Mountain Range, South Africa). **3** Tiger's-eye cabochon (Doorn, South Africa). 38 × 17 mm. **4** Polished section of ferruginous quartz (Hořovice, Czechoslovakia). 70 × 65 mm. **5** Aventurine quartz (Conquista, Brazil). 150 × 120 mm. **6** Rose quartz (Sahanibotri, Madagascar). 65 × 65 mm.

1

2

3

4

5

6

Chalcedony and **Jasper**

Silicon dioxide (silica) SiO_2*; both minerals are cryptocrystalline varieties of quartz; the name chalcedony is derived from a locality near the city of Kalchidon in Bythinia in Asia Minor, the name jasper is based on the Latin* jaspis, *a term used by Pliny the Elder; specific gravity: 2.59-2.61; hardness: 6.5; cleavage: none; fracture: conchoidal to hackly; tenacity: tough; colour: variable; streak: white to grey; transparency: translucent to opaque; lustre: vitreous to greasy; refractive index: ≅ 1.54; birefringence, dispersion and pleochroism: none (isotropic); main varieties: carnelian, plasma, sard, cacholong, chrysoprase, heliotrope.*

Chalcedonies are a special group of quartz varieties that differ from other quartzes in a number of properties as well as in their origin from a gelatinous siliceous mass. Outwardly they appear compact but under a microscope they reveal that they are aggregates of very fine and densely packed quartz fibres in layers or spherical aggregates (spherulites). The interstitial space between the fibres is usually filled with water or air. As a gemstone, chalcedony was very popular in classical times when it was one of the most sought-after and prized minerals.

In nature chalcedony usually forms layers with a reniform surface. It frequently occurs with an admixture of opal and various iron-containing mineral pigments such as haematite, limonite and chlorite. The fine pores between the individual quartz fibres, if big enough, enable chalcedony to be stained artificially. Chalcedony is translucent to opaque and occurs in many colours, the commonest being milky-grey, yellowish red and shades of green. The stones may also be mottled or spotted.

Chalcedony occurs mainly in cavities of amygdaloidal volcanic rocks in Brazil, Uruguay, India, Syria, Sri Lanka, Siberia and elsewhere. It also fills cavities in geologically younger igneous rocks, for example in Iceland and the Faroes Islands; it has also been known to occur as veins in some ore deposits.

Coloured chalcedonies are known under various names among collectors and jewellers but the names are often superfluous from the mineralogist's viewpoint. **Carnelian (cornelian)** is a translucent chalcedony tinted a reddish colour by haematite. Its name is derived from the Latin *carneus (=* fleshy*).* Localities include Akhaltsikhe in Georgian SSR, Idar-Oberstein in the Rheinland, FRG, Arabia, Egypt, Brazil and India. Nice carnelians are also found at Železnice in Czechoslovakia. **Plasma** is a chalcedony tinted green by admixtures of chlorite. The name is of Italian origin and used to be applied to all green cut stones from the ruins of ancient Rome. **Sard** is a reddish-brown chalcedony found in India, China and the USA. **Cacholong** is a chalk-white mixture of chalcedony and opal. The name is originally Mongolian and denotes a beautiful stone. It is known from localities for chalcedony and agate.

1 Translucent stalactites of chalcedony (Tri Vody, Czechoslovakia). Height 160 mm. **2** Pair of chalcedony candlesticks (late 19th century). Height 180 mm. **3** Polished section of plasma (Hrubšice, Czechoslovakia). 65 × 47 mm. **4** Carnelian seal stamp (first half of the 19th century). 30 × 25 mm.

1

2

3

4

The most valued chalcedony variety is the translucent green **chrysoprase**. Its colour may be apple green, yellowish green or a grass green, the depth of colour depending on the amount of hydrated silicates or nickel oxides present. The name is derived from the Greek *chrysos* (= gold). The specific gravity of chrysoprase is 2.59-2.65, its hardness 6.5-7. Chrysoprase is derived from weathered serpentinites. The classical locality of exquisite chrysoprase is at Kózmice near Ząbkowice in Poland, other important locations being Sarakul-Baldy in Kazakhstan and the Urals, USSR, and Tulare County in California, USA, and various places in the state of Goias in Brazil and in Queensland, Australia. The stone enjoyed a great popularity in the 14th century and Emperor Charles IV had the St Wenceslaus' Chapel in St Vitus' Cathedral in Prague, and the chapels in his Karlštejn castle decorated with chrysoprase. The chrysoprase decorations in the Sans-Souci Palace in Potsdam, GDR, are 18th century.

Jasper is a mixture of chalcedony, quartz and opal. It comes in a variety of colours including red, ochre, green, grey and even brown. The conspicuous colouring has always made the stone valuable. Jaspers originate mainly in cracks of amygdaloidal volcanic rocks. After the rocks solidified, the mineral constituents were once again separated out by hot solutions and the silica gel thus formed penetrated cracks in the rocks where it hardened. The best-known jasper localities are in the Urals where jasper boulders weighing several quintals (several hundreds of kilograms) have been found and later carved into art objects. The Ural jaspers are a mixture of red, white and brown colours and occur generally in the area around Orsk in the southern part of the range. Red-and-green jaspers occur in Kazakhstan, USSR. Top-quality jaspers are also extracted in many other localities, for example in the valley of the River Müglitz and near Karl-Marx-Stadt in Saxony, GDR, in Idar-Oberstein in the Rheinland, FRG, Dakkan in India, Brazil, USA, Italy, Egypt and many places in the foothills of the Krkonoše (Giant Mountains) in Czechoslovakia.

A green variety of jasper or chalcedony with numerous red spots caused by haematite is called **heliotrope**. Its specific gravity is 2.59-2.65 and its hardness varies between 6.75 and 7.0. Heliotrope is also a very popular gemstone. Its name is based on the Greek *helios* (= sun) and *tropos* (= turn, way or manner), because it was once used for observing the Sun in ancient times. Heliotrope is also known in English as **bloodstone**. The stone is found in India, the Urals, Australia, Brazil, China and the USA. In Europe it occurs in the Tirol and in the Krkonoše foothills in Czechoslovakia.

Being tough, chemically resistant, abundant, available in large uncracked lumps and attractive, chalcedony and jasper are suitable for carving decorative objects such as clasps, handles and holders, buttons, cameos and brooches, intaglio seal (signet) rings, earrings, necklaces and pendants. Indeed the popularity of coloured jaspers and chalcedonies dates very far back. The Egyptians and later the Greeks and Romans used to drill them and carve various symbols in them for wearing as amulets, and later started decorating these stones with carved portraits.

1 Chrysoprase veinlet in serpentine (Szklary, Poland). 110 × 55 mm. **2** Chrysoprase cabochons (Szklary, Poland). Height of drop 22 mm. **3** Polished section of heliotrope (Kozákov, Czechoslovakia). 60 × 40 mm. **4** Detail of a polished section of jasper (Kozákov, Czechoslovakia). Actual size.

1

2

3

4

Agate

Composed of layers of finely fibrous quartz, chalcedony and opal; amorphous; name derived from its first purported source — the ancient River Aghates (now R. Dirillo) in southern Sicily; specific gravity: fluctuates around 2.60; hardness: 6.5-7; cleavage: none; fracture: conchoidal; tenacity: tough; colour: variable; streak: white; transparency: translucent to opaque; lustre: vitreous to greasy; refractive index: ≅ 1.53; birefringence, dispersion and pleochroism: none (isotropic); main varieties: onyx, sardonyx, moss agate, araukarite.

Agates are more precious than chalcedonies proper from which they are derived. They occur mostly in amygdaloidal volcanic rocks. Agate is usually composed of various brightly coloured thin parallel bands that follow the contour of the cavity where the silica gel solidified. The concentric arrangement of the layers can be seen in sawed and polished agate sections. The bands may be sharply demarkated or they may merge imperceptibly one into another. Sometimes the original inlet hole through which the solutions and the tinting constituents penetrated the cavity can be observed. The arrangement of the individual coloured layers may also have been affected by later processes during the consolidation of the silica. The centres of incompletely filled agates may sometimes contain crystals of smoky quartz, rock crystal or amethyst.

The colours or the pattern gave agates their names, for example **cloud agate**, **ogle-eyed agate**, **ruin agate**, **fortification agate** and **star agate**. The black-and-white banded agate is known as **onyx**: **sardonyx** has bands of reddish brown and white. **Moss agate** (**mocha stone, dendritic agate**) contains dark-green moss-like or dendritic aggregates of chloritic minerals. The dendritic pattern may also be caused by rusty-red iron oxides and hydroxides or by black manganese oxides and hydroxides.

The banding gives agate a special character and it is therefore no wonder that it is one of the oldest-known minerals. It was greatly valued by the Sumerians and Egyptians who used it not only for adornment but also carved receptacles from it and wore it as amulets and charms. Classical artists in ancient Greece and Rome used agate for delicately carved cameos and intaglios (glyptography). The variety of colours and the individual pattern of each stone give every agate a unique character and it was this special feature that made agate a perfect material for carved *objets d'art* of enormous value. The *Gemma Augustea*, the famous sardonyx cameo dating from the first century AD, was singled out for special mention in the introduction (see p. 7).

1 Polished agate (Levín, Czechoslovakia). 50 × 50 mm. **2** Cut plates of Brazilian agate. 30 × 16 mm. **3** Cloud agate. 110 × 100 mm. **4** Tallow-topped agate cabochon (Idar-Oberstein, FRG). 80 × 50 mm. **5** Ruin agate (Schlottwitz, GDR). Actual size. **6** Agate with a bizarre pattern (Měděnec, Czechoslovakia). Actual size.

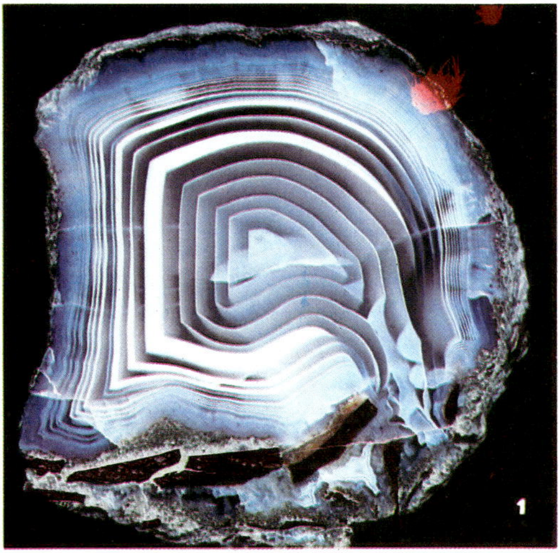
1

2

3

5

6

In ancient times an agate cameo would be worn around the neck suspended upside down to allow the wearer to pick it up and admire the carved motif. As was mentioned in the introduction, Romans were fond of intaglio seal (signet) rings made of agate and about 85 BC the first agate cameo and intaglio collection — the so-called *dactyliotheca* — was founded in Rome. An even richer and rarer collection, put together from war booty won by Pompey (Pompeius), was exhibited on the Capitol in Rome in 61 BC as a tribute to the gods for the Roman victory. After the fall of the Roman Empire the tradition of agate carving moved eastwards, mainly to Byzantium. Agate was also widely popular in medieval times. Agate is still used widely for jewellery and for such decorative objects as table-top inlays and inlaid boxes. It has an increasing industrial application in, for example, the manufacture of grinding equipment.

The most famous European agate localities are in the foothills of the Krkonoše (Giant) Mountains in Czechoslovakia (Lomnice nad Popelkou, Nová Paka and Kozákov). The once agate-rich localities near Idar-Oberstein in Rheinland, FRG, have been almost depleted. Many top-quality agates come from Brazil (especially the state of Rio Grande do Sul), Uruguay, Kathiavar in India, China, the Urals, Madagascar and the USA. Agates also come from the Georgian SSR, Crimea, Siberia, Mongolia, Morocco and Iceland, but the quality of these stones is somewhat inferior.

The rising demand for multicoloured agates and the scarcity of the natural stone led to the relatively early discovery of artificial staining of agates. The method was known to the ancient Greeks and Romans, but the art was perfected by the artisans of Constantinople. Nowadays, agate staining is an important and thriving business. Most suitable for staining are the Brazilian agates that are more porous and have more opal than others. If the fibres of the microcrystalline quartz are long and tapered, there is more space in the agate for the opal constituent and there is therefore more water. Such materials absorb the staining pigments better. Conversely agates with shorter and intertwined quartz fibres have less space for opal and can be stained only with difficulty. In gemmologists' jargon such stones are said to be 'hard'. Among hard agates are those from Bohemian localities, but these agates are usually naturally coloured.

1 Agate brooch (contemporary work). Width 48 mm. **2** Onyx chalice (material probably from Brazil, 19th century). Height 105 mm. **3** Classical carnelian cameo (ninth century; Želénka, Czechoslovakia). Height of cameo 23 mm. (Cameos were set in pendants upside down to allow the wearer to look down and admire the motif. Note also the exquisite gold work.) **4** Onyx cameo with portrait of Emperor Claudius (Roman, first century AD). Height 45 mm. **5** Moss agate (India). Detail slightly magnified. **6** Mocha-coloured dendritic agate (Asia Minor). 18 × 13 mm.

1

2

3

4

5

The modern agate-staining methods are based either on the direct penetration of the pigment into the permeable substance of the stone, or on the thermal decomposition of the absorbed chemicals. Agates are stained after cutting but before polishing. Some agate layers do not absorb the pigment at all and thus remain white.

A black agate is obtained if a thoroughly cleaned specimen is soaked in a hot saturated sugar solution or in honey for several weeks. After soaking the stone is washed in water, soaked in concentrated sulphuric acid and then annealed. The black colour is the result of the carbonization of sugar. Brown colours of various shades can be obtained by annealing agate impregnated with a diluted sugar solution. A black coloration may also be achieved if agate is soaked in a solution of cobalt nitrate and ammonium thiocyanate and then carefully heated. Blue-stained agates, also known as Swiss lapis or false lapis, are made by soaking agate first in potassium cyanoferrate to allow the chemical to permeate the mineral and then by boiling the stone in a solution of ferric sulphate. The resulting colour is a Prussian blue. The exact hue depends on the concentration of the solution and the pH values. Green and bluish green colours are produced by impregnating the stone with chromium salts, for example, potassium dichromate or chrome alum, and subsequently annealing. An apple-green hue is caused by nickel salts; red and various reddish brown shades can usually be achieved by annealing natural brown agates directly. These stones contain their pigment in the form of goethite (iron hydroxide). In another method, the agate to be stained is first soaked in iron salt and then annealed. Yellowish brown to yellow hues are produced if the cut face of the agate is first dipped in concentrated hydrochloric acid, dried and annealed.

Agates are mostly stained by inorganic pigments that retain their colourfastness for a long time, because stones stained with organic dyestuffs, such as aniline dyes, will be bleached by daylight after some time. The depth of the penetration of the staining agent depends on the porosity of the agate layers, on the water content (that is, on the amount of the opal constituent) and on the time of the effect of the agent. Usually only a very thin top layer is stained and this is why it is best to stain only those agates that have been already shaped and cut.

A special note must be made of the so-called **petrified wood**, which is valued for its hardness, resistance and durability, attractive colours and patterns. Woods of various geological ages become fossilized by jasper (jasperization), chalcedony, quartz and to a lesser extent also by opal. The wood retains its original structure and its colour is most often brown, grey or green. Its specific gravity varies between 2.60 and 2.65, and its hardness is 6.5-7. Although petrified wood appears compact, it is in fact a microcrystalline aggregate. The most famous locality is the Petrified Forest National Park near Holbrook in Arizona, USA, where a specimen of petrified **araukarite** dating from the Permian geological period and measuring 65 m long and 3 m thick has been found. Other petrified wood localities are in Nevada, Egypt, Patagonia in Argentina and the foothills of the Krkonoše Mountains in Bohemia, Czechoslovakia.

1 Artificially stained Brazilian agate; the rims are naturally coloured, the rest of the bands are stained with aniline dyes. 180 × 130 mm. **2** Detail of a cross-section of a fossilized (petrified) tree trunk (Permian; Žďár, Czechoslovakia). Actual size. **3** Fossilized vegetable debris — so-called fossilized peat (Stará Paka, Czechoslovakia). Detail actual size.

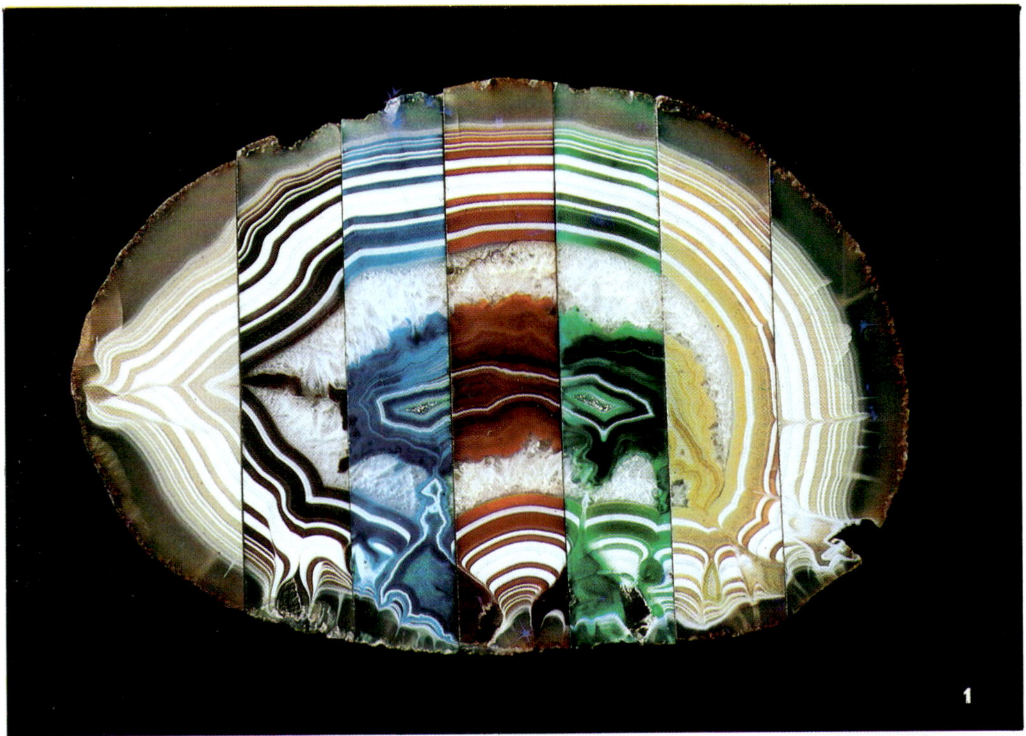

1

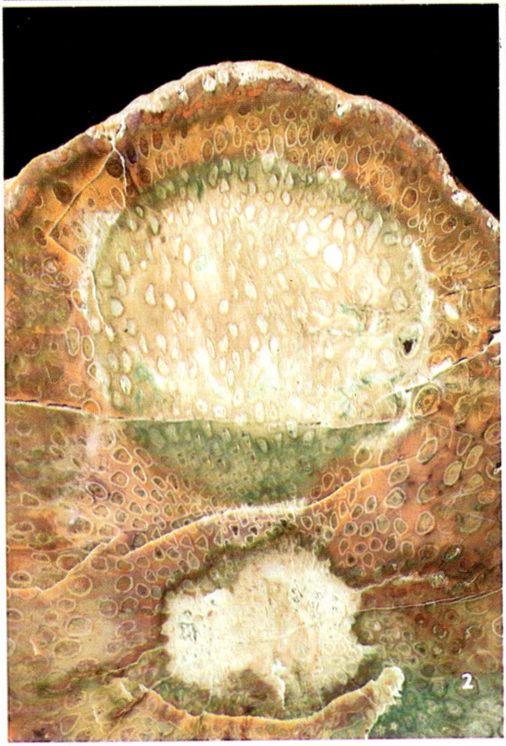

2

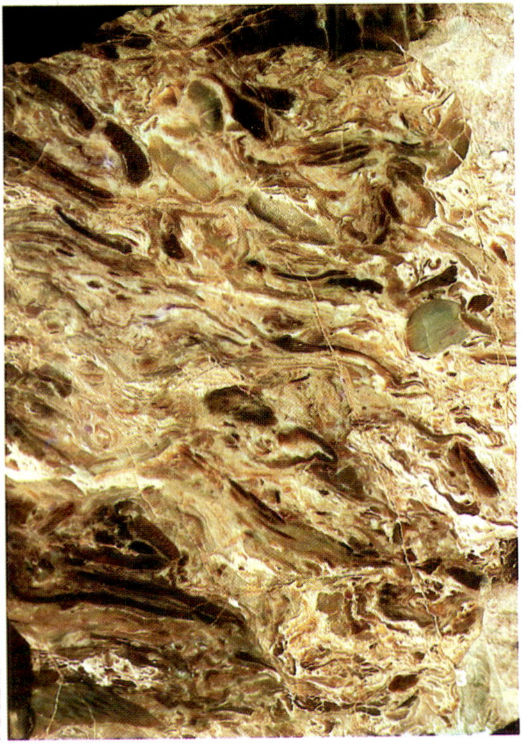

3

Opal

Hydrated colloidal silica, $SiO_2 \cdot nH_2O$*; amorphous; name derived from the Sanskrit* upala *(= precious stone), later the Greek* opallios*; specific gravity: 2.0-2.2; hardness: 5.5-6.5; cleavage: none; fracture: conchoidal; tenacity: brittle; colour: colourless or white, often tinted; streak: white; transparency: transparent (fire opal), usually translucent to nontransparent; lustre: vitreous, waxy, pearly or dull; refractive index:* n = *1.43-1.46; birefringence, dispersion and pleochroism: none (isotropic), but distinct iridescence (colour play); main varieties: precious opal, harlequin, fire opal, hyalite, prasopal, hydrophane, moss opal, wood opal, cacholong.*

Opal with its numerous varieties is a common and abundant mineral. The most precious and much sought-after variety is **precious opal**, which is noted for its play of exquisite delicate colour hues (iridescence). The beauty of precious opal has long been admired and the Greeks prized it as much as diamond. The magic properties of the stone were aptly characterized by Pliny the Elder who wrote about what he termed *opallus*: . . . 'because it possesses a fire finer than that of carbuncle, it has a purple sparkle of amethyst, the sea-green of emerald; in fact it has an unbelievable mixture of colours.'

Being an amorphous mineral, opal is reniform, spherical, botryoidal or stalactitic in habit. It often fills crevices and veins or forms layers in various rocks. Although opal is essentially amorphous it has been discovered to have a partially ordered internal structure. The atoms are not arranged in a regular three-dimensional lattice, as in a proper crystal, but are in groupings of tiny balls (spherulites) of silica in a hexagonal or dense cubic arrangement. The interstices between the spherulites contain either air or loosely bonded water. The diameter of the spherulites ranges from 0.15 to 0.3 µm, the size depending on the variety. Common ('potch') opal varieties have spherulites of different diameter arranged in regular small clusters or domains, or there are no domains at all. On the other hand, precious opal contains predominantly large domains with regularly arranged spherulites of a surprisingly identical diameter. In a scanning electron microscope these spherulites resemble layers of closely packed ping-pong balls. The symmetrical blocks of spherulites represent a diffraction lattice with dimensions corresponding approximately to the wavelengths of visible light. On such a lattice, diffraction and interference of light take place as well as the decomposition of light into the spectral colours that are observed on the surface of the opal as the unique rainbow effect called opalescence — a type of iridescence. The more regular and precise the arrangement of the individual spherulites, the livelier the colour play.

Opalescence is also affected by the water content of the mineral, which usually varies between 3 and 13 per cent although it can be as high as 21 per cent. If heated to 250 °C, an opal loses all its water, the typical opalescence disappears and the stone turns cloudy, or becomes 'blind'. It is therefore imperative not to overheat precious opals during cutting or polishing. Some opal varieties are also sensitive to soap, cosmetics and detergents.

Opals are usually translucent to nontransparent although some varieties may be perfectly transparent. Some opals emit a yellowish-green fluorescent light if illuminated with an ultraviolet lamp. Generally speaking, the colour of opals depends on the admixtures of metallic oxides and on the presence of foreign inclusions.

1 Precious opal on andesite (Dubník, Czechoslovakia). 80 × 72 mm. **2** Precious opal (Lightning Ridge, NSW, Australia). 60 × 45 mm. **3** Precious opal with parent rock (Bull's Creek, Queensland, Australia). Width 65 mm.

1

2

3

Opal is a secondary mineral and originates either as the result of the hydrothermal decomposition of silicates in various rocks or it is precipitated from hot waters and springs. It also fossilizes the remains of plants and animals. There are many opal varieties, which are distinguished by colour, transparency, lustre and general appearance.

Precious opal with its typical feature — opalescence — is classified into two types according to the basic colour: **white opal** (milky, yellowish, light grey) and **black opal** (dark, usually greyish black). The so-called **harlequin** has a mosaic-like arrangement of a great number of small irregular spots of different colours. A classical precious opal locality is at Dubník near Prešov in Czechoslovakia, where opal was mined from Roman times till 1923. The most important and richest modern localities were discovered in the latter half of the 19th century in New South Wales, Queensland and Victoria in Australia. Somewhat lower yields of opal are extracted from localities in Mexico and Nevada and Idaho, USA. The largest opal from Dubník found in 1775 weighs about 500 grams and is kept in the Museum of Sciences in Vienna. The largest Australian opal measuring some 50 × 15 cm is exhibited in the American Museum of Natural History in New York.

Fire opal is yellowish red to brownish red, mostly highly translucent to transparent. Some fire opal varieties called **girasols** exhibit fiery reflections, or colour play similar to that of precious opals. Fire opal is extremely sensitive to changes in temperature, humidity and light intensity. Their most important locality is at Zimapan in the state of Hidalgo, Mexico. It is also found at Kara-Agach in Kazakhstan, USSR.

Hyalite (from the Greek *hyalos* = glass) is a colourless, lucid opal forming botryoidal or stalactitic aggregates in the shape of a coronet, or reniform-surfaced incrustations in basalt cavities. It has a high lustre and luminesces in ultraviolet light. Hyalite is found in western Bohemia in Czechoslovakia, Mexico and Japan.

Prasopal (from the Greek *prasios* = leek green) is apple green, translucent and resembles chrysoprase. It is found in Polish Silesia but recently new localities have been opened up at Dudoma in Tasmania.

Hydrophane (*occulus mundi* or world's eye) is an opal turned cloudy owing to loss of water. It lacks lustre and colour play. If soaked in water it will regain its former opalescence and translucence. It is found in association with precious opal.

Moss opal is composed of a milky matrix that contains dendritic patterns, usually black. **Wood opal** is silicified wood and it retains the structure of the latter. **Cacholong (pearly opal)** derives its name from the Mongolian *cach-cholung* (= a beautiful stone). It is milky white, yellowish and nontransparent with a slight pearly lustre. It is usually porous and dull.

Opals are cut as tallow-topped cabochons of various shapes. Transparent opals like fire opal are often faceted. It is quite frequent to find genuine and imitation doublets composed of a thin plate of a pale precious opal with a cemented backing of black onyx or glass.

1 Pseudomorph of precious opal after calcite (White Cliffs, Australia). 80 × 60 mm. **2** Black opal (Yowah, Queensland, Australia). 38 × 24 mm. **3** Pendant with cabochon of the precious opal variety known as harlequin (material probably from Australia; contemporary work). Height of cabochon 12 mm. **4** Art Nouveau necklace with precious opal and Bohemian garnets set in gold (made by the School of Jewellery, Turnov, Czechoslovakia). **5** Cut fire opals (Zimapan, Mexico). Weight of largest stone about 11.3 carats. **6** Wood opal; the structure of the wood can be seen clearly (Clower Creek, USA). Detail slightly enlarged.

1

2

3

4

5

6

Spodumene

Lithium aluminium silicate, $LiAl[Si_2O_6]$, *of the pyroxene group; crystal system; monoclinic; name derived from the Greek* spodios *(= ash-coloured); specific gravity: 3.14-3.19; hardness: 6.5-7; cleavage: eminent; fracture: uneven to subconchoidal; tenacity: brittle; colour: colourless, greyish or greenish, yellowish green to emerald green (hiddenite) or purplish pink (kunzite); streak: white; transparency: transparent to translucent; lustre: highly vitreous; refractive indices:* $\alpha = 1.651\text{-}1.658$, $\beta = 1.665\text{-}1.675$, $\gamma = 1.676\text{-}1.681$; *birefringence: 0.015; dispersion: weak, 0.017; pleochroism: strong; main varieties: hiddenite and kunzite.*

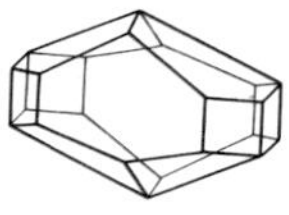

When yellowish-green crystals were found in North Carolina in 1879 they were first thought to be diopside and it was only later when W. E. Hidden discovered that the crystals were in fact a gemmy variety of spodumene that until then had been known only in its common ash-grey, nontransparent form. Then in 1902, a hitherto unknown and interesting mineral was found in California and was described by the gemmologist G. F. Kunz as 'a new, transparent, violet-coloured spodumene'. **Hiddenite** and **kunzite,** as these minerals becamé to be named, are relatively recent and quite fashionable stones. Gem-quality spodumene was discovered as late as 1971 in Brazil.

Crystals of hiddenite (Fig.) and kunzite are columnar or tabular and vertically striated. The ends of the crystals are often rounded and considerably etched by natural corrosion. Their eminent cleavage and splitting properties considerably hinder their cutting. The deep-coloured varieties of hiddenite are pleochroic and pleochroism in kunzite is so pronounced that it is visible to the naked eye. Pleochroism must be respected when selecting the cut. Double refraction is relatively high and doubling of the far facets may be observed with a magnifying glass. Gem-quality spodumene takes a good polish and possesses an intensive lustre.

Hiddenite is mostly yellowish green but the hue is pale and best prices are fetched by stones of a deep emerald green. The colour is caused by admixture of chromium and iron. If irradiated, hiddenite does not change colour and it does not fluoresce in ultraviolet light. It occurs in granite pegmatites at Stony Point, Alexander County in North Carolina, USA, in the states of Minas Gerais and Minas Novas in Brazil, and in Madagascar. The largest hiddenite crystal was found in 1958 in Brazil. In the rough it weighed 3,675 carats; cut into a 9.8 × 3.7 mm step cut it is a stone of 1,804 carats.

Unlike hiddenite, kunzite emits a strong orange-red luminescent light if treated with X-rays or ultraviolet light. Its purplish-pink colour is caused by an admixture of manganese. If irradiated, the purple colour will change into green but annealing at 200 °C will regenerate the original hue. Kunzite localities are chiefly in granite pegmatites at Pala Chief, San Diego County in California, USA, in the state of Minas Gerais, Brazil, and at Antsirabé in Madagascar. It is not rare to find large crystals of 10 cm or more in length. Kunzite is fashioned into high brilliants or table cuts.

Diopside is another mineral from the pyroxene group. It is calcium magnesium silicate, $CaMg[Si_2O_6]$, of monoclinic symmetry. Crystals are short and columnar. Diopside is mostly greenish to white. It occurs in contact metamorphosed rocks. Gem-quality stones are found in India.

1 Diopside crystal (Rothenkopf, Austria). Length 44 mm. **2** Cut diopsides (Itrongay, Madagascar). Weight of largest stone 2.4 carats. **3** Rough kunzite (Pala, California, USA). Height of crystals about 25 mm. **4** Step cut of kunzite (Brazil). 28.29 carats. **5** Jadeite elephant figurine (China, first half of the 20th century). 45 × 30 mm. **6** Jadeite figurine (Tibet, 19th century). Height 130 mm.

1

2

3

4

5

6

Nephrite and **Jadeite**

Two different minerals of similar appearance and properties sometimes embraced by the name **jade.**

Nephrite: *calcium magnesium iron silicate,* $Ca_2(Mg, Fe)_5[(OH, F)_2|Si_4O_{11}]_2$, *a variety of actinolite of the amphibole group; crystal system: monoclinic; name derived from the Greek* nephros *(= kidney), from the belief that it is a remedy for kidney disorders; specific gravity: 2.9-3.1; hardness: 6-6.5; cleavage: none; fracture: hackly; tenacity: very tough (elastic); colour: green, whitish, yellowish, brownish, blackish; streak: white; transparency: translucent; lustre: vitreous; refractive indices:* α*= 1.599-1.618,* β*= 1.613-1.633,* γ*= 1.625-1.641; birefringence: 0.03; dispersion: none; pleochroism: strong, but may be masked by aggregate structure.*

Jadeite: *sodium aluminium silicate,* $NaAl[Si_2O_6]$, *of the pyroxene group; crystal system: monoclinic; name derived from the Spanish* piedra de ijada *(= stone of the side), from the belief that it is a remedy for renal colic; specific gravity: 3.3-3.5; hardness: 6.5-7; cleavage: none; fracture: hackly; tenacity: very tough (elastic); colour: green yellow, white pink, purple, orange, bluish green, brown, blackish; streak: white; transparency: translucent; lustre: vitreous; refractive indices:* α*= 1.654,* β*= 1.659,* γ*= 1.667; birefringence: 0.02; dispersion and pleochroism: none.*

Nephrite and jadeite are undoubtedly minerals of a great cultural and historical significance. For Stone Age people, these minerals represented an indispensable material for stone axes, hammers and other tools and implements vital for their survival, as is shown by archaeological finds all over the world. For centuries, the two minerals, known under the common name **Yü stone**, have been popular with Chinese artists who carved them into beautiful objects of great value. Nephrite and jadeite still remain popular. At first look both minerals seem lumpy and compact but a microscope reveals that they are made up of a very fine mesh of acicular crystals or tiny grains. Essentially, they are finely fibrous, felted aggregates, in fact perfect natural laminates. This internal structure is the cause of their incredible toughness and strength. Nephrite and jadeite withstand pressures of up to 8,000 kg cm^{-2} without any damage and they are more elastic even than steel. On the other hand, their hardness is relatively low. Until the 19th century the two minerals were not differentiated and they can still be mistaken for each other, especially at first sight. Nephrite is usually spinach green but may be yellowish green. Generally, its coloration is more uniform than jadeite's, which has a much broader colour range. Jadeite also occurs spotted or striped. As compared with nephrite, jadeite is harder, has a higher specific gravity and melts more easily. A tiny sliver of jadeite partially melts or softens even in the flame of an alcohol burner.

Nephrite and jadeite occur as inclusions in serpentinites, at contact with gabbro intrusions and in crystalline schists associated with amphibolites. The most important jadeite localities are in Upper Burma, in the Yunan Province in China, in Tibet, Mexico and South America. Beautiful nephrites come from New Zealand, where it is known as **Maori stone** or **New Zealand greenstone**. The localities in the Bogotol mountain range near Lake Baikal and in Central Asia, USSR are also rich. A minor nephrite locality discovered in the 19th century is at Jordanow in Poland. Nephrite and jadeite are usually cut into various cabochons.

1 Polished plate of nephrite (Irkutsk region, USSR). Actual size. **2** Nephrite brooch in gold (1940s). 60 × 60 mm. **3** Polished section of nephrite pebble (New Zealand). 170 × 120 mm.

1

2

3

Vesuvianite (Idocrase)

Complex calcium magnesium silicate with iron and aluminium $Ca_{10}(Mg, Fe)_2 Al_4[(OH)_4|(SiO_4)_5|(Si_2O_7)_2]$; *crystal system: tetragonal; named after Mt Vesuvius where it was found in the extrusions, the name idocrase is derived from the Greek* idea *(= likeness) and* krasis *(= mixture), because of its likeness to other minerals; specific gravity: 3.35-3.47; hardness: 6.5-7; cleavage: poor; fracture: conchoidal to uneven; tenacity: brittle; colour: colourless or yellow, green, brown or blue; streak: white; transparency: translucent, rarely transparent; lustre: vitreous to greasy; refractive indices:* $\varepsilon = 1.700\text{-}1.746$, $\omega = 1.703\text{-}1.752$; *birefringence: 0.005; dispersion: weak, 0.019; pleochroism: weak, distinct in thick sections; main variety: californite.*

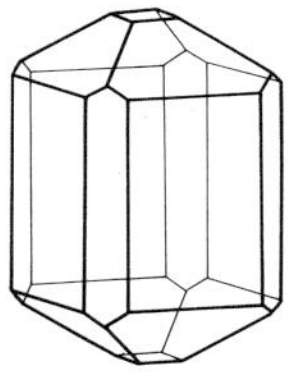

The green-coloured crystals found in the volcanic extrusions of Mt Vesuvius in Italy were first thought to be various other minerals, such as tourmaline, olivine or green garnet. Only later was it shown that it was a mineral in its own right and it was called **vesuvianite** after its original locality. Vesuvianite is quite widespread as a rock-forming mineral. Its transparent varieties may be used for jewellery stones.

Vesuvianite is only rarely perfectly transparent, mostly being merely translucent or nontransparent. It usually forms short and thick columnar or prismatic crystals (Fig.) or bladed and granular aggregates. The crystals are usually longitudinally striated, often with a multifaced termination.

It is usually colourless, but may also be yellow, brown, red, green or blue. It has several varieties, the names of which differ according to the colour and occurrence. **Californite** is a lumpy, fine-grained and green-coloured variety resembling jadeite in colour and toughness. The trade also knows it under the name **Vesuvian jade**. Jewellers seek mostly green and brown specimens with a reddish tint. Vesuvianite has a vitreous lustre, that is enhanced by cutting. Deep-coloured crystals are slightly pleochroic. The dispersion is low. Vesuvianite also does not fluoresce in ultraviolet light.

Vesuvianite occurs in metamorphosed rocks and is characteristic of contact-metamorphosed limestones and dolomites; it also occurs in cracks in crystalline schists, for example gneisses and amphibolites. It is found in association with garnets, wollastonite, diopside, epidote and albite. The fine-grained californite occurs in serpentinites.

There are many vesuvianite localities throughout the world, the major ones being at Zermatt in the Swiss Alps and Monzoni near Predazzo in the Ala Valley in Piedmont, Italy. Other well-known localities are Göpfersgrün in the Fichtelgebirge, FRG, Ciclova in Romania, Arendal in Norway and Akhmatovsk in the Urals, USSR. Gem-quality crystals are extracted at the Canadian localities of Litchfield in Pontiac County, Quebec and at Templeton in Ottawa County, Ontario. Compact californite is found in the counties of Siskiyou, Fresno and Tulare in California, USA. Recently, large vesuvianite crystals have also been found at the US localities of Magnet Cove, Garland County, Arkansas, and at Sanford, Maine. Other localities are in Mexico, Brazil and Kenya.

Transparent vesuvianites are fashioned into step and table cuts whereas the translucent californite is cut into cabochons. Larger pieces are carved into receptacles, figurines and small *objects d'art.* Vesuvianite may easily be confused with garnet, tourmaline, the zircon variety hyacinth, axinite, diopside, gem olivine (peridot) and other minerals of similar colour.

1 Vesuvianite crystals on blue limestone (Monzoni, Italy). Height of crystal 26 mm. **2** Vesuvianite crystal (Egg, Norway). Height 60 mm. **3** Brilliant cuts of vesuvianite (Kenya). 3.1 carats. **4** Vesuvianite cabochon (Utah, USA). 18 × 13 mm.

1

2

3

4

Pyrite and **Marcasite**

Both minerals are iron disulphides FeS_2.

Pyrite: *crystal system: cubic; name derived from the Greek* pyrites *(= in fire, sparking), because it produces sparks when struck; specific gravity: 4.9-5.2; hardness: 6-6.5; cleavage: none; fracture: uneven; tenacity: brittle; colour: gold yellow, brass yellow; streak: black with a greenish tint; transparency: opaque; lustre: metallic.*
Marcasite: *crystal system: orthorhombic; name derived from Old Arabic, the word formerly used to designate the so-called cockscomb pyrite; specific gravity: 4.85-4.90; hardness: 6-6.5; cleavage: none; fracture: uneven; tenacity: brittle; colour: brass yellow to greenish; streak: black with a greenish tint; transparency: opaque; lustre: metallic.*

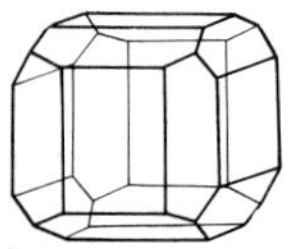
a

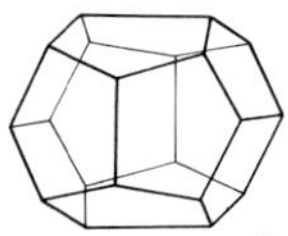
b

Both pyrite and marcasite are a yellow colour which is, however, slightly paler in marcasite and is characterized by a greenish tint. Pyrite crystallizes in cubic or pentagonal dodecahedral form (Figs a, b), the latter also being called a pyritohedron. Pyrite twin intergrowths known as iron crosses are frequent. Pyrite also occurs in lumps, granular aggregates and nodules with a radiating structure. It is a common and abundant mineral in nature.

Marcasite became ranked as a gemstone by mistake. Genuine marcasite must have been used only exceptionally in jewellery, if ever. Most probably it would have been used in the early 18th century when the two minerals could not easily be distinguished and were thus often mistaken for each other. In the jewellery trade, however, the word marcasite used to denote pyrite. Marcasite is not suitable for jewellery because it wears much more readily than pyrite does.

Together with quartz and calcite, pyrite is among the most abundant minerals in nature. It forms in almost any conditions and occurs in many parageneses. The richest deposits are in Spain, especially at Río Tinto; the locality is even mentioned in the Old Testament. However, the most exquisite crystal specimens come from the island of Elba. Other well-known localities include Gavorrano in Italy and Chalcidiké (Khalkidiki) in Greece. Another Greek locality Xanthi yields pyrite cubes up to 50 cm in size. For cutting, pyrite from the French Jura Alps, from the chalk sediments in Sussex, England and from Cyprus is used.

Cutting greatly enhances the metallic lustre of the mineral. In fact, polished pyrite was commonly used for earrings and pins in ancient Greek times, and the Greeks also used to wear it as an amulet. Pyrite tablets discovered in Inca tombs were most probably used as mirrors. Pyrite was formerly often cut into small roses displaying a high lustre and sheen. The outline of the rose was circular, with six low pyramids above the girdle, and a flat base. This type of cut was applied mainly to pyrites from Greece and Italy. As a gemstone pyrite was much admired by the famous Madame du Barry and regained its popularity again during the Victorian period. These so-called marcasites are usually set in silver because their colour does not go well with gold. Pyrite weathers in time and loses its lustre, becoming tarnished or 'blind'.

1 Pyrite cubic crystals (Světec, Czechoslovakia). Specimen 70 × 45 mm. **2** Radially divergent marcasite concretion (Sparta, Illinois, USA) and two pyrite crystals in the form of pentagonal dodecahedra known as pyritohedra (Elba, Italy). Diameter of marcasite 69 mm. **3** Pyrite. Top: a rose cut (Chalcidice, Greece). Diameter 15 mm. Bottom: a lozenge cut (Río Tinto, Spain). **4** Pyritized ammonites used as pendants, rough as well as in polished sections (Würtingen, FRG). Diameter of larger specimen 35 mm.

1

2

3

4

Feldspars (Felspar)

Aluminium silicates, predominantly of potassium, sodium and calcium — orthoclase and microcline, K$[AlSi_3O_8]$, *albite,* Na$[AlSi_3O_8]$ *and anorthite,* Ca$[Al_2Si_2O_8]$; *crystal system: monoclinic or triclinic; the name feldspar is derived from the German* Fels-spat *for spar stone or split stone, or from* Feld *(= field) and* spat *(= spar), because of the frequent occurrence of split stone in topsoil; specific gravity: 2.55-2.76; hardness: 6-6.5; cleavage: eminent; fracture: conchoidal to uneven; tenacity: brittle; colour: various pale shades; streak: white; transparency: mostly translucent or nontransparent; lustre: vitreous to pearly; refractive indices:* $\alpha = 1.518\text{-}1.575$, $\beta = 1.523\text{-}1.583$, $\gamma = 1.525\text{-}1.588$; *birefringence: 0.005-0.015; dispersion: very weak, 0.012; pleochroism: none; main types and varieties: orthoclase (adularia, sanidine, moonstone), microcline (amazonite), albite, oligoclase (aventurine or sunstone), labradorite (spectrolite), anorthite.*

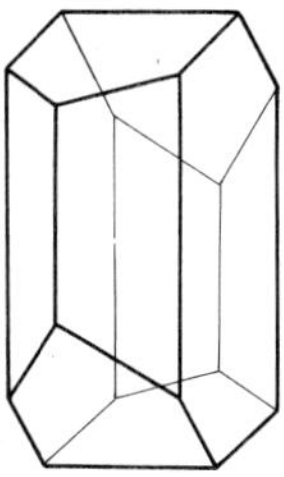

a

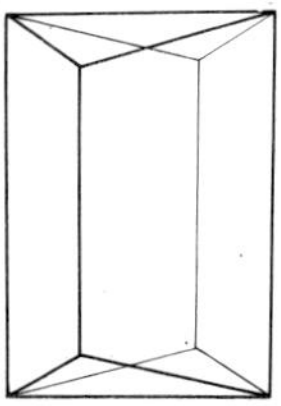

b

Feldspars constitute one of the most important and abundant groups of rock-forming minerals. The Earth's crust is composed of more than 50 per cent feldspar, and feldspars also form a considerable part of many rocks. In petrology, therefore, feldspars aid rock classification. However, only a few feldspar varieties are used in jewellery.

According to their chemical composition feldspars are grouped into potassium types, with the common representatives being the monoclinic **orthoclase** and the triclinic **microcline** and into the sodium-calcium types, the so-called **plagioclases** that constitute a continuous homogeneous series of triclinic mixed crystals from the sodium-containing **albite** to the calcareous **anorthite**. Intermediate members of the plagioclase group include **oligoclase**, which contains 70-90 per cent of albite and 10-30 per cent of anorthite, and **labradorite**, which contains 30-50 per cent albite and 50-70 per cent anorthite.

Feldspar crystals are usually tabular, platy or columnar (Fig. a) and may occur embedded in or grown in druse cavities. All feldspars are characterized by having two cleavage directions: the more perfect cleavage is oriented parallel to the base whereas the less perfect one occurs in the pinacoidal front-back direction. The cleavage properties are reflected in the name of some feldspar varieties, for example orthoclase (from the Greek *orthos* = straight, upright, vertical, and *klan* = to break), with the cleavage planes virtually perpendicular to each other, or plagioclase (from the Greek *plagios* = oblique, inclined) where the cleavage planes dissect at an acute angle. A very important feature of feldspars is their frequent twinnings — an important identification sign in the microscopic determination of plagioclases. Feldspars are usually pale-coloured; the common varieties are nontransparent or translucent. Some feldspars fluoresce weakly in ultraviolet light.

Among the potassium feldspars it is the noble, perfectly transparent **orthoclase** that is used for jewellery purposes. It has a straw-yellow to golden-yellow colour. The crystals are often strongly corroded. It occurs only rarely, for example in pegmatites at Itrongay in Madagascar. It is fashioned into faceted step and table cuts. Orthoclase may easily be mistaken for many other yellow stones. **Adularia** is a pure or nearly pure

1 Group of adularia crystals (Grimsel, Switzerland). Length of largest crystal 35 mm. **2** Cut moonstones (Sri Lanka). Length of largest cabochon 15 mm. **3** Group of amazonite crystals (Pikes Peak, Colorado, USA). Length of largest crystal 50 mm. **4** Amazonite cabochons (USSR). Length of largest stone 25 mm.

1

2

3

4

colourless variety of orthoclase (Fig. b). A variety of orthoclase, called **sanidine**, forms thinly tabular, platy crystals. Gem-quality sanidine was found only as late as 1967 in the volcanic tuff near Lake Laach in Eifel, FRG. The colour of its perfectly clear crystals resembles that of smoky quartz.

Moonstone is a variety of orthoclase with a small admixture of albite. It is usually colourless or slightly yellowish or greyish, almost perfectly transparent. A slight delicate cloudiness or opalescence is caused by diffraction and interference of light reflected from the very fine lamellae of albite. Moonstone was so named after its colour, which ranges from cloudy grey to bluish white to glittering silvery hues. The bluish iridescent glitter (schiller) of the stone can be observed best on specimens with suitably oriented tallow-topped cuts. The higher the dome, the narrower and more attractive is the glittering band that moves as the stone is tilted to and fro. Moonstone often contains foreign inclusions that are characteristic of the individual localities. The most important occurrences of moonstone are in Sri Lanka, southern India, Upper Burma and various US states. The mineral is also found in Brazil, Tanzania, Madagascar and Australia. Imitations are made from strongly annealed, slightly milky, decolorized amethyst or from glass.

Amazonite received its name because it was mistaken for the green jadeite and nephrite that used to be found earlier in the Amazonian Basin. Amazonite is a variety of the triclinic potassium feldspar known as **microcline** (from the Greek *micro* = small, and *klino* = tilt) on account of the minute angular deflection of the cleavage planes away from 90°. Amazonite forms perfectly developed crystals that can be tens of centimetres in size. It is often lumpy, nontransparent or slightly translucent, dark green to bluish green. The colouring may sometimes be nonuniform, the green being interlaced with white or yellow bands. Amazonite occurs in various places throughout the USA, in the Urals, Canada, Madagascar, Brazil and India. Its most common cuts are either flat, thin plates or cabochons of various profiles.

Aventurine is a gem variety of oligoclase. It is nontransparent and its usual colour is reddish brown or reddish orange, with a live, sheeny metallic lustre that gave it its second name **sunstone**. The glitter is caused by oriented inclusions of fine, flaky crystals of iron-bearing minerals (such as haematite and goethite). It is found in southern Norway, Canada, the USA and the USSR. Aventurine feldspar is cut into cabochons and could be confused only with glass imitations.

Another member of the plagioclase group, **labradorite**, is named after its first-known locality in Labrador, Canada. Although it is basically grey, when it is tilted at certain angles the cleavage planes come alive with spots of different sizes and colours resembling the wings of a tropical butterfly. This form of iridescence is called labradorescence after the mineral. Apart from Canada, the major occurrences of labradorite are in the USA, the USSR and Finland where the stone is also known as **spectrolite**. It is cut into extremely low-domed cabochons. Labradorite is impossible to confuse with any other mineral.

1 Sunstone oligoclase (Norway). 70 × 40 mm. **2** Necklace from aventurine feldspar (contemporary work). **3** Labradorite (Ojamo, Finland). 130 × 54 mm. **4** Labradorite cabochons (Finland). Length of largest stone 35 mm.

1

2

3

4

Haematite (Hematite)

Ferric oxide, Fe_2O_3*; crystal system: trigonal; name derived from the Greek* haíma *(= blood) or* haimatites *(= bloody stone, bloodstone, but bloodstone in English usage means a red-spotted green quartz); specific gravity: 4.90-5.30; hardness: 5.5-6.5 but hardness of the ore varieties may be as low as 1; cleavage: none: fracture: uneven, or affected by the aggregate structure; tenacity: brittle; colour: steel grey or red; streak: reddish brown; transparency: opaque; lustre: metallic, dull; mean refractive index ~ 3.0; main varieties: specular iron, kidney ore, iron mica.*

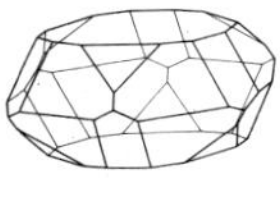

Haematite is primarily an iron-rich ore. In ancient times it was commonly used to stop haemorrhages. The name haematite is usually applied to the crystallized and crystalline varieties (**specular iron**) of a greyish-black colour and a metallic lustre that are harder than the varieties known, for example, as **kidney ore** and **pencil ore**, which are lumpy, granular, fibrous to earthy, nonlustrous, usually red to dark red. The fibrous and earthy varieties streak easily because their hardness is as low as that of talc. The American Indians used it as war paint before engaging in combat. In its pure, finely ground form it is known as **rouge** and is used for polishing in the gem trade.

The most beautiful haematite crystals (Fig.) come from Rio Marino and Rio Albano, Elba, which Vergil praised in his *Aeneid* for their rich iron ore deposits. **Iron mica** is a flaky haematite occurring in aggregates, often together with quartz. Beautiful groups of crystals shaped like blossoms and known as **iron roses** come from Ticino and Grison in Switzerland. If stratified and rock-forming, haematite is designated as iron mica schist or **itabirite**. Fibrous haematite occurs most commonly in reniform shapes, radially divergent inside, with a spherical, reniform or dish-like external contour. The reniform aggregates (kidney ore) come from Cleator Moor in Cumbria (formerly Cumberland), England, from Ning-hsia (now Yinchuan) Province in China, and beautiful, highly lustrous kidney ore also used to be found abundantly in the vicinity of Horní Blatná in Bohemia, Czechoslovakia. Large kidney ore specimens have recently been discovered in local fluorite deposits at Kadaň in Czechoslovakia. The mineral is also known from Brazil and Bangladesh. **Oolitic haematite** consists of flattened lenticular grains interspersed with the matrix. The earthy varieties are also known as **red ochre** or **reddle** (alternatively ruddle or raddle) and are used as pigments. The common feature of these varieties is the blood-red colour of their fine powder.

Haematite originates in various ways in nature. Its deposits are usually of a sedimentary origin. Crystals, often with an iridescent surface, and reniform aggregates are found in some ore lodes and veins. The mineral is often a constituent of metamorphosed rocks.

The stone is carved for signet rings, but it is also cut into cabochons or laterally faceted table cuts and brilliants. Haematite stones, often engraved, are set into rings and pendants and carved into seal stamps. The black varieties used to be cut for mourning jewellery. Cut haematite used to be a specialty of Horní Blatná in Czechoslovakia but today the bulk of the haematite jewellery production comes from Idar-Oberstein, FRG, where material imported from Cumbria in England is cut and polished.

1 Group of haematite crystals (Rio Marina, Elba, Italy). 80 × 60 mm. **2** Haematite known as Alpine rose (St Gotthard, Switzerland). 60 × 45 mm. **3** Kidney ore used for cutting (Hradiště near Kadaň, Czechoslovakia). 120 × 80 mm. **4** Seal ring stones from haematite material (Horní Blatná, Czechoslovakia). Both about 20 mm high.

1

2

3

4

Titanite (Sphene)

Calcium titanium silicate, $CaTi[O|SiO_4]$*; crystal system: monoclinic; named after its high content of tianium, the other name, sphene, derived from the Greek* sphen *(= wedge), on account of its wedge-like crystals; specific gravity: 3.40-3.55; hardness: 5-5.5; cleavage: poor; fracture: conchoidal; tenacity: brittle; colour: yellow, green or brown; streak: white; transparency: transparent or translucent; lustre: greasy to adamantine; refractive indices:* $\alpha = 1.843\text{-}1.950$*,* $\beta = 1.870\text{-}1.970$*,* $\gamma = 1.940\text{-}2.093$*; birefringence: 0.13; dispersion: strong, 0.051; pleochroism: strong in deep-coloured stones.*

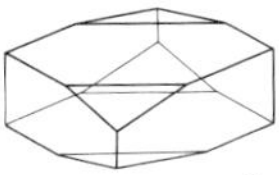

a

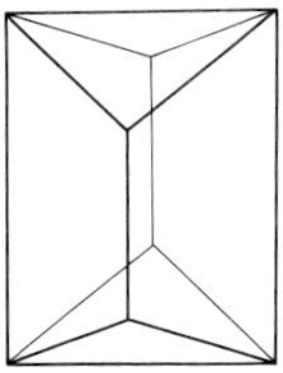

b

As a subsidiary, accessory constituent of many igneous rocks titanite is quite abundant in nature although its crystals are mostly so small and flat that they can only rarely be cut into gems of more than one or two carats. Transparent, nicely coloured crystals are relatively rare and titanite is therefore seldom used for jewellery.

Titanite crystals are thinly or thickly platy or tabular, with a wedge-like termination (Figs a, b). Crystals embedded in igneous rocks have a characteristic 'envelope' appearance. Edged crystals are sometimes also columnar or prismatic. Crystal twinnings with zonal coloration in bands parallel to the twinning plane are quite frequent.

Titanite is characterized by a high birefringence and dispersion. The birefringence can be observed on cut stones with the naked eye. The deeper-coloured crystals are pleochroic. Some brown titanites can be annealed to various hues of reddish brown or orange-brown. Titanite does not fluoresce in ultraviolet light. Inclusions and ingrowths of other minerals are extremely rare.

Titanite occurs in acid intrusive rocks, for example, granites and granodiorites, in alkaline syenites and in phonolites. It is also quite common in metamorphic rocks such as gneiss, amphibolite and chloritic slate and in metamorphosed limestones. Perfectly developed transparent crystals occur in cracks and druse cavities in Alpine parageneses; the crystals have a beautiful green or yellow colour.

The classical titanite localities are in the Alpine region. Larger crystals are also found at Bridgewater, Bucks County in Pennsylvania, USA. Recently titanite localities have been opened at Pino Solo, Baja California Norte in Mexico, yielding material for gems of up to 10 carats. Other localities are in Canada, Madagascar and Upper Burma.

The magnificent sheen of titanite is enhanced on faceted cuts, especially brilliants. The mineral can be mistaken for topaz, yellow beryl, chrysoberyl, vesuvianite and demantoid garnet.

1 Titanite (sphene) crystals on parent rock (Binnatal, Switzerland). Crystals up to 8 mm long. **2** Titanite crystal fragment (Ofenhorn, Switzerland). Actual size. **3** Briolette cut of titanite (Brazil). 4.6 carats. **4** Cuts of titanite (Tirol, Austria). 3.2 and 2.8 carats.

1

2

3

4

Lazurite (Lapis lazuli)

Sodium calcium aluminium silicate with chlorine, sulphide and sulphate ions, $(Na, Ca)_8[(SO_4,S,Cl)_2|(AlSiO_4)_6]$; *crystal system: cubic; name derived from the Persian* lazhward *(= blue); specific gravity: 2.4-2.9; hardness: 5-5.5; cleavage: poor; fracture: uneven; tenacity: brittle; colour: blue, greenish blue; streak: blue; transparency: non-transparent; lustre: greasy to dull; refractive index:* n = *1.50; birefringence, dispersion and pleochroism: none (isotropic).*

Lazurite has long been admired throughout the world for its outstanding qualities — its beautiful blue colour of various hues and depths, its easy cuttability and polishability, and, last but not least, its colourfastness. The gemstone was known in the ancient world as early as the fourth millennium BC. It then equalled even gold in price.

The stone used for jewellery is not, however, composed only of lazurite. It is instead a polymineral rock better known under its Latin name **lapis lazuli** and contains, apart from lazurite, sodalite and haüyne (both complex aluminium silicates and grouped with lazurite in the feldspathoid family of minerals) and also calcite, pyroxenes (diopside, enstatite, augite), micas, amphiboles and small inclusions of pyrite grains.

The rock is fine-grained to solid, compact, and its occurrences are associated with contact-metamorphosed limestones or dolomites. The quality of gem material depends on the chemical composition, especially on the content of lazurite. Top-grade Afghan material contains 25-40 per cent lazurite. The golden-yellow pyrite grains make the stone very attractive, increase its commercial value and are a proof of the genuine character of the material.

The oldest and most famous lapis lazuli localities, without competition in both quality and quantity, are in Badakhshan Province in northeastern Afghanistan where mines at Sari-Sang high up in the mountains have been continually worked for some 6,000 years. Other important occurrences are in the USSR near Lake Baikal and in the Pamirs. The Andean localities in the province of Coquimbo in Chile are also quite rich.

Lapis lazuli is cut into various cabochons, flat platelets for rings or into beads for necklaces. Artificially stained jaspers are sometimes passed off as lapis lazuli, but jasper does not exhibit the marked luminiscence.

Sodalite

Sodium aluminium silicate and chloride, $Na_8[Cl_2| (AlSiO_4)_6]$; *crystal system: cubic; name probably derived from the English* sodium *(Na), which forms a substantial part of sodalite; specific gravity: 2.15-2.3; hardness: 5.5-6; cleavage: poor; fracture: uneven; colour: white, grey, blue or blue-violet; streak: white or bluish; lustre: glassy to greasy; refractive index* n = *1.48; birefringence, dispersion and pleochroism: none (isotropic).*

Sodalite, a rock-forming mineral, is found in nature as a component of certain igneous rocks. The rough, azure-blue or lavender-blue aggregates can occasionally be used as gemstones. It strongly resembles lazurite but has a pronounced pale-violet hue. In ultraviolet light it shows an orange fluorescence. The most important locality is the Princess Sodalite Mine in Canada; it is also found in the USA and USSR. It is sometimes cut into cabochons or table cuts.

1 Polished section of lazurite (lapis lazuli) (Andes de Ovales, Chile). 120 × 100 mm. **2** Polished section of lapis lazuli with pyrite (Badakhshan, Afghanistan). 100 × 50 mm. **3** Detail of lapis lazuli rosary (made in Prague, *c.* 1600). Height of medallion 70 mm. **4** Polished section of sodalite (Timmings, Canada). Detail actual size.

1

2

3

4

Turquoise (Callaite)

Hydrated copper aluminium phosphate, $CuAl_6[(OH)_2|PO_4]_4 \cdot 4\,H_2O$*; crystal system: triclinic; name derived from the French* pierre turquoise *(= Turkish stone) because turquoise reached Europe via Turkey; the other name derived from the Greek* kallos lithos *(= beautiful stone); specific gravity: 2.6-2.9; hardness: 5-6; cleavage: good; fracture: conchoidal to uneven; tenacity: brittle; colour: blue, blue green or green; streak: white; transparency: nontransparent; lustre: greasy; refractive indices:* $\alpha = 1.61$, $\beta = 1.62$, $\gamma = 1.65$*; birefringence: 0.04; dispersion: none; pleochroism: weak.*

The blue turquoise, its colour resembling that of a forget-me-not, has been used as a gemstone for several thousand years. The usage dates back to ancient Egypt where the stone was greatly prized and admired for its beauty which gave it its Greek name. In the ancient Orient, turquoise was praised by poets and it was believed to possess magical powers and was therefore worn as an amulet. Tablets of turquoise were later inscribed with verses from the Koran. In the New World too, the American Indians used the stone for their typical silver jewellery and the craft still thrives.

Turquoise was originally thought to be an amorphous mineral. It forms solid cryptocrystalline masses or reniform and botryoidal compact tubers and lumps; it may be encrusting or stalactitic or it may fill cracks in rock forming veins and veinlets. The small but well-developed turquoise crystals are rare and were discovered for the first time in Virginia, USA in 1911.

Turquoise is nontransparent and only very thin splinters and slivers will show some translucence. The coloration is not uniform and may vary from purely sky blue and blue-green to a greyish green, the green colour being caused by admixtures of iron. Turquoise is often mottled, with brown veinlets of limonite or black stripes of manganese oxides. It is sensitive to excessive temperatures and if heated to 250 °C its blue colour will turn into an unattractive green. Great care must therefore be taken when the stone is polished to prevent overheating by means of excessive friction. Some turquoise stones also deteriorate in sunlight, and other varieties may be sensitive to soap, water, grease and perspiration. If a jewel decorated with a turquoise is worn for a long period of time, the blue becomes a dirty green and the stone loses its attractive appearance. The original colour may sometimes be restituted with organic solvents.

Turquoise originated as a secondary mineral in the weathering zone of volcanic rocks in arid areas. It forms crusts on the surface of the weathered rocks, or it fills cracks and cavities in brecciated trachyte.

The oldest classical turquoise sites on the Sinai Peninsula have been long exhausted but rich localities are worked today near Neyshabur in Iran, and in the US states of New Mexico, Nevada, Arizona, Utah and Colorado. The mineral also occurs in Queensland, Victoria and New South Wales in Australia. Recently, mining operations have started in the valley of the River Umba in Tanzania.

Turquoise is generally cut into cabochons, rounded or oval tables or smoothed into grains, beads and irregular pebbles. The major imitations are artificially stained fossilized ivory or stained bone or teeth. It may be confused with other mineral aluminium phosphates, such as variscite, wardite and lazulite.

1 Turquoise (Anatolia, Turkey). 50 × 40 mm. **2** Drop-shaped cabochon of turquoise (Iran). Height 14 mm. **3** Turquoise and gold pendant (made in Prague, 1840). Width 35 mm. **4** Turquoise and rock crystal brooch (made in 1850). Height 50 mm.

1

2

3

4

Brazilianite

Sodium aluminium phosphate, $NaAl_3[(OH)_2|PO_4]_2$*; crystal system: monoclinic; named after Brazil where discovered; specific gravity: 2.980-2.995; hardness: 5.5; cleavage: eminent; fracture: conchoidal; tenacity: brittle; colour: yellow green; streak: white; transparency: transparent to translucent; lustre: vitreous; refractive indices:* $\alpha = 1.602$, $\beta = 1.609$, $\gamma = 1.623$*; birefringence: 0,02; dispersion: weak, 0.014; pleochroism: weak.*

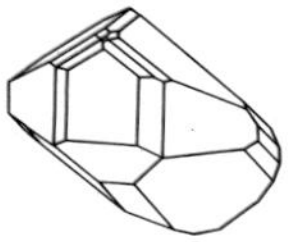

In 1945, the American mineralogist F. H. Pough received from a Brazilian locality a nice yellowish-green crystal originally thought to be a chrysoberyl. Although the colour and lustre resembled the latter, the symmetry and hardness did not. When further specimens of crystals were obtained, a detailed study of the mineral was made and the crystals were identified to be a new, hitherto unknown phosphate of sodium and aluminium. The authors of the first detailed study, Pough and E. P. Henderson, suggested that the new mineral be named in honour of its 'native' country. However, as one variety of baddeleyite had already been called brazilite, the two scientists coined the name brazilianite.

Brazilianite crystals are of two types, either low columnar (Fig.) to almost isometric, or elongated and pointed. Some crystals with a multifaced termination may be tens of centimetres long. The prismatic faces are densely longitudinally striated, which facilitates the proper orientation of the crystals and even fragments for the selection of the cuts. Brazilianite is transparent or merely translucent if clouded by minute cracks. It is brittle and parts easily in the direction of eminent cleavage. Cutting therefore requires great care but the stone takes a good polish with tin buffing skaifes.

Brazilianite has a pleasant yellowish or yellow-green colour which resembles the Chartreuse liqueur or Mexican apatite. It displays a very weak pleochroism and dispersion. Brazilianite does not fluoresce in ultraviolet light. As regards foreign inclusions, only tin crystals of the green tourmaline and muscovite have been observed in brazilianite. It occurs in hydrothermally altered granite pegmatites as druse crystals. Its associated minerals are quartz, beryl, apatite, tourmaline and mica.

The classical localities are in Minas Gerais in Brazil, near Conselheiro Peno and Manteno. In 1947, new rich sources were discovered in the USA — in the Palermo Mine at North Groton in Grafton County, and the Smith Mine, Newport in New Hampshire.

The first Brazilian specimens were cut into stones of 19 and 23 carats, respectively, and are kept in the museum collections of the Divisão do Geologia e Mineralogia in Rio de Janeiro, and in the American Museum of Natural History in New York, which also keeps an exceptionally large crystal weighing 975 grams.

Brazilianite is cut into oblong step cuts and circular or oval brilliants. It is a fashionable stone, greatly valued by collectors. It may be confused with chrysoberyl, apatite, topaz and other minerals of a similar colour.

1 Brazilianite (Mendes Pimental, Brazil). Length of crystals up to 15 mm. **2** Brazilianite crystal (Minas Gerais, Brazil). 60 × 35 mm. **3** Cut brazilianite (Minas Gerais, Brazil). 16 carats. **4** Two cuts of differently coloured brazilianites (Minas Gerais, Brazil). Weight of larger stone 8.3 carats.

1

2

3

4

Rhodonite

Manganese calcium silicate, $CaMn_4[Si_5O_{15}]$, *usually with iron, magnesium or zinc; crystal system: triclinic; named after its pinkish red colour from the Greek* rhodon *(= rose); specific gravity: 3.4-3.7; hardness: 5.5-6; cleavage: good; fracture: conchoidal to uneven; tenacity: brittle, but lump varieties tough; colour: rose red, but greenish or yellowish when impure; streak: white to pinkish; transparency: translucent; lustre: vitreous, pearly on cleavage faces; refractive indices:* $\alpha = 1.715\text{-}1.733$, $\beta = 1.716\text{-}1.737$, $\gamma = 1.724\text{-}1.747$; *birefringence: 0.014; dispersion: none; pleochroism: distinct; main variety: fowlerite.*

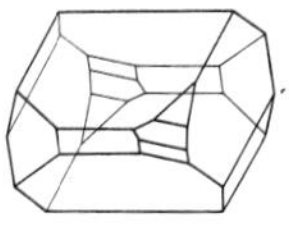

Rhodonite occurs as a common mineral in ore veins and in some metamorphic deposits. It occurs in great quantities in some places but it is not an economic manganese ore. Since the 19th century, it has been used for decorative purposes because of its pleasant pinky-red colour. Together with the paler rhodochrosite, rhodonite is one of the minerals that have recently become fashionable as gemstones.

Its crystals are thickly tabular to columnar (Fig.), often imperfectly developed and rounded on the edges. The lumpy, compact rhodonites in fine-grained cryptocrystalline aggregates have the greatest use in jewellery. The coloration is not uniform and the ground mass is often interwoven with black spots, bands or fine veinlets. The polished stones display dendritic, sometimes quite bizarre patterns that contrast nicely with the red colour. The black constituents are manganese oxides and hydroxides, which are secondary weathering products. Compact rhodonites are nontransparent or translucent at best. Larger cuttable transparent crystals are rare. Unlike lump rhodonite which possesses a considerable toughness, the crystals are extremely brittle and sensitive to impact and must be handled with utmost care during fashioning. The transparent-red or orange-red crystals are pleochroic and do not fluoresce in ultraviolet light. Rhodonite is never found in its pure form because it also contains admixtures of calcium, magnesium, iron or zinc. The zinc-rich variety is called **fowlerite** and occurs in the form of large crystals that may sometimes be tens of centimetres long. Fowlerite is occasionally used as a gemstone.

Rhodonite occurs in metamorphic deposits of manganese and iron ores in crystalline schists, quartzites and crystalline limestones.

Large deposits of rhodonite are in the Urals at Sverdlovsk (Sedélnikovo) USSR, where the mineral enjoys a wide popularity as a gemstone. Major deposits occur also in New South Wales in Australia where, apart from the lump variety, beautiful reddish brown crystals are occasionally found at Broken Hill. Gems of several carats have been cut from these crystals. Other important localities are in Sweden, Mexico, Vancouver in Canada, and in many places throughout the USA. Fowlerite is found at Franklin Furnace in New Jersey, USA.

Lump rhodonite is cut into cabochons or into small necklace beads and is carved into small objects, such as paperweights. It is also used as a decorative stone for wall panelling. Transparent crystals are fashioned into faceted table cuts and brilliants. Because of its characteristic colour and black veining rhodonite is practically never confused with other minerals, with the possible exception of the pinkish-red variety of zoisite called thulite.

1 Ground plate of rhodonite (Urals, USSR). 120 × 65 mm. **2** Rhodonite (Urals, USSR). Detail actual size. **3** Rhodonite cabochon (USSR). Height of cabochon 32 mm. **4** Tallow-topped rhodonite cabochon (Urals, USSR). Height of cabochon 30 mm.

1

2

3

4

Dioptase

Hydrous copper silicate, $Cu_6[Si_6O_{18}] \cdot 6\,H_2O$*; crystal system: trigonal; name derived from the Greek* dia *(= through) and* optasis *(= vision) on account of the reflections visible inside the crystals on the cleavage cracks; specific gravity: 3.28-3.35; hardness: 5; cleavage: eminent along rhombohedral faces; fracture: conchoidal to uneven; tenacity: brittle; colour: emerald green; streak: green; transparency: transparent to translucent; lustre: vitreous; refractive indices:* $\varepsilon = 1.697\text{-}1.723$*,* $\omega = 1.644\text{-}1.667$*; birefringence: 0.053; dispersion: strong, 0.028; pleochroism: weak.*

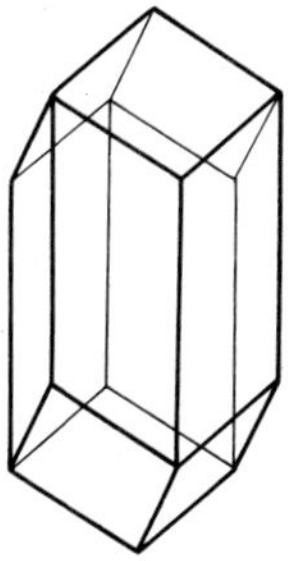

In 1780 a merchant from Bukhara named Akhir Mahmed brought from the Kirgiz steppes to Semipalatinsk in Kazakhstan crystals of an exquisitely beautiful green colour. At first nobody doubted that the crystals were emeralds. Then Mahmed obtained some more specimens and a few crystals were shipped to St Petersburg where Academy Member Ferber described them as a variety of emerald and called them **achrite.** It was only later in 1801 that the purported emeralds were identified as a new mineral. Because the species shows live internal reflections running transversely on the prismatic faces when the stone is viewed against the light and moved, the French mineralogist R.J. Haüy called it dioptase.

This emerald green mineral with a bluish or even blackish tint is relatively rare. Its major shortcoming is the low hardness, which is much lower than that of genuine emeralds and is one of the reasons why dioptase is not a common and more prized stone. It is valued mainly by collectors who sometimes call it copper emerald or emerald of the poor.

Dioptase usually forms low six-sided columns terminated in rhombohedra (Fig.). The rhombohedral faces are densely striated. Dioptase is transparent or translucent and is characterized by strong birefringence and dispersion. It is slightly pleochroic and does not fluoresce in ultraviolet light. Cut stones display a live fire play. The fine cleavage cracks inside the crystals sometimes cause a pearly lustre and interesting internal reflections that emit from within the stone. Admixtures and inclusions are relatively rare but traces of iron cause a darker coloration.

Dioptase originates in the oxidation zone when copper ore deposits undergo weathering. Its crystals fill cracks in limestones and dolomites, or grow in irregular druse cavities. It is often associated in weathering zones with malachite and smithsonite. Because it is chemically quite stable and resists corrosion it is sometimes also found in alluvia.

The now classical localities are on Mt Altyn-Tyube in Kazakhstan, USSR. Larger cuttable crystals are found at Renéville in Zaire. The mineral is also found in minor amounts in the Otavi Range at Guchabo in Namibia, at Baiţa in Romania, Copiapo in Chile, Peru, and Pinal County, Arizona, USA.

Only the perfectly transparent ends of larger crystals are used for cutting. Step and table cuts are fashioned only with difficulty because of the eminent cleavage. Compact, fine-grained lumps are sometimes cut into cabochons. Dioptase may be confused with emerald or green tourmaline but low hardness will always reveal its identity.

1 Druse of dioptase crystals (Mindouli, Zaire). 70 × 60 mm. **2** Cut dioptase (Africa). 0.2 carat. **3** Druse incrustation of dioptase crystals on limestone (Altyn-Tyube, USSR). Length of crystals up to 3 mm.

1

2

3

Obsidian

Volcanic glass of varying composition with a silica content ranging from 65 to 77% and with low water content; amorphous; name said to be derived from Obsidian, a Roman reported to have been the first to bring it from Ethiopia to Rome; specific gravity: 2.33-2.60; hardness: 5.5-7; cleavage: none; fracture: conchoidal; tenacity: brittle; colour: black, dark grey, red or brown; streak: white; transparency: translucent to semi-transparent or opaque; lustre: vitreous; refractive index: n = *1.48-1.53, sometimes reaching up to 1.6; main variety: marekanite.*

Obsidian is a natural volcanic rock, that is one formed by rapid solidification of the molten magma that reached the Earth's surface and was extruded during periods of volcanic activity. There are large obsidian outcrops in southern Italy and islands such as Lipari off the Italian coast, in Iceland, the US states of Oregon, Arizona and Utah, in the Caucasus and the Urals, in Hungary and eastern Slovakia. Although obsidian is glassy in general appearance, in thin section under the microscope a multitude of minute crystals, called crystallites, can be seen. In obsidians from certain localities — especially Mexico, the USA and some volcanic areas of the USSR (for example, the Lake Sevan district in the Armenian SSR) — these crystallites give the mineral an outstanding sheen and a chatoyant silky lustre.

The sharp edges of obsidian made it a very useful material for prehistoric people who fashioned from it knives, scrapers, arrowheads and spearpoints. It was widely used by the pre-Columbian Indians of Central America who admired it not only for its technical qualities but also for its magnificent silvery sheen. The Mexican Indians have long been famous for their production of obsidian decorative objects and amulets as well as necklaces and bracelets composed entirely of the so-called **Apache tears**.

As a gemstone, obsidian is cut in various ways. Perfectly transparent specimens are faceted, mainly into step cuts, but brilliants are also quite common. Materials of lower transparency are fashioned into cabochons or table cuts. Irregular cabochons are often cut from jet-black obsidians containing groups of pale and even white tiny crystals of tetragonal silica **cristobalite** known from Mexico and some localities in North America. A very attractive obsidian with grey, eye-like spots in the red, haematite-coloured groundmass comes from Gyumushskoe in the Armenian SSR.

Marekanite is the name for a smoky-brown to black perlitic obsidian (one with concentric, onion-like cracks in it) from the basin of the River Marekanka near Okhotsk in Siberia; the same name is also applied to some Mexican obsidians. Obsidian resembles the more acid **pitchstone** occurring, for example, in the Meissen district of Saxony, GDR and the more basic basalt glass called **tachylyte**, which is found, for example, in the Hawaiian Islands.

1 Obsidian (Caucasus, USSR). 60 × 45 mm. **2** Obsidian with silvery silky sheen (Erivan, Armenian SSR). 120 × 80 mm. **3** Obsidian Neolithic tool (Cejkov, Czechoslovakia). 140 × 100 mm. **4** Obsidian rhinoceros figurine (Russian work, Carl Fabergé, *c.* 1900). Length of figurine 60 mm.

1

2

3

4

Moldavite

Acid natural glass in the tektite group, average chemical composition SiO_2 *(78.82 wt %),* Al_2O_3 *(10.62%),* Fe_2O_3 *(0.25%),* FeO *(1.61%),* MgO *(1.84%),* CaO *(2.08%),* Na_2O *(0.56%),* K_2O *(2.61%); amorphous; named after the River Vltava (German — Moldau) in Bohemia; specific gravity: 2.3-2.4; hardness: 5.5-6.5; cleavage: none; fracture: conchoidal, sharp-edged; tenacity: brittle; colour: depends on the constituents, but usually dark green; streak: white; transparency: transparent; lustre: vitreous; refractive index:* n = *1.488-1.503*

The origin of moldavite is possibly explained by a fall of a huge meteorite into what is now the Ries area near Stuttgart FRG. It is thought that upon impact of the meteorite, the top strata in the immediate area were remelted and catapulted into southern Bohemia and southwestern Moravia. The occurrence of this variety of tektite is almost entirely limited to Czechoslovakia, with the exception of a few specimens found near Dresden, GDR and in Palaeolithic cultural strata near Krems and Willendorf in Austria.

Moldavites are very attractive. They have an intensive vitreous lustre, sometimes of a glossy lacquer character, unless the original lustre has been worn off as the result of a lengthy transport by streams or of being in topsoil for a long time. The surface of moldavites is strikingly sculptured by circular or elliptical pits, or by striae and incisions. This sculpturing was probably caused by the etching of the less resistant parts of the moldavite surface by permeating waters, together with the activity of humic acids, while the glass lay embedded in sediments.

Moldavites may occur in curious shapes such as discs, drops, ovals or rods, or they may be irregular. Their size usually does not exceed a few centimetres; the average weight of a moldavite is roughly 8 grams.

Some moldavites from southern Bohemia contain bubbles. These are usually extremely small, with volumes of just a few tenths of a cubic millimetre, but larger bubbles may occur. The colour, chemical composition, content of bubbles and shape of moldavites vary according to locality.

Moldavites from Radomilice and its vicinity in southern Bohemia occur mainly in only slightly flattened shapes; they have few internal bubbles, contain almost no lechatelierite (a silica glass) and are usually pale green to bottle green in colour. They have the highest content of silica of all moldavites, but compared with other types have a lower content of alumina, total iron and alkalis.

Moldavites from other southern Bohemian localities are mostly a bottle-green colour, their shapes are flattened, they contain many bubbles and are rich in lechatelierite. In their content of silica, iron and aluminium, they constitute an intermediate type between moldavites from Radomilice and those from Moravia.

Moldavites from southern Bohemia, Czechoslovakia.

1 Flat drop, partially smoothed (brook alluvial deposit, Slavče). 40 × 20 mm. **2** Moldavite of a bottle-green colour (Ločenice). 25 × 12 mm. **3** Moldavites with water-worn surfaces (Malešice near Vodňany). Largest stone 26 × 18 mm. **4** Moldavite (Ločenice). 24 × 15 mm.

1

2

3

4

Moldavites from Moravia are mainly an olive-green to brown colour, they have only slightly flattened shapes, a lower content of lechatelierite and they contain relatively few bubbles. In comparison with moldavites from southern Bohemia they are on average richer in alumina and total iron as attested also by the colour, and on average contain less silica.

As can be seen, moldavites are stones of a highly exceptional character and it is no wonder that they attract so much interest. Prehistoric people were the first to notice their striking appearance and started collecting them, using the sharp fragments for various tools and most probably saving the unbroken specimens for amulets.

There is no record of moldavite use in medieval times but the country folk were probably familiar with the stones. Moldavites were described in 1787 by J. Mayer and popular interest in them culminated at the time of the Bohemian Jubilee Exhibition in 1891 where moldavites were shown and sold as gemstones, cut and set in gold. Cut moldavites have a pleasant green to olive-green colour but their lustre is low and the hardness does not exceed that of glass, which moldavite strongly resembles. Unfortunately, interest in moldavites soon dropped because the cutters preferred to use the more available bottle glass.

In recent years interest in moldavites has picked up. The stone has again become popular for jewellery and pendants, earrings, rings, bracelets and cufflinks are made from it. Nowadays the stone is usually left in its rough uncut form and just set in gold, gold-plated silver or plain silver. Uncut moldavites are actually more valuable than cut stones. The striking sculptured surface, the vitreous and even lacquer-like lustre, the unusual shapes and the pleasant colour of moldavite gemstones make them very attractive for jewellery.

The other tektites are used only rarely for jewellery purposes. Quite recently, however, an attempt was made to engrave and cut some indochinites, and some australites were cut into oval cabochons and used in rings.

1 Table-cut moldavites. Top: pale-green stone from Bohemia (Ločenice). Bottom: darker stone typical of Moravian localities (Dukovany). **2** Two clasps with cut moldavites (Bohemia, second half of the 19th century). Width of clasp 50 mm. **3** Silver pendant with rough moldavite with richly sculptured surface (contemporary work of K. Valter). Length of stone 14 mm. **4** Gold set with rough moldavites (contemporary work). Length of largest specimen 45 mm.

1

2

3

4

Azurite (Chessylite)

Copper carbonate, $Cu_3[OH|CO_3]_2$*; crystal system: monoclinic; name derived from the Persian* lazhward *(= blue); specific gravity: 3.7-3.9; hardness: 3.5-4; cleavage: good; fracture: conchoidal to uneven; tenacity: brittle; colour: sky blue, blackish blue; streak: blue; transparency: translucent to nontransparent; lustre: highly vitreous; refractive indices;* $\alpha = 1.730$, $\beta = 1.758$, $\gamma = 1.838$*; birefringence: 0.11; dispersion: none; pleochroism: weak; main variety: azurmalachite.*

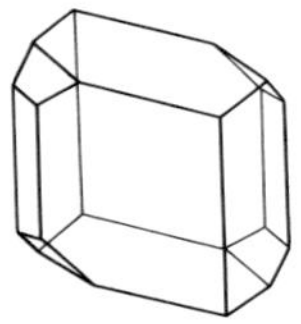

Ancient writers used many different names for azurite, among them *lasur, lasurit, lapis armenium, caeruleum montanum* and *cuprum lazureum.* The mineral was widely used in the ancient Orient as an important colourfast pigment for various blue paints used for murals and is still used as a base in modern paint production. Its low hardness is the main reason why it is not more widely used in jewellery even though its rather small, perfectly homogeneous crystals are transparent and cuttable.

The crystals are short-to-long columnar, tabular (Fig.), sometimes pseudorhombohedral in appearance, and almost isometric. Columnar crystals may be tens of centimetres long and their prismatic faces are transversely striated. Azurite also occurs as fine-grained lumps or spherical, radially divergent aggregates. It often forms pseudomorphs after other minerals but may be 'pushed back' by malachite, which is more stable in nature. Azurite is usually nontransparent or translucent at best, but small crystals may sometimes be perfectly transparent. Transmitted light is pleochroic in various shades of blue. Azurite does not fluoresce in ultraviolet light. Proper fashioning will enhance its vitreous lustre to an almost adamantine one. Cutting of azurite is hindered by its relatively high brittleness.

Azurite is a secondary mineral formed by weathering in the upper oxidation zone of ore deposits. Like malachite, its frequent associate, it is formed by the effect of waters containing carbon dioxide on primary copper-bearing minerals. It also forms when cupric salts react with limestones. Experimental synthesis of azurite and malachite shows that the major decisive factor in their formation is the pressure of carbon dioxide. A drop in the pressure results in the precipitation of malachite. A mixture of azurite and malachite, called **azurmalachite**, occurs in spherical, stalactitic or reniform masses. A suitably polished stone will show a concentric banding of deep-blue and emerald-green resembling the eyes of the peacock's tail. A popular form of azurite with malachite comes from the Copper Queen Mine in Bisbee, and from Morence in Arizona, USA.

Azurite occurs world wide. Large, beautiful crystals come from Tsumeb in Namibia, and Burraburra near Adelaide in Australia is another important locality. The once famous locality at Chessy near Lyon in France (**chessylite**) has been exhausted.

Azurite crystals are fashioned into thin table cuts; the compact azurmalachite appears as smoothed plates of tallow-topped cabochons.

1 Spherically radial aggregate of azurite crystals (Chessy, France). Diameter 50 mm. **2** Azurite crystals (Tsumeb, Namibia). Length of crystals 100 mm. **3** Azurite pendant (made by the School of Jewellery, Turnov, Czechoslovakia, 1920s). Height 35 mm. **4** Azurmalachite (Chessy, France). 75 × 50 mm.

1

2

3

4

Malachite

Copper carbonate, $Cu_2[(OH)_2|CO_3]$; *crystal system: monoclinic; name derived either from the Greek* malache *(= mallow) after its green colour or from the Greek* malakos *(= soft) because of its low hardness; specific gravity: 3.75-3.95; hardness: 3.5-4; cleavage: eminent; fracture: uneven, conchoidal to hackly; tenacity: brittle; colour: green (banded); streak: green; transparency: opaque to semitransparent; lustre: vitreous in crystals, silky to dull in aggregates; refractive indices:* $\alpha = 1.655$, $\beta = 1.875$, $\gamma = 1.909$; *birefringence: 0.254; dispersion: none; pleochroism: weak; main variety: azurmalachite.*

The history of malachite as a gemstone is very old. Although a relatively soft mineral, its harmoniously matching greens made it very popular with the ancient Greeks and later also the Romans; some exquisite malachite cameos, sculptures and vases have survived to testify to the artistic skills of the ancient carvers. Malachite used also to be worn as an amulet to fend off various evils. For centuries it has been worked as a copper-rich ore and miners of old knew its conspicuous colour to be a sure indicator of outcrops of copper veins and ore deposits. More than a century ago rich malachite localities were discovered in the Central Urals and malachite soon became a fashionable decorative stone at the court of the Czars. The great popularity of malachite is attested by the beautiful specimens in the Hermitage and by the majestic columns of St Isaac's in Leningrad, USSR. Malachite's noble qualities have made it an extremely fashionable stone even today.

In nature malachite occurs in lumps, in the form of cryptocrystalline aggregates composed of tiny acicular crystals. Larger crystals are rare. In some places malachite forms thick beds or irregular tuberous masses. The aggregates may be dish-shaped, spherical, reniform, botryoidal or stalactitic, with a radially divergent structure. As is the case with agate, malachite sections show layers or bands of all conceivable shades of green ranging from the palest hues to a black green. A suitably oriented cut will show on the polished surface various curves, concentric circles, bands or parallel lines, which form a beautiful intricate pattern.

Malachite is nontransparent and only thin slivers are translucent. It does not fluoresce in ultraviolet light. It is a product of weathering in the oxidation zone of the upper horizons of various copper ores and is often associated with other oxidized copper minerals, such as azurite or chrysocolla.

The once famous Ural deposits where malachite used to be quarried in blocks weighing several tons have been practically depleted. Among present important localities are those in southern Zaire, Tsumeb in Namibia and Broken Hill in New South Wales, Australia. Gem-quality malachite suitable for jewellery is mined at Eilat in Israel.

Malachite is exclusively cut into rounded shapes such as various cabochons and necklace beads.

1 Polished section of malachite (Urals, USSR). Detail actual size. **2** Detail of malachite set (first half of the 19th century). Height 42 mm. **3** Rough stone and three cabochons of malachite (Shaba, Zaire). Rough specimen 140 × 110 × 50 mm.

1

2

3

Aragonite

Calcium carbonate, $CaCO_3$*; crystal system: orthorhombic; named after the province of Aragon in Spain; specific gravity: 2.9-3.0; hardness: 3.5-4; cleavage: none; fracture: subconchoidal; tenacity: brittle; colour: yellow, honey gold or brown, also white or yellowish green; streak: white; transparency: transparent, translucent or opaque; lustre: vitreous to greasy in crystals, almost dull in aggregates; refractive indices:* $\alpha = 1.530$, $\beta = 1.681$, $\gamma = 1.685$*; birefringence: 0.155; dispersion and pleochroism: none; main varieties: onyx marble, erzbergite, sprudelstein, peastone.*

As far as chemical composition is concerned, aragonite is identical with the much more common **calcite**. However, their crystal symmetry differs (calcite is trigonal) and the two minerals can easily be distinguished as aragonite has no cleavage.

Nicely formed columnar or acicular crystals of aragonite are quite rare in nature and occur mainly in cavities in basalt. Thick clusters and aggregates of beautiful crystals are the pride of the Sicilian sulphur deposits. A fascinating variety of aragonite occurs as fine, snow-white shrub-like aggregates — the so-called 'iron flowers'. These are tiny, mutually interweaved aragonite stalactites in cavities in iron ore deposits. The most famous locality for these aragonite clusters is Eisenerz in Austria where the stone is fashioned into decorative objects. Similar **flos ferri** are found at Lake Baikal, USSR, and in Mexico. The mother-of-pearl in the shells of many molluscs and the material from which pearls are built is also basically aragonite.

Aragonite crystals are very popular among collectors but only compact varieties are of any practical use as decorative stones. A popular compact variety is known as **onyx marble** (also simply called onyx or golden onyx). This is a layered or banded form of aragonite. The bands are of various colours ranging from white and pink to ochre and brown or from apple green to deep dark-green. The coloration is mainly caused by precipitated oxides and hydroxides of iron, manganese and other colouring constituents. Note, however, that most so-called onyx marbles are not made up of aragonite but of calcite into which aragonite changes when heat or pressure is applied to it.

For millennia, aragonite onyxes have been precipitating from hot water springs. The water in such springs contains large amounts of dissolved mineral constituents and gases, mainly carbon dioxide. As the solution nears the surface it gets colder and minerals are precipitated, forming deposits of various forms of aragonite onyx.

Layered varieties of aragonite are known from hot water spring areas in the USA, New Zealand and Kamchatka, USSR. **Erzbergite** comes from Austria and **sprudelstein** (spring stone) and **peastone** come from Karlovy Vary (Carlsbad) in Bohemia. Greenish, translucent aragonite onyx is known from the Kel'badzher district in the Azerbaidzhan SSR and a brown-and-white striped variety comes from Turkmenia, USSR.

1 Polished section of spring stone (sprudelstein) (Karlovy Vary, Czechoslovakia). Detail actual size. **2** Polished section of erzbergite (Erzberg, Austria). Detail actual size. **3** Peastone (Karlovy Vary, Czechoslovakia). Detail actual size. **4** Sections of aragonite pisolites — peastone (Karlovy Vary, Czechoslovakia). 35 × 25 × 24 mm. **5** Brooch inlaid with sprudelstein and rimmed with Bohemian garnets (second half of the 19th century). Height 45 mm. **6** Bouquet incrusted with sprudelstein (Karlovy Vary, Czechoslovakia). Height 160 mm.

1

2

3

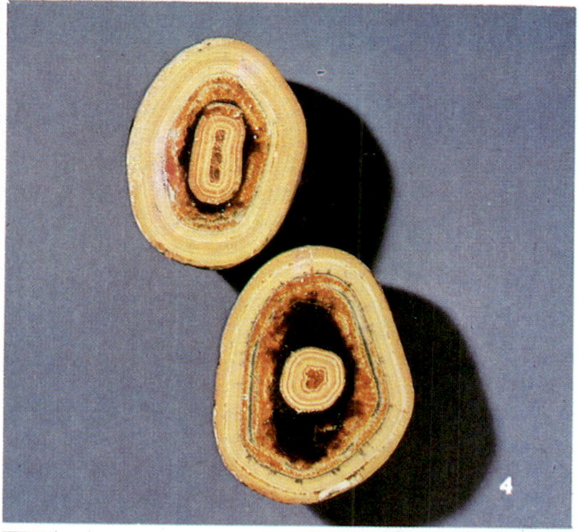

4

5

6

Fluorite (Fluorspar, Fluor)

Calcium fluoride, CaF_2*; crystal system: cubic; name derived from the Latin* fluere *(= to flow), on account of its use as a flux in ore smelting; specific gravity: 3.1-3.2; hardness: 4; cleavage: eminent along octahedral faces; fracture: conchoidal; tenacity: brittle; colour; colourless, but tinted by impurities giving many colours; streak: white; transparency: transparent to translucent; lustre: vitreous; refractive index:* n = *1.433; birefringence and pleochroism: none (isotropic); dispersion: 0.007; main variety: blue-john (Derbyshire spar).*

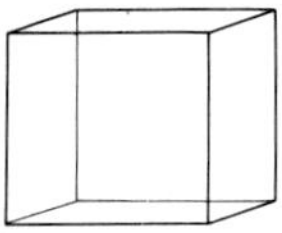
a

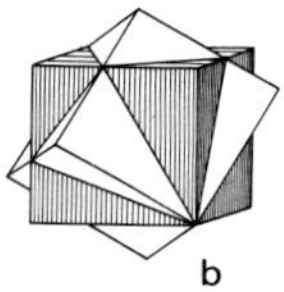
b

Ancient miners named the druses of beautifully coloured crystals they saw in their mines 'ore flowers'. In 1529, Georgius Agricola described what he termed *fluores* as minerals similar to gemstones but less hard. Still later, the famous Anselmus Boetius de Boot (1609) put their hardness between that of gemstones and that of minerals.

Fluorite crystals form mostly cubes (Fig. a); octahedral forms are rarer. Interpenetrant twinning in the form of an octahedral intergrowth of two cubes (Fig. b) is typical for fluorite. In some places fluorite, or **fluorspar**, forms huge deposits of coarse-to-fine crystalline or compact aggregates. Some crystals can be tens of centimetres long.

The coloration may be uneven; lumpy aggregates are often banded in various colours like agates and even single crystals may be multicoloured. **Blue-john (Derbyshire spar)** is a massive violet-blue and white or yellowish banded variety from Derbyshire in England. When observed against light, some fluorite crystals appear green, and are violet if seen in an incident light. This type of colour change, first seen in fluorite, has been termed fluorescence after the mineral. When heated to temperatures exceeding 100°C fluorite emits light in darkness — it thermoluminesces. In ultraviolet light some varieties of fluorite are strongly fluorescent and may even be phosphorescent. A careful heating of some deeply coloured crystals to temperatures above 250 °C causes a colour change, but irradiation will restitute the original hue. The perfect cleavage calls for utmost care when fluorite is being cut or polished.

Fluorite is a very common mineral in nature. It crystallizes from hydrothermal solutions in ore veins and occurs in granites, syenites and pegmatites; it may also be found in limestones, dolomites and other sedimentary rocks in which it may form independent deposits in certain places. It is mined in vast quantities as an important raw material used as the base of various fluorine compounds.

Attractively coloured fluorite crystals occur in England at Weardale near Durham and at Alston and Cleator Moor in Cumbria (formerly Cumberland). Blue-john comes from Castleton in Derbyshire. Beautiful green crystals are found at Westmoreland in New Hampshire and in Jefferson County in New York State, USA. Other classical localities are Wölsendorf, FRG, Kongsberg in Norway, Freiberg in Saxony, GDR, and in the Alps. Huge deposits of sedimentary origin are in the USA, China, the USSR (for example, Bek-Pak-Dal in Kazakhstan) and Bulgaria.

Transparent fluorites are fashioned into trap cuts and brilliants; cutting into cabochons is less frequent. Irregular pebbles and kernels are tumbled for necklaces.

1 Interpenetrant twin of fluorite cubes (Durham, England). 20 × 20 mm. **2** Group of fluorite crystals (Slavkov, Czechoslovakia). Length of largest crystal 18 mm. **3** Druse of fluorite crystals (Durham, England). Detail actual size. **4** Step-cut green fluorite (unknown locality). 22.4 carats.

1

2

4

Serpentine

Hydrous magnesium silicate, $Mg_6[(OH)_8|Si_4O_{10}]$*; crystal system: monoclinic; name derived from the Latin* serpens *(=snake) after the colour which resembles snakeskin; specific gravity: 2.5-2.8; hardness: 2.5-4; cleavage: good; fracture: conchoidal, uneven or hackly; tenacity: soft to splintery; colour: green, yellow, brown, often veined and spotted with various colours; streak: white; transparency: translucent to opaque; lustre: greasy, waxy, silky or dull; refractive index: 1.56 (mean); birefringence, dispersion and pleochroism: none (usually almost isotropic); main varieties: bowenite, williamsite, verd-antique.*

As a rock-forming mineral serpentine occurs in two different aggregate forms: the flaky **antigorite** (named after the locality of Antigorio in Italy) and the finely fibrous **chrysotile** (from the Greek *chrysos* = gold, and *tilos* = fibre). Serpentine is relatively abundant in nature and is the prevailing constituent (especially in the flaky antigorite form) of the rock serpentinite. It is the snakeskin-like serpentinite — not the pure mineral serpentine — that has been used for centuries as a popular decorative stone.

Macroscopically serpentinite appears massive and compact and is composed of cryptocrystalline, leaf-like, flaky or fibrous aggregates. It originates in nature as the result of hydrothermal alteration of magnesium-rich ultramafic rocks, especially peridotites, forming thick beds, veins and in some places even massives.

Serpentinite is mostly nontransparent and only rare varieties are translucent in thin slivers. It cuts well, takes a good polish and feels smooth and even greasy to the touch. Its greatest shortcoming is its excessive softness. Serpentinite is characteristically a greyish-green colour, but siskin-green and even reddish-brown shades occur. The coloration is often nonuniform and stones may even be mottled with darker irregular spots, veinlets and smudges, or they may be striped, streaked or marbled. Serpentinite containing the fibrous chrysotile has weakly glittering, silky lustrous spots on polished surfaces.

According to the colour several varieties of serpentinite are distinguished: **bowenite,** a fine-grained, yellowish green serpentinite with pale spots which is sometimes even translucent and resembles jadeite, occurs in the USA, China, South Africa and New Zealand; **williamsite** is dark green with black spots and occurs in Pennsylvania, USA; **verd-antique** is a massive, marbly, green variety with veinlets of white calcite or dolomite, occurring in Italy and Greece. Other important localities for top-grade material are in Saxony, GDR, England, Romania, Norway and the USSR.

Attractively coloured stones are occasionally fashioned into cabochons or flat plates or they are carved into various decorative objects — paperweights, ashtrays, receptacles, and such like.

1 Serpentine (Zöblitz, GDR). 90 × 70 mm. **2** Serpentine cabochon (Hrubšice, Czechoslovakia). 43 × 21 mm. **3** Serpentine (Cornwall, England). 90 × 80 mm. **4** Serpentine cabochon (unknown locality). Diameter 30 mm.

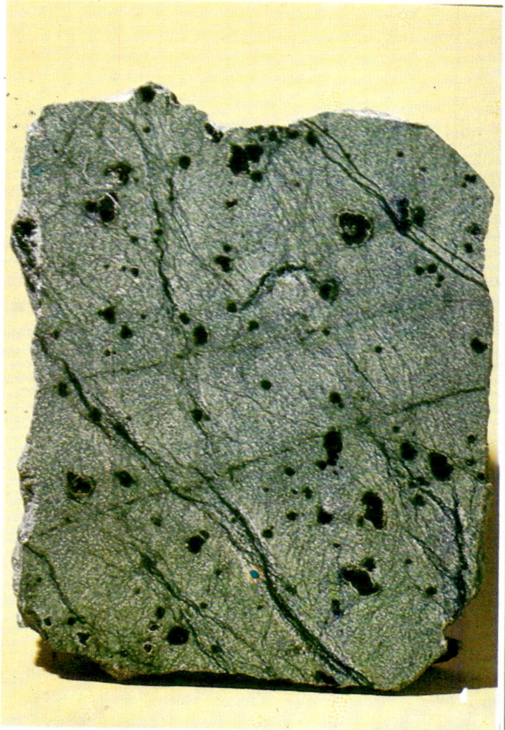
1

2

3

4

Jet and **Cannel**

Jet: *a hard, tough compact bituminous variety of brown coal or lignite; amorphous; name derived from the Old French* jyet *or* jaiet *based on the Latin* Gagates, *from Gagas, an ancient town and river in Lycia in Asia Minor from where the Romans obtained it; specific gravity: 1.30-1.38; hardness: 2.5-4; cleavage: none; fracture: conchoidal; colour: black; transparency: opaque; burns like coal; refractive index:* n = *1.66.*

Cannel: *a compact, fine-grained sapropelitic coal; amorphous, name refers to the fact that it burns with a smoky flame like a candle; fracture: conchoidal; colour: black or greyish black; transparency: opaque.*

Basically jet is nothing but the fossilized remains of woody plant material (branches, twigs and such like) that decomposed in anaerobic waterlogged environments such as bogs and swamps. The plant debris became saturated with organic slime, formed peat and this in time changed into lignite in conditions of increased temperature and pressure (see p. 18). Jet occurs in tubers of various sizes, not seams, in Jurassic sediments and one of the main localities for it is in the vicinity of Hawsker and Robin Hood's Bay near Whitby in Yorkshire, England. It is mined from galleries driven inside the coastal cliffs. Lumps of jet are also found lying on the seashore.

Jet mining in England has had a very long history that started about 1500 or 1400 BC and reached its peak in the latter half of the 19th century. During the Roman occupation of Britain jet was even exported to Rome. Jet is also mined at Villaviciosa in Spain and at Aude in France. Some deposits also occur in the Henry Mountains in Utah, USA, in the USSR and at Würtenberg, FRG. However, none of these localities is worked systematically. Deposits of similar substances in the Alpine Jurassic are thought to be the carbonized remains of marine algae.

Jet jewellery has enjoyed considerable popularity especially during the Victorian period when it was used for carved crosses, highly intricate ornaments and other, mainly ecclesiastical and mourning jewellery. Today, however, the demand for jet as a gemstone is low and the stone is used mainly for figurines and various curios and souvenirs.

As a substitute for jet, **cannel** from Scotland and Pennsylvanian or Vietnamese **anthracite** were sometimes used. Both are glossier than jet, especially anthracite which is the richest in carbon of all coals as it represents the last stage in the coalification process. Anthracite has a very high vitreous lustre, sometimes even of a metallic character.

The brownish black tough, dully lustrous, highly bituminous claystone (sapropelite) known in Czech as **švartna** and in German as **schwarten-kohle** that forms a 10-20-cm thick stratum at the top of the Kounov seam in the Rakovník and Slaný districts in Bohemia, was used in prehistoric times for the making of bracelets.

1 Anthracite (Donetsk Basin, USSR). 80 × 70 mm. **2** Cannel coal (Donetsk Basin, USSR). 75 × 35 mm. **3** Sapropelitic coal disc (from a Celtic necklace workshop) re-used as a pendant in a contemporary piece of jewellery (Nové Strašecí, Czechoslovakia). Diameter 34 mm. **4** Anthracite lion figurine (material from Tonkin Basin, Vietnam). 250 × 160 mm.

1

2

3

4

Amber

A fossil resin, average chemical composition 78% carbon, 10% hydrogen, 11% oxygen, with small amounts of sulphur and ash matter; amorphous; name derived from the Latin ambar *(=perfumed substance), which was taken from the Arabic* anbar *for ambergris; specific gravity: 1.03-1.1; hardness: 2.-3; cleavage: none; fracture: conchoidal; tenacity: brittle; colour: yellow, brown, reddish or whitish, occasionally black; streak: white; transparency: transparent to translucent; lustre: greasy; melting point: 300-375 °C; refractive index:* n = *1.542 ± 0.003; main varieties: succinite, rumanite, simetite, burmite, valchovite.*

The properties of amber were known in ancient times. In the sixth century BC, the Greek philosopher Thales of Miletus discovered that when he wiped amber with a dry cloth, it attracted tiny particles and lint. Today it is, of course, known that friction gives amber a negative electrical charge — it is triboelectric — and electricity actually received its name from amber after the Greek name *elektron* (= sun-made) for it.

In Tertiary times the area around what is known today as the Baltic Sea used to be covered with vast primeval forests of tall conifers, especially the pine *Pinus succinifera* that thrived mainly during the Oligocene, some 30 million years ago. These trees were rich in resin and cracked or wounded parts of the trunks bled profusely. The exuded resin coagulated into drops and larger blobs and eventually fell to the ground where it was buried in the soil.

Amber occurs in tubers, pebbles and grains and usually has an attractive yellow or reddish colour. It often contains parts of plants such as conifer needles or perfectly preserved insects or even inorganic inclusions which were trapped on the sticky surface of the resin before it hardened.

Today in the Baltic region amber is excavated from Tertiary sediments of the so-called 'blue clay', or is fished from the sea with dragnets — or even collected on beaches where it has washed up. The major occurrences are on the Baltic coast near Kaliningrad at Yantarnyi in the USSR. It is collected and pit-mined on the Polish coast on the Hel Peninsula. Amber is also found on the coasts of Norway and Denmark; it used to be washed up on the eastern coast of England. Baltic amber is sometimes called **succinite** because it contains succinic acid. Materials resembling Baltic amber but of a slightly different chemical composition are known from Romania (**rumanite**, from Buzau and Prahov), from Sicily (the reddish-brown **simetite** from the Simeto River basin near Catania), Burma (the reddish-yellow to reddish-bronze **burmite** mined occasionally in the Bhamo district) and from other places. The largest piece of amber weighing 10.5 kg was found by a fisherman on the Swedish coast in October 1969. **Valchovite** is amber from Upper Cretaceous sediments in Czechoslovakia. It is occasionally used for decorative objects.

According to their clarity, ambers are classed as clear, cloudy, misty, bony and foamy. Amber cuts well and when polished it has a high lustre. Smaller pieces and amber cutting waste are heat-processed under increased pressure into the so-called pressed amber or **ambroid.** It can be recognized by margins of varying translucence and internal bubbles that are elongated owing to the pressure.

1 Amber tuber (Baltic coast of the USSR). 80 mm. **2** Amber with enclosed insect (Baltic coast of Poland). Enlarged detail. **3** Bracelet made from smoothed amber pebbles (contemporary Polish work). **4** Valchovite, a tuber of Cretaceous resin (Hřebeč, Czechoslovakia). 93 mm.

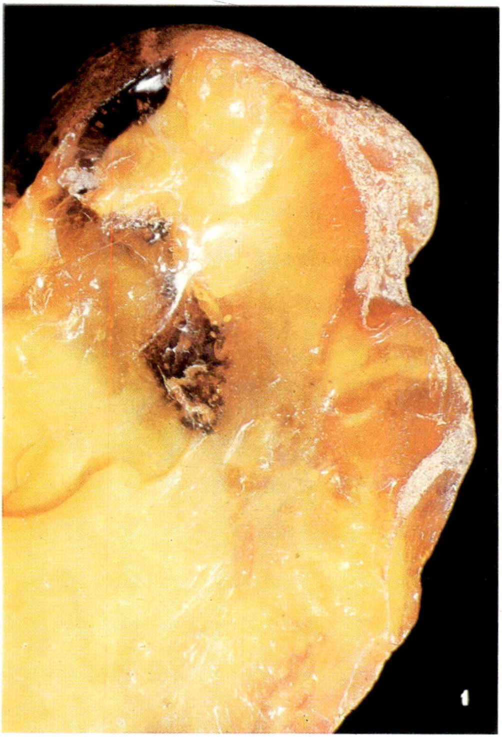

1

2

3

4

Pearls

Organic material composed of calcium carbonate in the form of orthorhombic aragonite and trigonal calcite, the protein conchiolin and water; name derived from the French perle, *which in its turn came from the Latin* perla; *but the precise derivation of this word is unknown; specific gravity: 2.60-2.85; hardness: 3.5-4; cleavage: none; fracture: uneven; tenacity: tough; colour: white, yellow, pink, reddish, greenish, bluish, brown, grey or black; streak: white; transparency: translucent; lustre: pearly; refractive index: 1.60 (mean).*

Pearls are products of various bivalve molluscs living in warm subtropical and tropical seas as well as in freshwater streams. The body of these molluscs is protected by a double shell consisting of two halves (valves). The shell is essentially composed of three layers: the outer layer is formed by dark, horn-like conchiolin; the intermediate or prismatic layer, which is the thickest, is formed by extremely tiny columnar crystals of aragonite and calcite bonded with conchiolin; the inner mother-of-pearl (nacre) layer is composed of thin flaky crystals of aragonite bonded with calcium albuminate or conchiolin. Pearls are nothing else but spherically developed bivalve shells — the individual concentric layers of varying thickness can easily be observed in cross-section.

A pearl starts developing when a foreign particle, such as a sand grain or a larva of some parasite, penetrates the fluid-filled cavity between the protective inner covering layer (mantle) and the shell of the bivalve and sets up an irritation. The epithelial cells of the mantle then react by secreting layer upon layer of nacre around the irritating foreign body. The process continues for up to seven years by which time a pearl has formed. Pearls sometimes grow attached to the nacreous lining of the shell. These **blister pearls**, as they are called, have to be cut from the mollusc. The part that was joined to the shell is rough and is not covered with nacre, but the pearl can still be used in jewellery if suitably mounted. Blister pearls are usually irregular in shape. Pearls that grow within the tissue of the mollusc and are completely formed are called **cyst pearls** — these are obviously more valuable than blister pearls.

Pearls come in sizes ranging from a mere millimetre to the size of a pigeon's egg, and occasionally even larger. They are sorted by size on pearl sieves, the size being given in the so-called *pp* value — a figure corresponding to the size of the mesh. Pearl weight is given in grains (1 grain = 0.25 carat = 0.05 gram). Pearls may be round, drop-shaped, pear-shaped, barrel-shaped, button-shaped (button pearls or **boutons**) or irregular (**baroques**) and are valued in that order. Those weighing less than one quarter-grain are known as **seed pearls**.

The chemical composition and specific gravity of pearls vary and depend on the species of mollusc and the environment. On average pearls contain 73-92 per cent calcium carbonate, 4-6 per cent conchiolin and 2-4 per cent water. Pearls are soluble in weak acid and because human perspiration is slightly acid, pearls should always be wiped clean after wearing to prevent corrosion. The conchiolin layers are also attacked by alkaline lyes.

1 Freshwater pearl in shell (southern Bohemia, Czechoslovakia). Diameter of pearl 6 mm. **2** Freshwater pearls (River Otava, Horažďovice, Czechoslovakia). Diameter about 2.5 mm. **3** Blister pearl (Indian Ocean). Diameter of shell 190 mm. **4** Group of pearls of different colours and origins. First row (top): freshwater pearls; second row: sea (salt water) pearls; third row: blister pearls; fourth row: pearl cross-sections; the one in the middle is a cultured pearl, the other two are natural pearls. Diameter of largest pearl 9 mm.

1

2

3

4

Lower-grade pearls usually have a lower specific gravity; the highest specific gravity (2.84-2.89) has been observed in pink pearls. The hardness of pearls roughly corresponds to that of aragonite; black pearls are the hardest. Because of their zonal structure pearls have a considerable toughness and are even slightly elastic. Undrilled fresh pearls are quite difficult to break; their internal cohesion is much greater than one would expect on the basis of their chemical composition.

A pearl's colour depends not only on the species of mollusc secreting the pearl but also on the environmental conditions and the composition of the water in which the animal lives. White pearls with a weak bluish tint and cream-white pearls are produced by various pearl oyster species (especially of the genus *Pinctada*) living in the Indian Ocean, the Persian Gulf and in the seas surrounding Ceylon. *Pinctada margaritifera* lives in the waters around Australia and produces silvery white or yellow pearls. Pearls of a bronze or gun-metal colour — the so-called black pearls — are dived for in the Gulf of Mexico and grey and orange pearls come from the coast of California. Pink pearls are produced by a univalve (single-shelled) mollusc called the Great Conch (*Strombus gigas*) and come from the Caribbean. Pearls are also found in various species of freshwater clam and mussel, for example *Margaritana margaritifera*, which lives in clean rivers and streams in Europe.

The fine colour play or iridescent surface sheen shown by pearls and mother-of-pearl is caused by the interference and diffraction of light falling on the thin overlapping outer layers of nacreous material. These surface layers also determine the pearl's characteristic lustre and glitter. Best prices are fetched by perfectly spherical pearls with a bright silverish lustre and a weak rainbow colour play. The pink conch pearls are not nacreous and so do not have the iridescent sheen of true pearls.

Apart from natural pearls, the jewellery trade also uses cultured pearls. A lengthy period of research in pearl cultivation was successfully concluded about 1920 by K. Mikimoto of Japan. The process is based on the introduction into the body of a three-year old oyster of a very small bead ground from mother-of-pearl enclosed by a piece of mantle epithelium. The inoculated pearl oysters are then cultivated for up to four years in special cages suspended from rafts floating in the water of sea farms.

The quality of cultured pearls depends on the ratio of the dimensions of the nacreous nucleus and the encasing mantle layers whose thickness is usually 0.5-2.0 mm. If the nucleus is small and the encasement thick enough, the properties of the outer layers are essentially the same as those of natural pearls. If, however, the covering of nacre in pearls is too thin it tends to peel off and the surface shows dark conchiolin blemishes. The market price for cultured pearls averages one-fifth of the price of natural pearls.

Outstanding specimens of pearls are set in many famous jewels. The largest pearl, the so-called Hope Pearl (owned once by Henry Thomas Hope), is a pear-shaped baroque with a diameter exceeding 5 cm and a weight of over 90 grams. It is kept in the British Museum (Natural History) in London. Unusually large pearls are in the Coronation Treasury in Vienna and exquisite specimens of baroque pearls can be seen in the Grünes Gewölbe Treasury in Dresden and in the Loretto Treasury in Prague.

Pearls intended for jewellery are either partially drilled on one side to a depth of two-thirds or three-quarters of the pearl's diameter and then fixed to pegs, or they are drilled through for stringing; the drilled hole diameter should be 0.3 mm. Smaller pearls are also split in half and set in jewels like other gems.

1 Gold and pearl monstrance with baroque pearls (Baroque period). **2** Pendant with amethysts and freshwater pearls (19th century). Height 60 mm. **3** Pendant with ruby and pearls (19th century). Height 28 mm. **4** Ring of white gold, pearl and diamonds (early 20th century).

1

2

3

4

Coral

Irregularly branched organogenic material composed of calcium carbonate, $CaCO_3$, *in the form of the trigonal calcite; name derived from the Greek* korállion *for the hard calcareous skeleton secreted by coelenterate polyps; specific gravity: 2.6-2.7; hardness: 3-4; cleavage: none; fracture: uneven to hackly; tenacity: brittle; colour: red, pink, white or black; streak: pale red; lustre: waxy; refractive indices:* $\varepsilon = 1.49$, $\omega = 1.65$.

Coral's bright scarlet colour and easy fashioning have long aroused Man's interest. For instance, coral was used to decorate bronze objects of the La Tène culture in Europe as long as 500-55 BC. Ancient caravans delivered coral to China, Japan and India where coral was highly prized as a precious material. During medieval times coral amulets were believed to ward off sickness and ill fortune. Coral has retained its popularity and it is still in very great demand as a gem material.

Coral is formed from the calcareous supporting skeletons of myriads of tiny coelenterate polyps that live in colonies in warm shallow seas. Many types of coral exist. Some corals build huge compact calcareous masses that become coral reefs and islands. Most of these reef-building corals belong to the coelenterate order Zoantharia. The precious coral species (*Corallium*), however, produce quite a different skeleton; it is feathery or tree-like and these corals are grouped with the so-called soft corals or Alyconaria. The branches of the skeleton may be 20-40 cm high and taper towards the tip. They are usually round in cross-section with a diameter of 2-4 cm. In places on the branch there are knot-like growths. The surface is longitudinally striated or helically fluted, a characteristic feature of rough unsmoothed corals. The branches have no internal hollows. Under a microscope, a section of the coral branch reveals the concentrical dish-shaped structure of the calcite grains.

Coral dissolves in acids with effervescence. It is also attacked by lyes and its colour and appearance may be affected by the wearer's perspiration. Discoloured, dull corals can sometimes be reconstituted by immersion in hydrogen peroxide. The colour of precious corals differs according to the species, but the deep-red corals produced by *Corallium rubrum* or *Corallium nobile* are the most popular. Corals are sometimes unevenly coloured, mottled and may have a pink or even a white colour.

The classical region of coral growth and fishing is the Mediterranean, especially the coastal waters of Italy, Sicily, Algeria and Tunisia. The Indian and Pacific Oceans are also important sources of coral.

Once dredged from the sea, the live crust is removed from the surface of the coral and the individual branches are polished and cut into lenticular or spherical beads; small branches and fragments are strung and worn as necklaces and necklets. Larger pieces are carved into decorative objects and cameos.

1 Tuft of natural red corals (Šibenik, Yugoslavia). Height 160 mm. **2** Necklace of red corals (contemporary work, Yugoslavia). **3** Detail of coral diadem (mid-19th century). **4** Cut cameo with Bacchus' head made of pink coral (19th century). Height 50 mm.

1

2

3

4

Novelty stones

Novelty stones are synthetically produced monocrystals of various chemical compounds that either do not exist as minerals in nature or are unsuitable for jewellery in their natural form. These stones are mainly oxides of rare elements and most crystallize in the cubic system, so are singly refractive (isotropic). They have a high refractive index and a high specific gravity, they come in various colours and are sold under different trade names. All synthetically produced crystals meet the requirements of gem material intended for jewellery, that is they have good mechanical properties that permit easy and perfect fashioning. Novelty stone crystals are produced by the Czochralski method of pulling crystals from the melt or by the Verneuil process (see p. 70).

Yttroaluminate, $Y_3Al_5O_{12}$, is sometimes called yttroaluminium garnet or '**YAG**', but the only thing that this compound has in common with genuine garnet is its cubic symmetry and a similar crystal structure. Its specific gravity varies between 4.57 and 6.69 depending on its chemical composition, its hardness exceeds 8 and its refractive index *n* is 1.83-1.87. A pure yttroaluminate is clear and colourless but the stones can be coloured by admixtures of rare earth elements such as terbium (pale yellow), dysprosium (yellowish green), holmium (golden yellow), erbium (yellowish pink), thulium (pale green), ytterbium and lutetium (both pale yellow). If exposed to ultraviolet light yttroaluminate emits a yellow fluorescence. The presence of foreign inclusions depends on the method of synthesis and may distinguish these stones from natural stones of similar colour. Yttroaluminate is marketed under the name **'Diamonair**.

'Zirconia' is a successful imitation of diamond also called Watten diamond. It is a double-oxide of zirconium and yttrium. $ZrO_2 + Y_2O_3$, and has cubic symmetry. Its specific gravity is 5.7, its hardness is 8.5 and its refractive index *n* is 2.20. The stones are clear and colourless and have a strong dispersion. Zirconia is cut into brilliants; some stones are up to 10 mm in diameter.

'Djevalite' is another oxide of zirconium, this time stabilized with calcium, $ZrO_2 +$ CaO, and is also cubic. Its specific gravity is 5.60-5.71, its hardness is 8-8.5 and its refractive index *n* is 2.17. The stones are clear and colourless, they have a strong dispersion and their facets have a diamond-like lustre. Djevalite does not fluoresce in ultraviolet light. Although colourless stones are usually marketed, various coloured Djevalites are also available. A great shortcoming of this synthetic diamond imitation is its brittleness combined with a considerable hardness. Excessive pressure or impact can easily damage the cut facet, especially when the stone is being set.

'Fabulite' strontium titanate, $SrTiO_3$, is another cubic novelty stone. Its specific gravity is 5.13, its hardness is 6 and its refractive index *n* is 2.41. Its dispersion is five times as high as diamond's. It is a lucid, perfectly colourless stone and brilliants cut from it display a much livelier fire and colour play than those from natural diamonds. Fabulite does not fluoresce in ultraviolet light. Under a microscope its growth zones can be seen. Fabulite was once called 'Starilian' or 'Diagem'.

'Titania', titanium dioxide, TiO_2, is a synthetic rutile which crystallizes in the tetragonal system. Its specific gravity is 4.25, its hardness is 6.5 and its refractive indices ε and ω are 2.90 and 2.62 respectively. It possesses a strong birefringence and its dispersion is about six times as high as diamond's. It is usually a pale-yellow colour, but other colours (red, orange, blue and brown) have been produced. The greatest shortcoming of synthetic rutile is its relatively low hardness.

1 Crystals of yttroaluminates (YAGs) of different colours, synthetized by the Czochralski method. Height of the largest 80 mm. **2** Group of cut YAGs of various colours. **3** Rough Zirconias. Actual size. **4** Cut Zirconias of various colours. Actual size.

1

2

3

4

Other gem minerals and ornamental stones

Agalmatolite (Pagodite)

A massive variety, mainly of **pyrophyllite** (a hydrous aluminium silicate), but it may also be formed by, for example, talc (steatite) and mica. Its specific gravity is 2.7-2.9, its hardness is 1.5-2.5 and its refractive index is around 1.57. It is greyish green, apple green, greenish white or yellowish in colour. It comes from the borderland between China and Tibet, from Sutherland in Scotland and Ochsenkopf in Saxony, GDR. Europe knew it at first only from finished products such as figurines and statuettes, not in its rough natural state as the sources were a closely guarded secret. Once the localities had become known the stone rapidly lost its former precious character.

Alabaster

Hydrated calcium sulphate, $Ca[SO_4] \cdot 2\ H_2O$, a fine-grained, compact and massive variety of **gypsum**. In ancient times the term alabaster was also used for fine-grained limestone. The specific gravity of alabaster is 2.30-2.33, the hardness is 2.0-2.3 and the refractive index ranges between 1.52 and 1.53. It is white, pinkish or brownish in colour and it is translucent. Practically all alabaster comes from Castellino Maritimo near Volterra in Tuscany, Italy, but alabaster from southern Spain and Derbyshire and Staffordshire in England is also often fashioned. On the southern coast of Wales the pink Welsh alabaster is mined at Glamorgan but it has no special importance in the trade. Alabaster was known to the Assyrians, Egyptians and Phoenicians and outstanding examples of alabaster vases and amphoras made by these ancient peoples have survived to the present day. Alabaster was once used as a medium for both direct and indirect illumination.

Apatite

Calcium phosphate with fluorine, chlorine and hydroxyl, $Ca_5(F, Cl, OH)[PO_4]_3$; hexagonal. Its name is derived from the Greek *apataó* (=deceit) because apatite occurs in different colours depending on the admixtures and ancient people mistook it for other minerals. The specific gravity of apatite is 3.2, the hardness is 5 and the refractive indices range from 1.63 to 1.64. The colour is usually yellow, yellowish green, green, violet, blue, brown, grey or white. The stone has a weak birefringence. Attractively coloured varieties are used as gemstones, which are usually cut into cabochons but Swiss apatites are cut into beautiful brilliants. The translucent yellow-green apatites from Murcia Province in Spain are called **asparagus stones** because their colour resembles that of asparagus tips. **Apatite cat's-eye** comes from the Mogok in Burma and from Sri Lanka and Brazil. **Moroxite** is a bluish-green variety from Arendal in Norway. Other gemmy varieties of apatite are known from Czechoslovakia, India, Madagascar, Mexico and Maine and California, USA.

Axinite

Complex calcium aluminium borosilicate with iron, manganese and magnesium, $Ca_2(Fe, Mg, Mn)\ Al_2[BO_3|OH|Si_4O_{12}]$; triclinic. Its specific gravity is 3.27-3.29, its hardness is 6.5-7 and its refractive indices range from 1.674 to 1.699. It occurs in various brown, honey-yellow, plum-purple and blue colours and it displays a strong pleochroism from olive green to reddish brown to yellowish brown. Gem-quality axinites come from the Isère region of France; reddish-brown varieties are found at Mina la Olivia in Baja California, in Mexico, Cornwall in England and in the USA.

1 Agalmatolite clasp (Chinese work, 19th century). Diameter 50 mm. **2** Alabaster necklace (late 19th century). **3** Honey-yellow crystals of apatite (Durango, Mexico). Length of larger specimen 35 mm. **4** Gem-quality axinite crystal (Baja California, Mexico). 45 × 40 mm.

1

2

3

4

Benitoite

Barium titanium silicate, $BaTi[Si_3O_9]$; trigonal. Its specific gravity is 3.65-3.68, its hardness is 6-6.5 and its refractive indices range from 1.757 to 1.804. It occurs in colour shades ranging from pale to dark sapphire blue, it is strongly pleochroic (colourless to deep blue) and has an exceptionally strong dispersion. Benitoite is named after the locality of San Benito County in California, USA.

Cassiterite (Tinstone)

Tin dioxide, SnO_2; tetragonal. Its specific gravity is 6.8-7.1, its hardness is 6-7 and its refractive indices range from 1.997 to 2.093. It is usually black and opaque but exceptionally reddish brown crystals are found with a sufficient translucence to permit cutting. Stones suitable for cutting come from Spain and from Erongo in Namibia. Cassiterite's major use is as a rich tin ore. Collectors appreciate its twins.

Charoite

A complex hydrated silicate of calcium, potassium, sodium, boron and strontium, $(Ca,Na,K,Sr,B)_3[Si_4O_{10}](OH,F)\cdot H_2O$, named after the River Chara, Yakutia, USSR, where it was first found. Its specific gravity is 2.54, its hardness is about 6 and its refractive indices range from 1.550 to 1.559. Charoite is an unimportant rock-forming mineral of metamorphic rocks. It forms massive, finely fibrous aggregates of a lilac colour that makes it an attractive material for vases, paperweights, rings, pendants and cufflinks.

Chrysocolla

Hydrated copper silicate, $Cu_4H_4[(OH)_8|Si_4O_{10}]$ a cryptocrystalline mineral with a specific gravity of 2.0-2.6, a hardness of 2-4, a refractive index of around 1.5, a greasy vitreous lustre, and a conchoidal fracture. It has a green, bluish-green or turquoise colour and is usually semitransparent to nontransparent. Chrysocolla forms lumpy encrustations and stalactites; it also develops secondarily in copper ore deposits. The major localities are in Chile, Peru, in the Urals and in the US states of Arizona, Nevada and New Mexico and in Zaire.

Cuprite

Cuprous oxide, Cu_2O; cubic. Its specific gravity is 5.85-6.15, its hardness is 4 and its refractive index n is 2.85. It is crimson-red in colour, transparent to translucent, and it has a metallic lustre. Only some crystals from Santa Rita in New Mexico, USA and Onganyo in Namibia are suitable for cutting into brilliants.

1 Group of blue benitoite crystals with dark neptunite. (San Benito, California, USA). Detail actual size. **2** Cassiterite twins (Araca, Bolivia). 60 × 50 mm. **3** Cut cassiterite of unusual shape (Czechoslovakia). 12 mm. **4** Ground plate of charoite. (Chara River, USSR). Detail slightly enlarged. **5** Reniform incrustation of chrysocolla (Poloma, Czechoslovakia). 92 × 70 mm. **6** Step cut of cuprite (Namibia). 7.2 carats.

1

2

3

4

5

6

Danburite

Calcium borosilicate, $Ca[B_2Si_2O_8]$; orthorhombic. Its specific gravity is 3.0, its hardness is 7-7.5 and its refractive indices range from 1.630 to 1.636. It is mostly colourless but grape-yellow or pinkish varieties also occur. The colourless crystals are lucid. Danburite is named after its place of discovery — Danbury in Connecticut, USA — but material from this locality has probably never been cut. Gem-quality danburites come from Mogok in Burma, Madagascar, Bungo in Japan and several localities in Mexico, especially in the state of San Luis Potosí.

Dumortierite

Aluminium borosilicate, $Al_7[O_3|BO_3|(SiO_4)_3]$; orthorhombic but mostly forms fibrous to massive aggregates. Its specific gravity is 3.26-3.41, its hardness is 7 and its refractive indices range between 1.686 and 1.723. Its colour is blue, purplish blue or reddish brown, it is strongly pleochroic and has a vitreous lustre. Dumortierite is found in Brazil, Sri Lanka, Madagascar, Canada, near Lyon in France, at Tvederstrand in Norway and in Nevada, USA. Gem-quality specimens from Nevada and India are impregnated with quartz.

Kornerupine

A complex magnesium aluminium borosilicate, $Mg_4Al_6[(O, OH)_2|BO_4|(SIO_4)_4]$; orthorhombic. Its specific gravity is 3.28-3.35, its hardness is 6.5.-7 and its refractive indices range from 1.665 to 1.682. Its colour is pale green, green or greenish brown. Kornerupine is relatively rare but cuttable crystals occur in Sri Lanka, Madagascar, Greenland, Lac Ste Marie in Quebec, Canada and Mogok in Burma where kornerupine cat's eyes are occasionally found.

Lazulite

Magnesium iron aluminium phosphate, $(Mg, Fe)Al_2[(OH)PO_4]_2$; monoclinic, but crystals are quite rare. Its specific gravity is 3.1-3.2, its hardness is 5-6 and its refractive indices range from 1.615 to 1.645. Lazulite is a rare ornamental stone (not to be confused with lapis lazuli) with an interesting blue colour ranging from deep blue to whitish blue. It is translucent to nontransparent, strongly pleochroic (colourless to azure blue) and it has a white streak and vitreous lustre. The major localities of top-quality stone are Bhandara in India, Minas Gerais in Brazil, the US states of North Carolina and Maine, Lobito Bay in Angola, Salzburg in Austria and Sweden.

Lepidolite

A lithium-bearing **mica**, massive, fine-grained and pink to purple in colour. Its specific gravity is 2.8-2.9, its hardness is 3.5 and its mean refractive index is 1.55. Massive lumps of lepidolite come from the Urals, Madagascar, the US states of Maine, California and Connecticut and the Karibib district of Namibia. Lepidolite is sometimes carved into vases, stands, ashtrays and similar objects; stone from Rožná in Czechoslovakia has been cut into cabochons.

Natrolite

Hydrated sodium aluminium silicate, $Na_2[Al_2Si_3O_{10}] \cdot 2\,H_2O$; orthorhombic. Its specific gravity is 2.20-2.25, its hardness is 5.5 and its refractive indices range from 1.48 to 1.49. Its colour is white or yellowish but it can also be colourless. If colourless, it is transparent, otherwise it is merely translucent. Massive material is sometimes fashioned into table cuts but the practice is rare and is usually dictated only by collectors' interests. Natrolite is a zeolite; the raw material for cutting comes from Norway and Scotland.

1 Danburite crystal (Tatyukha, USSR). Height of crystal 45 mm. **2** Dumortierite (Arizona, USA). 80 × 60 mm. **3** Cut kornerupine (Fugada, Madagascar). 3.6 carats. **4** Polished section of lazulite (Stickelberg, Austria). 75 × 70 mm. **5** Lepidolite cabochon (Rožná, Czechoslovakia). Length 30 mm. **6** Natrolite (Kola, USSR). 150 × 80 mm.

1

2

3

4

5

6

Prehnite

Hydrous calcium aluminium silicate, $Ca_2Al_2[Si_3O_{10}](OH)_2$; orthorhombic. Its specific gravity is 2.88-2.93, its hardness is 6.0-6.5 and its refractive indices range from 1.61 to 1.64. It is yellowish green, brownish yellow or apple green in colour with a white streak and a vitreous to pearly lustre. It is usually translucent even in compact aggregates so that it can be cut into cabochons. Some cabochons are chatoyant like cat's eye. Prehnite is also facet-cut. The best-known localities are near Sydney in Australia, Renfrew, Dunbarton and Stirling in Scotland, in China, South Africa and New Jersey, USA. The salmon-pink and green stones from the Lake Superior region are mixtures of prehnite and chlorite.

Rhodochrosite (Dialogite)

Manganese carbonate, $MnCO_3$; trigonal. Its specific gravity is 3.30-3.70, its hardness is 4 and its refractive indices range from 1.600 to 1.820. The crystals and the fine-grained massive aggregates have a characteristic delicate pinkish red colour and they have a white streak. Like malachite, rhodochrosite is often banded in various hues. It is usually translucent but transparent crystals may occur. The lustre is vitreous. Compact forms of rhodochrosite are used for decorative objects and only a few cabochons are known to have been cut from exceptionally clear crystals. The main source of this beautifully coloured mineral is at San Luis in Argentina where the local silver mines were known to the Incas who worked them as early as the 13th century. Other Argentinian localities are Capillitas near Andalgala and Catamarca, east of Tucumán. Deep-red crystals of rhodochrosite have been found near Alma in Colorado, USA.

Rutile

Titanium dioxide, TiO_2; tetragonal. Its specific gravity is 4.2-4.4, its hardness is 6-6.5 and its refractive indices range from 2.62 to 2.90. It is normally reddish brown in colour and translucent, but exceptionally it has a yellowish or greenish tint. Rutile is highly birefringent; it also disperses light six times as much as diamond, but the fire is much faded by the dark hues of the mineral. Dispersion is one of the outstanding properties of synthetic rutiles (see page 210), which are often cut as brilliants. Collectors appreciate the twins and multiple intergrowths of natural rutile. The natural stones are rarely cut because of their dark colour and low translucence and because of the presence of fine internal cracks caused by the good cleavage along the prismatic faces. In the past, dark-brown and blackish rutiles were cut for mourning jewellery. The yellowish brown, yellowish green and occasionally transparent rutiles from Minas Gerais in Brazil are sometimes cut and are extremely rare gems. Needle-like inclusions of rutile are sometimes present in rock crystal forming the quartz variety known as **sagenite** or **needlestone**.

1 Prehnite (West Patterson, USA). 100 × 70 mm. **2** Rhodochrosite (Cappillitas, Argentina). Slightly enlarged. **3** Rhodochrosite (Rosia Montana, Romania). 130 × 80 mm. **4** Contact twins of rutile (Chapadas, Minas Gerais, Brazil). Length of the longer specimen 9 mm. **5** Rutile in rock crystal — sagenite (Swiss Alps). Slightly enlarged. **6** Sagenite cabochons (Val Tremola, Switzerland). Height 15 mm.

1

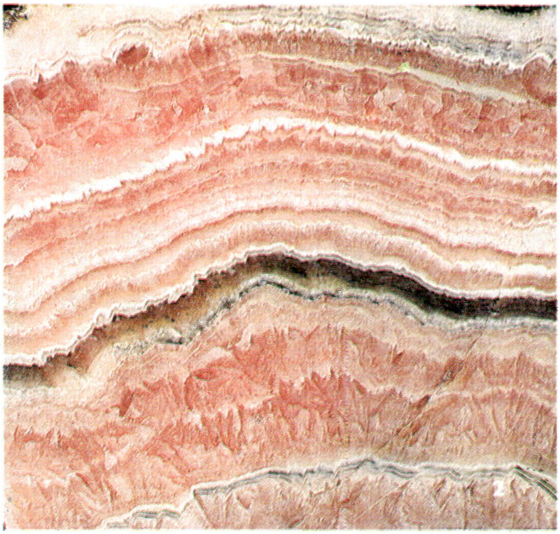
2

3

4

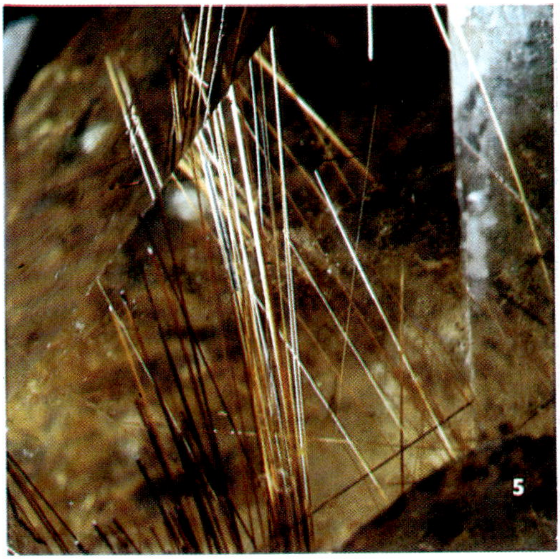
5

6

Sepiolite (Meerschaum)

Hydrated magnesium silicate, $Mg_4[Si_6O_{15}] \cdot (OH)_2 \cdot 6\,H_2O$; orthorhombic, but it is actually microcrystalline — under the microscope the material is seen to be composed of fine fibres embedded in a groundmass of the same composition. Sepiolite occurs in compact, foam-like masses. Its specific gravity is usually 1.0-2.0, it is porous and when dry it floats on water. Its hardness is 2.0-2.5 and its mean refractive index is 1.53. It can be white, yellowish, greyish or reddish in colour and has a white streak. Sepiolite is used for making smoking accessories such as cigarette holders and pipe bowls, which are often richly decorated. Rings with ornamental sepiolite stones are in vogue today. The main sources of the mineral are Eski Shehir in Turkey, Thebes in Greece, Morocco, Spain and the USA.

Sillimanite (Fibrolite)

Aluminium silicate, $Al_2[O|SiO_4]$; orthorhombic. It is polymorphic with andalusite and kyanite and usually fibrous, hence its other name. Its specific gravity is 3.14-3.25, its hardness is 6-7.5 and its mean refractive index is 1.65-1.68. Gem-quality sillimanite is rare. Blue, transparent sillimanite is found at Mogok in Burma and greyish-green varieties occur in gravels in Sri Lanka. The massive fibrous sillimanite cobbles from the Clearwater River Valley in Idaho, USA, used to provide material for carved figurines and souvenirs.

Smithsonite

Zinc carbonate, $ZnCO_3$; trigonal. Its specific gravity is 4.3-4.5, its hardness is 5 and its refractive indices range from 1.621 to 1.849. It is often translucent, of a pale-green, pale-blue or pink colour, with a white streak. The lump varieties have a greasy to pearly lustre and are cut into cabochons. The main occurrences of smithsonite are in Attiki in Greece, Tsumeb in Namibia, Sardinia, Santander in Spain, Cananea in Mexico and the US states of Arkansas, New Mexico and Utah.

Sphalerite (Blende, Zinc Blende, Black Jack)

Zinc sulphide, ZnS; cubic. Its specific gravity is 4.08-4.10, its hardness is 3.5-4 and its refractive index *n* is 2.368-2.371. Its most common colour is dark brown to black, but translucent crystals with a yellowish-brown or orange tint are known. Greenish or almost colourless sphalerite is very rare. The streak is yellowish to pale brown. Sphalerite cleaves perfectly along the faces of a rhombic dodecahedron (in six directions) so that cutting the mineral is quite difficult; light-coloured stones are sometimes faceted. Transparent sphalerite comes mainly from the Chivera mines in Mexico and from the vicinity of Santander in the Picos de Europa in Spain. Otherwise sphalerite is quite a common zinc ore.

1 Sepiolite (meerschaum) pipe bowl with figurative scene (first half of the 19th century). Height 150 mm. **2** Sillimanite cabochon (České Budějovice, Czechoslovakia). Length 14 mm. **3** Smithsonite (Sardinia). 60 × 60 mm. **4** Cut sphalerites (Picos de Europa, Spain). 41.5 and 23.2 carats.

1

2

3

4

Staurolite

Iron aluminium silicate, $Al_4[Fe(OH)_2|O_2|(SiO_4)_2]$; monoclinic. Its specific gravity is 3.65-3.78, its hardness is 7-7.5 and its refractive indices range from 1.739 to 1.792. Even more admired than the facet-cut, dark-brown transparent crystals are the interpenetrant twins in the form of a cross. Staurolite occurs in crystalline schists and is of a metamorphic origin. It is found in the vicinity of Ticino and St Gotthard in Switzerland, in France, England, the USSR, Brazil and the USA.

Thomsonite

Hydrated sodium calcium aluminium silicate, $NaCa_2[Al_2(Al, Si)Si_2O_{10}]_2 \cdot 6H_2O$; orthorhombic. Its specific gravity is 2.3-2.4, its hardness is 5-5.5 and its refractive indices range from 1.52 to 1.54. It is usually a translucent, milky-white, yellow, reddish, brownish or greenish colour and forms columnar radial aggregates. It has a porcelain lustre, which is improved by cutting. Gem-quality thomsonite comes from Arkansas (snow-white variety), Michigan and Minnesota, USA. It is a zeolite.

Variscite (Utahlite)

Hydrated aluminium phosphate, $Al[PO_4] \cdot 2H_2O$; orthorhombic. Its specific gravity is 2.4-2.6, its hardness is 4-5 and its refractive indices range from 1.55 to 1.59. Its colour is yellowish green, deep green, bluish green or greenish blue. Gem-quality variscite is often massive and is composed of finely fibrous crystals. It is often translucent and has a vitreous lustre and a white streak. Variscite suitable for cutting comes from nodules called **utahlite** that occur in Tooele County, Utah and in Nevada, USA. Another locality is Dayboro in Queensland, Australia.

Wardite

Hydrated sodium aluminium phosphate, $NaAl_3[(OH)_4|(PO_4)_2] \cdot 2H_2O$; tetragonal. Its specific gravity is 2.81, its hardness is 5 and its refractive indices range from 1.590 to 1.599. It is a pale bluish-green colour. The principal locality for wardite, which is cut into cabochons, is Cedar Valley in Utah, USA.

Zoisite

Complex hydrous calcium aluminium silicate, $Ca_2Al_3[SiO_4]_3(OH)$; orthorhombic. Its specific gravity is 3.2-3.4, its hardness is 6-7 and its refractive indices range from 1.691 to 1.700. It is either greyish white, greenish, brown, pinkish red **(thulite)** or blue **(tanzanite)**. The lustre is vitreous, almost pearly on the cleavage faces. The streak is white. Zoisite commonly forms lumpy, coarse- to fine-bladed or fibrous aggregates. The pink thulite from Norway (*thule* is an old Greek and Roman name for the far-northern countries) was used in the past for jewellery. Recently the greyish-green zoisite from California has become quite fashionable. Thulite occurs near Trondheim and at Arendal in Norway; it is also found in the Austrian Tirol, Western Australia, Namibia and North Carolina, USA. In 1967 transparent, bluish-violet crystals were found near the town of Arusha in Tanzania. The mineral was later identified as a variety of zoisite and called tanzanite. At the time of the discovery, the press described it as the 'blue treasure of Africa'. The largest tanzanite specimen found so far weighs 126 carats.

1 Staurolite twins (Sobotín, Czechoslovakia). Length up to 10 mm. **2** Thomsonite (Doubice, Czechoslovakia). 60 × 60 mm. **3** Variscite (Utah, USA). 70 × 50 mm. **4** Wardite with pseudowavellite and variscite (Levingstone, Utah, USA). Diameter 60 mm. **5** Cut tanzanite (Tanzania). 3.2 carats. **6** Thulite (Lexviken, Norway). 190 × 140 mm.

1

2

3

4

5

6

Minor gemstones

The following minerals occur only rarely as gemstones or are cut mostly because of collectors' interest — or they have only a local popularity:

Amblygonite: lithium aluminium fluoro-hydroxy phosphate, $LiAl[(F, OH)PO_4]$
Analcime (Analcite): hydrated sodium aluminium silicate, $Na[AlSi_2O_6] \cdot H_2O$
Anatase: titanium dioxide, TiO_2
Arandisite: a tin silicate, probably a mixture of green hydrous cassiterite and quartz
Augelite: hydrous aluminium phosphate, $Al_2[(OH)_3PO_4]$
Barite (Barytes): barium sulphate, $Ba[SO_4]$
Beryllonite: sodium beryllium phosphate, $NaBe[PO_4]$
Boracite: magnesium chloroborate, $Mg_3[Cl|B_7O_{13}]$
Brookite: titanium dioxide, TiO_2
Cancrinite: hydrated sodium calcium aluminium silicate with carbon dioxide, $(Na_2, Ca)_4$ $[CO_3(H_2O)_{0-3}(ALSIO_4)_6]$
Celestine (Celestite): strontium sulphate, $Sr[SO_4]$
Cerrusite: lead carbonate, $PbCO_3$
Colemanite: hydrated calcium borate, $Ca[B_3O_4(OH)_3] \cdot H_2O$
Crocoite: lead chromate, $Pb[CrO_4]$
Datolite: calcium borosilicate, $CaB[OH|SiO_4]$
Durangite: sodium aluminium fluorarsenate, $NaAl[(F)AsO_4]$
Ekanite: potassium calcium sodium thorium silicate, $K(Ca,Na)_2\ Th[Si_8O_{20}]$
Epidote: hydrous calcium aluminium ferric iron silicate, $Ca_2(Al, Fe)_3[OH(SiO_4)_3]$
Eudialyte: hydrous sodium, calcium, ferrous iron, zirconium silicate, $(Na, Ca, Fe)_6Zr[(OH, Cl)|(Si_3O_9)_2]$
Friedelite: manganese iron chloro-hydroxy silicate, $(Mn, Fe)_8[(OH, Cl)_{10}Si_6O_{15}]$
Gahnite: zinc aluminium oxide, $Zn[Al_2O_4]$
Hambergite: beryllium borate, $Be_2[(OH)BO_3]$
Howlite: calcium borosilicate, $Ca_2[(BOOH)_5SiO_4]$
Kurnakovite: hydrated magnesium borate, $Mg[B_3O_3(OH)_5] \cdot 5\,H_2O$
Microlite: complex calcium sodium tantalum and niobium oxide with hydroxyl and fluorine, $(Ca, Na)_2(Ta, Nb)_2O_6(O, OH, F)$
Painite: complex calcium boro-aluminium silicate, $5\ Al_2O_3 \cdot Ca_2[(Si, BH)\ O_4]$
Petalite: lithium aluminium silicate, $Li[AlSi_4O_{10}]$
Phosgenite: lead chlorocarbonate, $Pb_2[(Cl_2)CO_3]$
Pollucite: hydrated caesium sodium aluminium silicate, $(Cs, Na)\ [AlSi_2O_6] \cdot H_2O$
Proustite: silver arsenic sulphide, Ag_3AsS_3
Purpurite: manganese ferric iron phosphate, $(Mn, Fe)[PO_4]$
Rhodizite: complex potassium alkali aluminium beryllium borate, $KNaLi_4Al_4[Be_3B_{10}O_{27}]$
Scapolite: isomorphous group of aluminium silicates whose compositions form a series between marialite, $Na_8[(Cl_2,SO_4,CO_3)\ (AlSi_3O_8)_6]$ and meionite, $Ca_8[(Cl_2,SO_4,CO_3)_2(Al_2Si_2O_8)_6]$
Scheelite: calcium tungstate, $Ca[WO_4]$
Scorodite: hydrated iron arsenate, $Fe[AsO_4] \cdot 2\,H_2O$
Sinhalite: magnesium aluminium borate, $MgAl[BO_4]$
Stibiotantalite: tantanium niobium antimonate, $Sb(Ta,Nb)O_4$
Stichtite: hydrated magnesium chromium hydroxy carbonate, $Mg_6Cr_2[(OH)_{16}CO_3] \cdot 4\ H_2O$
Taafeite: magnesium beryllium aluminium oxide $MgBeAl_4O_8$
Tugtupite: sodium beryllium silicate with chlorine $Na_8[Cl_2(BeAlSi_4O_{12})_2]$
Ulexite: hydrated socium calcium borate $NaCaB_5O_6(OH)_6 \cdot 5\,H_2O$
Vivianite: hydrated iron phosphate, $Fe_3[PO_4]_2 \cdot 8\,H_2O$
Wavellite: hydrated aluminium phosphate, $Al_3[(OH)_3PO_4]_2 \cdot 5\,H_2O$
Willemite: zinc silicate, $Zn_2[SiO_4]$
Wulfenite: lead molybdate, $Pb[MoO_4]$
Zincite: zinc oxide ZnO

Gemlore

Originally, stone served prehistoric people only as a tool. Then one day — we don't know when — somebody stumbled on a stone that attracted him or her with its beauty. Prehistoric people were not, of course, able to explain the existence of such an extraordinary stone; they could not understand how it happened to be there and why it looked the way it did. The occurrence of such a stone was for them a unique phenomenon and thus they started believing that these beautiful stones possessed some supernatural, magic or healing powers. In fact at this stage of their cultural development people had to explain everything in terms of magic because they had no objective understanding of nature and the laws governing it. No wonder then that they ascribed magic powers to such extraordinary stones of breathtaking beauty.

As early as 4000-3000 BC, the people of Mesopotamia used gemstones for personal adornment or wore them as talismans to bring them luck, happiness and success. Gems were also buried with their owners in tombs. In ancient Egypt the scarab beetle was regarded as a symbol of the soul's immortality and the image of the beetle was often carved into gems. Ancient Indian peoples also knew and valued the many precious stones found abundantly on their territory. The Indians believed that gems protected one's life and that they were powerful remedies for all kinds of diseases.

The Persians and the Arabs have also worn talismans made from gemstones for a long time. During their captivity in Babylon and Egypt, the Jews gained their knowledge of gemstones and it was they who started giving meanings to particular gemstones. The origin of this very old custom is based on the twelve stones on the robe of the Jewish high priest. The Second Book of Moses describing the exodus of the Israelites from Egypt stipulates precisely in Chapter 28 how the golden breastplate worn by Aaron should look like. It was to be decorated with twelve gemstones: carnelian, olivine, emerald, ruby, lazurite, onyx, sapphire, agate, rock crystal, topaz, beryl and jasper to symbolize the twelve united tribes of Israel. However, the original Hebrew words for the individual stones as well as their order gradually became so confused in the different translations of the Bible that in some cases, like that of the so-called *Lynkurion* (ligurion), the identity of the stone cannot be determined with certainty. Some authorities give it as amber, some zircon. Three times each year when the high priest entered the Holy of the Holies in the Tabernacle (later the Temple) in Jerusalem, he adorned himself with diamond, which was even then valued as the most precious of all gemstones. Even after the Temple had been destroyed by Roman troops led by Titus in AD 70 and the office of the Jewish high priest lost its importance, the belief in the special magic of Aaron's shield and its gems did not die and Charlemagne is reputed to have had a copy of the shield set in his crown.

The astrologers also contributed to the symbolism of the twelve stones of Aaron's shield and quite early on the stones were related to the twelve zodiacal symbols. Then came the medieval age with its Christian faith and the twelve stones were related to the twelve apostles and later to the twelve months of the year, thus starting the tradition of the twelve birthstones. A different stone was worn each successive month but some people wore all twelve stones simultaneously all the year round just to be on the safe side. People believed that the magical and healing powers of the stones depended on the season of the year so in time a whole number of combinations were devised, with one or more stones for each astronomical month (see Table 11).

The Greeks learned about gemstones from Phoenician merchants and from ancient Greece the knowledge of gemstones spread to Rome. The magical powers of gemstones are mentioned in the works of classical Greek and Roman philosophers and naturalists, such as Herodotus, Plato, Aristotle and the latter's disciple, Theophrastus. The Romans, especially during the Imperial period, used gemstones widely not only for jewellery but also to decorate their robes, weapons and armour and they also wore them as amulets.

The belief in the healing power of gemstones is often reflected in the fantastic tales concerning their origin that appear in many ancient writings. For instance, Plutarch of Chaeronea (AD *c.*46-*c.* 120), the Greek historian and philosopher who summarized all the known knowledge of gemstones, held that carbuncle (a collective term for rubies, spinels and garnets) was the fiery eye of an extinct dragon. The first who opposed such tales was the great naturalist Pliny the Elder. Pliny mastered an immense knowledge of rocks and minerals. In his extensive 37-volume work *Historia Naturalis* he energetically disputed some of the gemlore. But he still maintained that diamond was invincible and indestructible, saying that it would break both the anvil and the hammer used to strike it with great force. He believed that only if placed in the still-warm blood of a billy goat that had been fed for six weeks on parsley and wine, would the diamond turn soft and lose its invincibility. So, although Pliny did uproot some of the superstitions and beliefs, he himself was unable to overcome the limitations of non-materialistic thought. Similar tales survived well after Pliny and new ones were added to gemlore during the Middle Ages.

Some medieval treatises deal with the healing powers ascribed to gemstones. For example, the learned Albertus Magnus, Bishop of Regensburg (1193-1280) describes the healing magic of gemstones in his five-volume work *De Mineralibus et Rebus Metalicis*. Some of the believed effects of the gemstones discussed by the Bishop are such powerful remedies that we should be sorry that these miracles cannot happen. The treatise is, nevertheless, a valuable survey of older thought on minerals.

The growing interest in science did not dispel the superstitions. In fact, alchemy and astrology blossomed on the belief that gemstones had miraculous powers. The so-called philosopher's stone and elixir of life (*elixir vitae*) were incessantly sought after. Even Anselmus Boetius de Boot, the Dutch mineralogist and personal physician to Emperor Rudolf II, was unable to purge his book *Gemmarum et Lapidum Historia* (1609) entirely of superstitious lore.

Magical properties were ascribed mainly to conspicuous, coloured minerals. It was believed that all white stones protected the eyesight; in Italian lore white stones put on the roof were supposed to protect the house against lightning. Red stones, also called blood stones, were used to stop haemorrhages and to heal wounds. Black stones were said to drive away melancholy and in India they were worn as a protection against evil spells; green gemstones promoted fertility and increased crops. The Indians living near the River Orinoco in South America still wear pieces of amazonite around their necks as a protection against spells and evil forces. The Javanese believe that violet stones protect children from spasms and make them love their parents. All yellow stones are said to prevent yellow jaundice and gall bladder disorders.

Agate is reputed to prolong the life of its owner, win people's favour, bring success and to make men attractive to women. Moss agate is believed to bring good crops and to ward off evil spells. The Babylonians deemed agate to be a lucky stone for those born under Taurus whereas medieval astrologers ascribed this luck to Taurus, Gemini and Capricorn.

Amethyst was believed to protect the wearer from intoxication and poisoning. Medieval gemlore held that amethyst had a positive influence on one's reason and on trade. The Babylonian astrologers related it to Aries, the Greeks to Capricorn.

Beryl was always used as a healing and protective stone. Pagan priests used it as an accoutrement when preparing their rituals. It was also indispensable to alchemists. The Babylonian astrologers related it to Gemini, the Greeks to Leo.

Diamond was universally regarded as magical. It was believed to help overcome difficulties, protect against poisoning, make one rich and be a remedy for all sicknesses and wounds. The Babylonians related it to Libra, the Greeks to Cancer and the Byzantines to Aries.

Garnet is supposed to bring good humour and drive away nightmares. The Bohemian folklore held that garnet protected against evil spells and country women often wore strings of Bohemian garnets. Astrologers related garnet to Leo (Greeks) and Capricorn (Byzantines).

The precious ruby protected against the scheming of the devil and warded off black plague. A mere touch of it would stop all bleeding. The Babylonians related ruby to Leo, the Greeks to Scorpio and the Byzantines to Virgo. Sapphire was a ticket to immortality and it was popular with ancient rulers.

In ancient Greece haematite was known as *haimostates*, an arrester of haemorrhage, and was therefore worn as a talisman against bleeding. Medieval astrologers deemed it a lucky stone of those born under Aquarius.

Rock crystal was a remedy for internal disorders. In practice it was used as a thirst quencher because placed under the tongue it felt pleasantly cool. Rock crystal balls were an indispensable property in all oracles and later fortune-telling businesses. Rock crystal was a guardian of the soul's purity and was supposed to bring joy. Astrologically, it is a lucky stone of Capricorn.

Opal was very popular in both ancient and medieval times. It was generally believed to secure happiness. For the Romans it was a symbol of dignity and power. In the Reformation, however, opal was regarded as a stone of ill fortune for a time. The eastern nations regard opal as a sacred stone in which the spirit of truth dwells. The Babylonian astrologers related it to Capricorn, the Byzantines to Libra.

Emerald was said to sharpen one's wit, help foresee the future and cure a number of diseases. The Babylonians put it under the sign of Cancer whereas the Greeks and Byzantines deemed it a lucky stone for those born under Taurus.

The gemlore of various nations and periods is inexhaustible. Today, the magical powers of gemstones are generally things of the past; we value more the intrinsic beauty of precious stones and the use to which they can be put in modern technology.

Table 11 Basic combinations of birthstones

Month	Hebrews	Romans	Arabs	Isidore, Bishop of Seville AD 635	Russians	Italians	19th and 20th centuries, generally
January	Garnet	Garnet	Garnet	Hyacinth	Garnet Hyacinth	Hyacinth Garnet	Garnet
February	Amethyst	Amethyst	Amethyst	Amethyst	Amethyst	Amethyst	Amethyst Pearl
March	Jasper	Haematite	Haematite	Jasper	Jasper	Jasper	Jasper Hyacinth
April	Sapphire	Sapphire	Sapphire	Sapphire	Sapphire	Sapphire	Sapphire Diamond
May	Chalcedony	Agate	Emerald	Agate	Emerald	Agate	Agate
June	Emerald	Emerald	Agate Chalcedony	Emerald	Agate	Emerald	Emerald Turquoise
July	Onyx	Onyx	Carnelian	Onyx	Ruby	Onyx	Onyx
August	Carnelian	Carnelian	Sardonyx	Carnelian	Alexandrite	Carnelian	Topaz
September	Olivine	Sardonyx	Olivine	Olivine	Olivine	Olivine	Olivine Sapphire Diamond
October	Aquamarine	Aquamarine	Aquamarine Beryl	Aquamarine	Beryl	Beryl	Opal Sapphire
November	Beryl Topaz	Beryl Topaz	Topaz	Beryl Topaz	Topaz	Topaz	Topaz
December	Ruby	Ruby	Ruby	Ruby	Turquoise Chrysoprase	Turquoise Ruby	Ruby Haematite

Legend to maps of gem localities

European gem localities
Bergen
S. Norway
Cumbria
Yorkshire
Baltic coast
Saxony
Kozákov
Schneckenstein
Szkla
Idar-Oberstein
Třebenice
Spessart
Hof
Třebíč
České Budějovice
Grimsel
Tirol
(moldavite)
Adula
ALPS
Traversella
Val Malenco
Carrara
Elba
0
500
1000
1500 km

1
Kol'skiy Poluostrov
(Kola Pen.)
(chiastolite)
POLAR URALS
N. URALS
URALS
Murzinka
Nizhniy Tagil
Belaia
Sysert'
Tokovaya
Miass
Orsk
Orijärvi
Volhynia
Kiyev (Kiev)
Dubník
armarosch
Moldova
Mikhaylovo
Cyprus

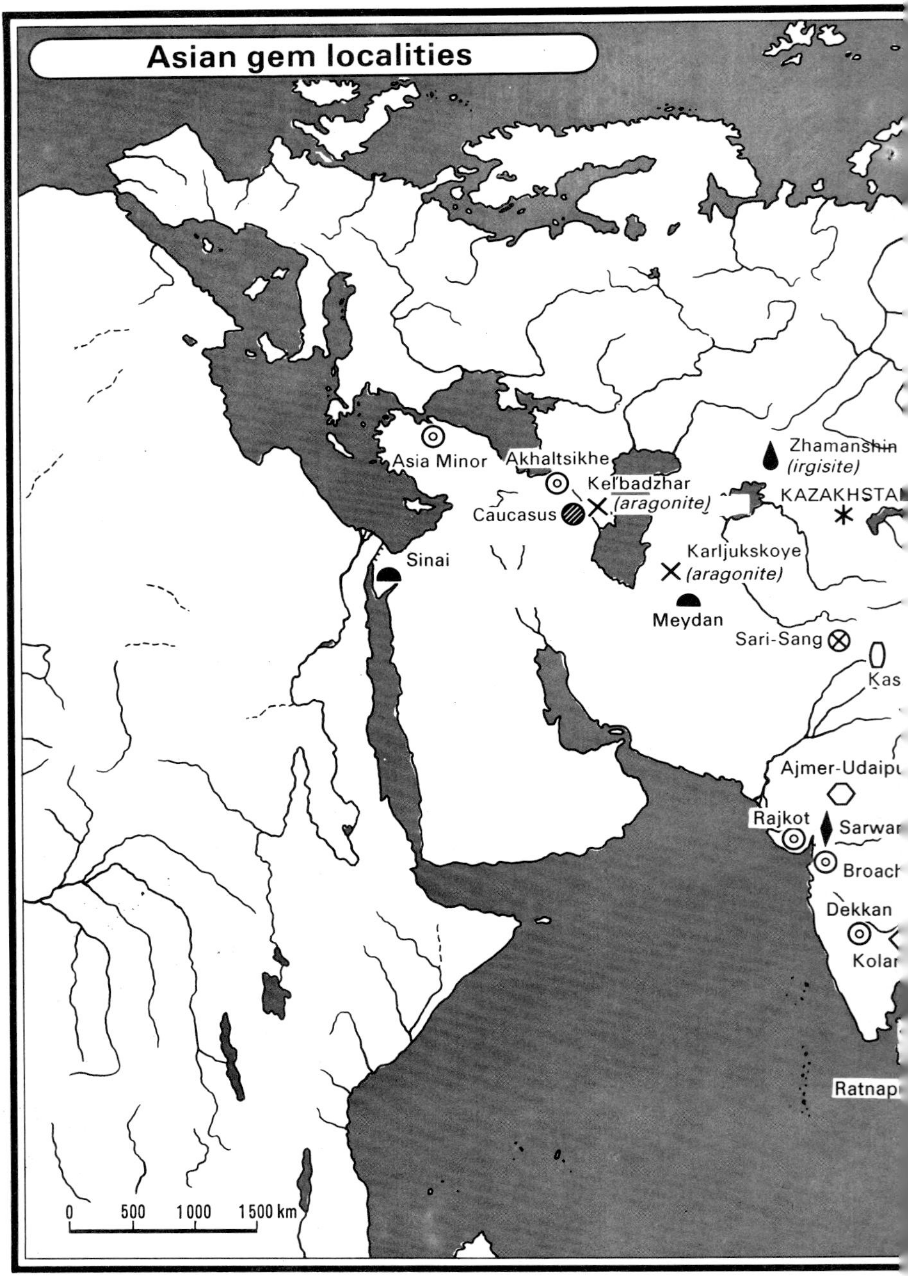
Asian gem localities
Asia Minor
Akhaltsikhe
Kel'badzhar
(aragonite)
Caucasus
Sinai
Zhamanshin
(irgisite)
Karljukskoye
(aragonite)
Meydan
Sari-Sang
Rajkot
Dekkan
Kolar
0 500 1000 1500 km

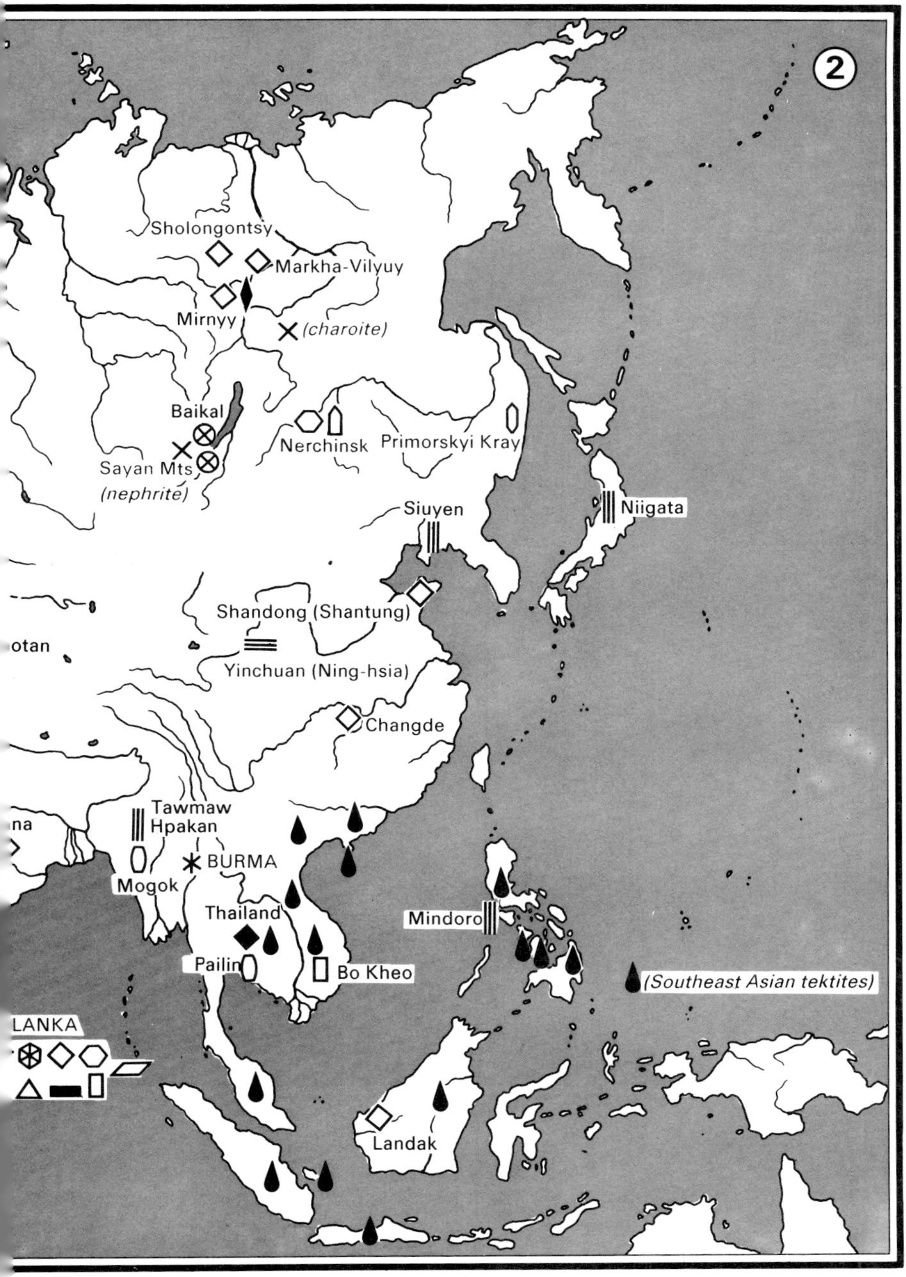

2
Sholongontsy
Markha-Vilyuy
Mirnyy
(charoite)
Baikal
Sayan Mts
(nephrite)
Nerchinsk
Primorskyi Kray
Siuyen
Niigata
Shandong (Shantung)
otan
Yinchuan (Ning-hsia)
Changde
Tawmaw
Hpakan
na
BURMA
Mogok
Thailand
Mindoro
Pailin
Bo Kheo
(Southeast Asian tektites)
LANKA
Landak

North American gem localities
3
Labrador
Bancroft
Maine
Yogo-Gulch
Virgin Valley
Pikes Peak
Pala
Holbrook
North Carolina
Arizona
Los Cerillos
Georgia
(georgianite)
Texas
(bediasite)
Zimapan
0
500
1000
1 500
km

4
South American gem localities
Mazaruni
Muzo
Maraba
Boi Morto
Rio Machado
Chapada Diamantina
Cristalina
BRASILIEN
PARAGUAY
Minas Gerais
Bahia Conquista
Tibagi
Artigas
Capillitas
(rhodochrosite)
Rio Grande do Sul
Ovalle
0 500 1000 1500 km

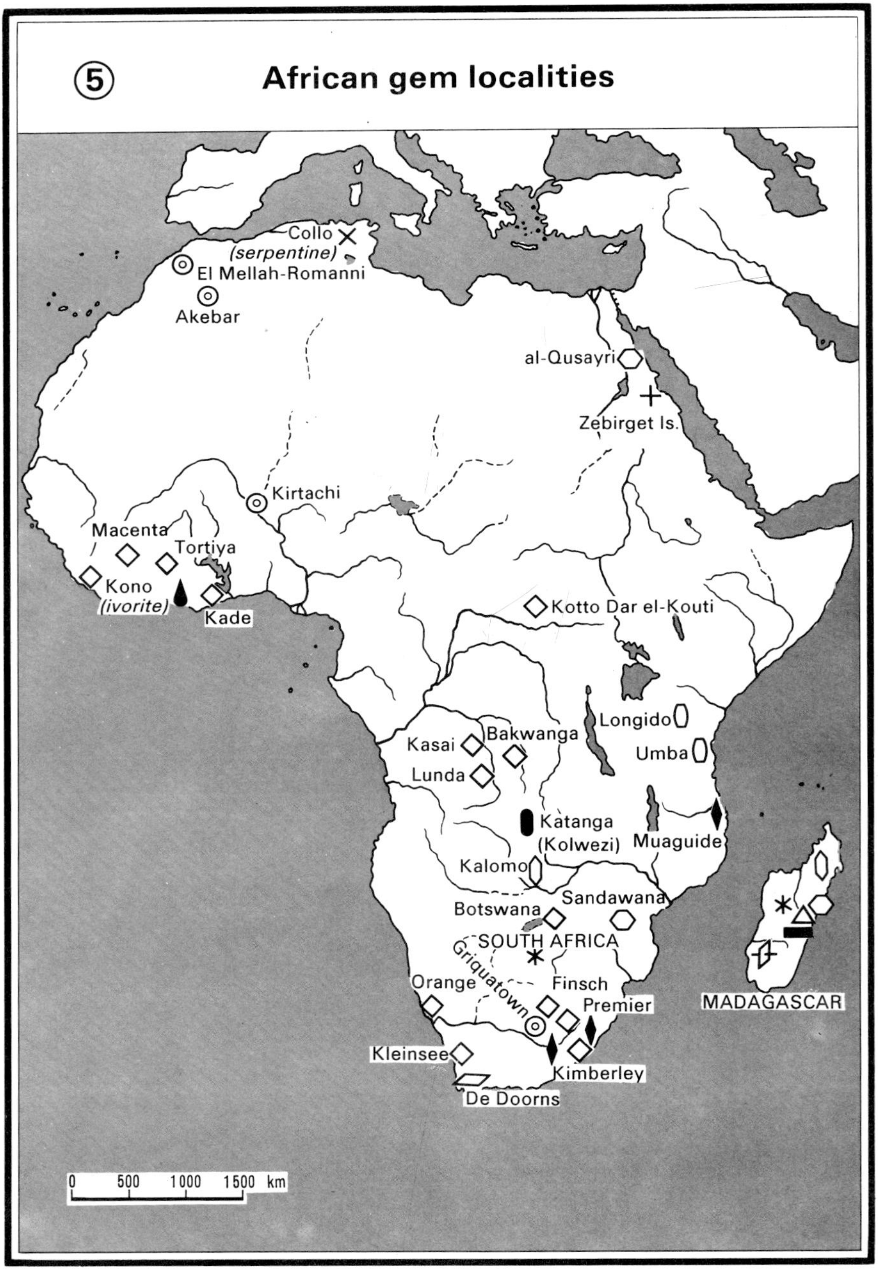

5
African gem localities
Collo
(serpentine)
El Mellah-Romanni
Akebar
al-Qusayri
Zebirget Is.
Kirtachi
Macenta
Tortiya
Kono
(ivorite)
Kade
Kotto Dar el-Kouti
Longido
Umba
Kasai
Bakwanga
Lunda
Katanga
(Kolwezi)
Muaguide
Kalomo
Sandawana
Botswana
SOUTH AFRICA
Griquatown
Orange
Finsch
Premier
Kleinsee
Kimberley
De Doorns
MADAGASCAR
0 500 1000 1500 km

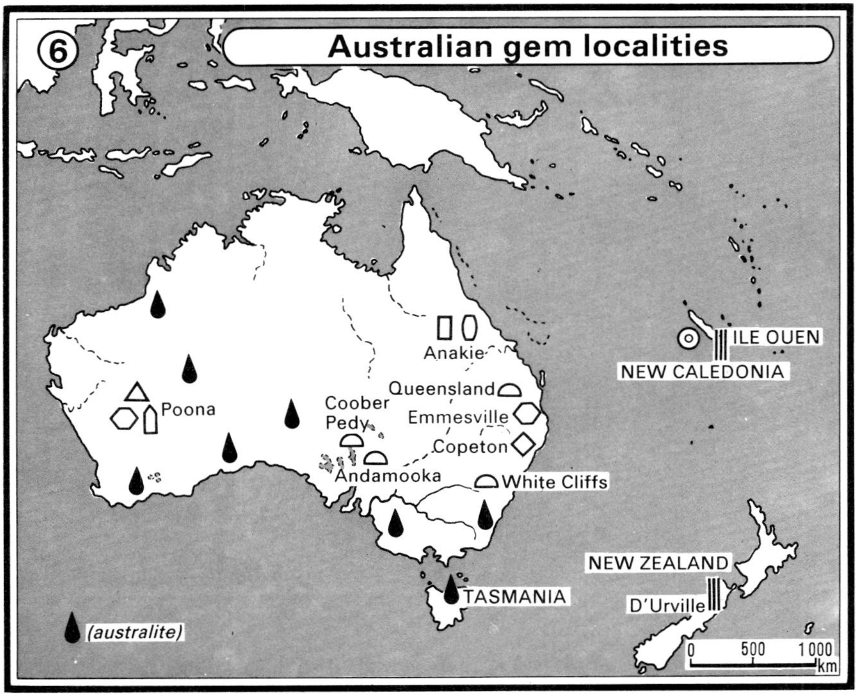

Gemstone groups

A **Gemstones from Burma** (except those marked on Map 2) Amber, apatite, beryl, chrysoberyl, danburite, jadeite, olivine (peridot), quartz and its varieties, sillimanite, spinel, topaz, zircon

B **Gemstones from Sri Lanka** (except those marked on Map 2) Andalusite, apatite, diopside, kornerupine, quartz and its varieties, sillimanite, titanite (sphene)

C **Gemstones from South Africa and Madagascar** Agate, amber, beryl (aquamarine, emerald, morganite), chalcedony, chrysoberyl, cordierite, corundum (ruby, sapphire), danburite, diamond, dumortierite, feldspar (amazonite, orthoclase), fluorite, garnet (almandine, pyrope, spessartite), jadeite, jasper, kornerupine, malachite, opal, prehnite, quartz and its varieties, rhodonite, serpentine, sodalite, spinel, spodumene (kunzite), titanite (sphene), topaz, tourmaline, zoisite

D **Gemstones from Kazakhstan, USSR** Chalcedony (chrysoprase), fluorite, jasper, opal (fire opal), quartz and its varieties, pyrite

E **Gemstones from the Urals, USSR** Beryl (aquamarine, emerald), chalcedony, chrysoberyl (alexandrite), cordierite, corundum (leucosapphire, ruby, sapphire), diamond, euclase, feldspar (amazonite), garnet (demantoid, hessonite, spessartite, uvarovite), gypsum (alabaster), kyanite, malachite, phenakite, quartz and its varieties, rhodonite, serpentine, topaz, vesuvianite, zircon (hyacinth)

F **Gemstones from Brazil** Agate, andalusite, beryl (aquamarine, emerald, morganite), brazilianite, chalcedony, chrysoberyl, diamond, dumortierite, euclase, feldspar (amazonite), garnet (almandine, pyrope, spessartite), haematite, opal, phenakite, quartz and its varieties, sodalite, spodumene (kunzite), titanite, topaz, tourmaline

Further reading

ANDERSON, B. W. *Gemstones for everyman.* Faber:London, 1976.
ANDERSON, B. W. *Gem testing,* 9th edn. Butterworths:London, 1980.
BARIAND, P. *Marvellous world of minerals.* Abbey Library:London, 1976.
BATTEY, M. H. *Mineralogy for students,* 2nd edn. Longman: London, 1981.
BAUER, J. *A field guide in colour to minerals, rocks and precious stones.* Octopus Books: London, 1974.
BOEGEL, H. *A collector's guide to minerals and gemstones.* Thames & Hudson:London, 1971
CLARK, A. *Minerals* (Hamlyn nature guides). Hamlyn:London, 1979.
DEESON, A. F. L. (ed.) *The collector's encyclopedia of rocks and minerals.* David & Charles:Newton Abbot, 1973.
FIRSOFF, V. A. *Gemstones of the British Isles.* Oliver & Boyd:Edinburgh, 1971.
HURLBUT, C. S. *Dana's manual of mineralogy,* 18th edn. Wiley:New York, 1971.
HURLBUT, C. S. & SWITZER, G. S. *Gemmology.* Wiley:New York, 1979.
KIRKALDY, J. F. *Minerals and rocks,* 3rd edn. Blandford Press:London, 1976.
KOUŘIMSKÝ, J. *The illustrated encyclopedia of minerals and rocks.* Octopus Books: London, 1977.
LIDDICOAT, R. T. *Handbook of gem identification,* 10th edn. Gemmological Institute of America, 1975
MITCHELL, R. S. *Mineral names: what do they mean?* Van Nostrand Reinhold:New York, 1979.
PHILLIPS, W. J. & PHILLIPS, N. *An introduction to mineralogy for students.* Wiley: Chichester, 1980.
POUGH. F. H. *A field guide to rocks and minerals,* 4th edn. Constable:London, 1981.
READ, H. H. *Rutley's elements of mineralogy,* 26th edn. Allen & Unwin:London, 1970.
READ, P. G. *Beginner's guide to gemmology.* Newnes Technical Books (Butterworths): London, 1980.
READ, P. G. *Gemmological instruments.* Butterworths:London, 1978.
READ, P. G. *Gems.* Newnes Technical Books (Butterworths):London, 1981.
SCHUMANN, W. *Minerals and rocks: identified and illustrated with colour photographs* (Chatto nature guides). Chatto & Windus:London, 1978.
SINKANKAS, J. *Gem cutting,* 2nd edn. Van Nostrand Reinhold:New York, 1963.
SMITH, G. F. H. *Gemstones,* 14th edn. Chapman & Hall:London, 1972. (Contains extensive bibliography.)
SORREL, C. A. & SANDSTROM, G. F. The rocks and minerals of the world. Collins: London, 1977.
WEBSTER, R. *Gems: their sources, descriptions and identification.* 3rd edn. Butterworths: London, 1975.
WEBSTER, R. A. *Gemmologists' compendium,* 6th edn. Van Nostrand Reinhold:New York, 1980.
WEBSTER, R. A. *Practical gemmology,* 6th edn. NAG Press:London, 1979.

Useful addresses

The Gemmological Association of Great Britain
St Dunstan's House, 2 Carey Lane, London EC2 8AB.
The Gemmological Institute of America
1660 Stewart Street, PO Box 2110, Santa Monica, California 90406 USA.
The Canadian Gemmological Association
Box 1106, Station Q, Toronto, Ontario, Canada.
The Gemmological Association of Australia
Box 75, Broadway 4000, Queensland, Australia.
The Mineralogical Society of South Africa
PO Box 4206, Capetown 8000, South Africa.

Index

(numbers in italics refer to illustrations)